AF531219

DEVELOPING YOUR LATENT POWERS

MAN

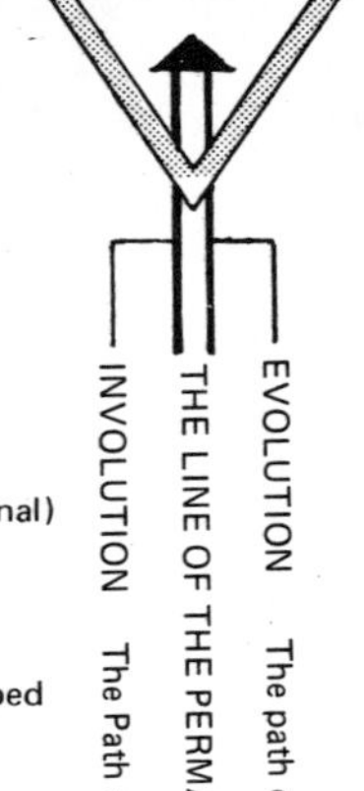

THE OVERSOUL
Synthesis of personality lives, reached through the Crown Chakra

Initiates, controls and integrates all personality factors

BUDDHIC (spiritual)
'Persian Saddle'
Pituitary and Pineal

The summation and integration of *each* personality life
Recognition of past lives on occasion

HIGHER EMOTION (non-personal)
Throat Chakra

Imagination and visualisation as dual ways
Most ESP powers

HIGHER MENTALITY (developed personality)
Heart Chakra

Inspiration: leadership, to develop, must be attached to non-personal drives

LOWER MENTAL (personality)
Navel Chakra

Conflict
Earth attractions and repulsions always work with lower emotional: fame, sex, all earth pulls

LOWER EMOTIONAL (personality)
Spleen Chakra

Conflict and tensions (which can escape control). All desires, fears. Works with lower mental to create 'day dreams' and personas

PHYSICO-ETHERIC
Root Chakra combines with Unconscious for 'Kudalini'

The 'yolk' of the egg. The etheric is the mould and is affected by Unconscious
It is from experiences and purification starting at this vehicle that man develops

The Unconscious bearing Karmic influences good or bad: the repressions of present life and can be affected by elemental urges. The cause of conditioned reflexes

DEVELOPING YOUR LATENT POWERS

Thirty Practical Steps to Spiritual Satisfaction

Frederick R. Gould

ROBERT B. LUCE Co Inc

Washington New York

To those Pilgrim Souls who on
earth were my loved Wife, my
Father and my Mother,
and to my sons Dennis and Bob

Library of Congress Catalog Card Number 76-4445

ISBN 0 88331 085 6

Published in the United States 1976

Printed in Great Britain

CONTENTS

LESSON 1
Introductory

Exercise One Breathing (Low, Middle and High)

Read not to contradict and confute nor to believe and take for granted but to weigh and consider. Francis Bacon

I envisage a method whose aim would be to reconcile contraries in a synthesis incorporating a rational understanding and a mystical experience. Wolfgang Pauli, Nobel Prize Winner, 1945

This survey of man from the points of view of biology, psychology, Western and Eastern philosophy and religion . . . enables us to arrive at certain conclusions. From the point of view of science we see man as an elaborate piece of mechanism, his actions determined by man's endocrine glands, his central nervous system, his hereditary endowments and his environment. From philosophy we learn that his capacity for knowledge is strictly limited, so that by means of the sense organs alone he can never know reality. This is confirmed by Eastern philosophy but a new idea is added.

Man, as he is, can see no more and do no more, but by right effort and right method, he can gain new powers; understand and achieve more. Finally we have confirmation of this view by religion . . . from the point of view of all religions man is a being in whom are lying latent powers.

Kenneth Walker. *Diagnosis of Man*

Introduction for the Student

The writer is also a student, a humble student, who believes the kind of thinking this course provides is urgently needed in our own purposeless age—which is the headache that follows on a night of materialistic intoxication, producing hallucinations which have reduced man to the servant of a machine in his daily life and the status of a machine in his spiritual one.

There is another path and a higher outlook; this the writer has tested and it has illumined his life.

The writer has for many years headed groups of occult (the word simply means 'hidden') seekers and he feels there is a great need for a simple statement of the nature of that search: for tried and proven exercises on its path and of suggested reading and allied thinking. This is an attempt, feeble but sincere, to proffer such assistance. He has been urged by several of the seekers in such groups to enumerate his own qualifications for this writing. Please accept that he sincerely believes that 'the proof of the pudding is in the eating'—if the work is worthy it will not need data about the author. *Prove the work* for yourself—that is the touchstone.

The method throughout will be practical in the larger sense of that word. Each lesson will be in two parts: (a) a theory statement and (b) practical exercises with explanations of what they aim to achieve. In other words we shall proceed in scientific methodology, stating (a) a hypothesis, (b) collecting and classifying information in support or disproof, (c) experimentation, and (d) formulating a law (to be discarded as are scientific 'Laws' when new truths render them obsolete or incomplete). The hypothesis we shall try to prove is the following.

1 *That man is an immortal creature.* Words are always difficult: indeed T. S. Elliot has written delightfully and explicitly about 'the intolerable wrestle with words and meanings'. For example, the word 'Man' in the above heading does not mean the 'forked radish', as Carlyle loved to call him. This is merely his body. Man, in this thinking, is 'a mind', or, in mystical phraseology, 'a spark from the light of God'. Equally, 'immortal' has the meaning of 'everlasting' only according to any concept our finite minds can hold.

2 *That as man is immortal mind incarnated, it follows that he had pre-existence and will have existence after the discarding of the physical body.* Life, as seen through the physical body, is only a day in a larger lifetime. Accepting the premise that Man is indeed, an immortal mind, according to our concept of such words, then it equally follows that his immortality is present at the moment, was present in the past, and will be present in the future. The thing that is mortal, that dies, is the vehicle which Man uses.

3 *That 'whole' man is conscious on many planes other than the physical.*

We know that Man can only use a few vibrations, of which science is aware. These vibrations, which titillate his physical senses, are used by his physical body to become conscious of what we call 'physical things'. If a diver wished to explore the bed of the sea, he would, and does, put on a special suit adapted to that purpose. Within that suit he can be sustained in a varying element by his native air. The suit limits and impedes his movements, and has special organs of perception which he would not want to use on land, but it is the only way in which he can explore the ocean bed. Equally the only way in which the Oversoul can explore the earth is by putting on a physical body.

4 *That by understanding the laws governing the states of consciousness, we can get out of the physical vehicle (the diver's suit) and use other vehicles on other planes or states of consciousness for limited periods.* It is the purpose of the writer to help people to think about this—to awaken to their latent powers.

Gurdjieff said that most people were merely sleeping machines, by which he meant that they lived their lives as behaviourist psychology teaches, like push-button automata giving responses in accordance to impulses, and his system was designed to make Man awaken.

It may very well be that, at first reading, our hypothesis appears ludicrous, but if the reader will continue, he will be amazed at the amount of verificatory detail that can be educed in its support. There cannot help but be some repetition: the writer has had students say, 'Oh, I have heard all that before, I know all that'. The first part of the statement is probably true—great truths have a habit of presenting themselves again and again for our consideration. The second part is more doubtful: if they really 'know' their subject they will also know that it is inexhaustible and that every day brings to light a new facet of the truth which they 'know'—but only partially.

You must live your occultism to get the fullness thereof, and you will do this best by knowing that its wonders are beyond finite knowledge, so that we have never exhausted them, we never know them fully.

We shall consider the need for integration as the psychologist sees it; through this we shall proceed to the work of Dr Carl Gustav Jung, which has done so much to unify the wisdom of Eastern theory and the knowledge of Western science. From this standpoint we shall attempt to consider some of the factors like Time and Dreams, and the vast mass of parapsychological and super-normal experience which is available. The search is a long one, but it is so very well worth the doing.

To develop, we need to exercise both physically and spiritually—the Law of Duality is one that permeates our world. It is in accord with this Law that we have devised our lessons, each of which will have *two* parts. The first, and to the writer's mind the most important, is psycho-philosophic — a statement of the thinking behind the practice. The second consists of a series of carefully graded exercises that will develop your 'I', so that you will understand more and more of the occult thinking behind what you are attempting.

A warning must be given about haste. Aim to consider each sentence and its meaning: to accept some statements as true *for you* and to build them into your thinking; to put some into a 'pending tray' for further consideration later in the course; or perhaps to reject some as not true statements for you. *Your aim* is to make you *own* philosophy as a basis for all your life and those thereafter.

The practical exercises, the 'doing' as Gurdjieff called it, means using methods with understanding until they become part of your daily life: eg in breathing the writer has so long practised the 'complete breath' that he uses it automatically and can vary the vibratory rhythms and rates to suit the circumstances of his immediate environment without effort. It has taken him some 50 years to learn this, but he counts them well spent. *The moral is* 'Hasten slowly', be 'thorough' in what you do, and results cannot fail to accrue, but do not pass one lesson until you have gathered from it what you need, and what it has to tell.

It is suggested that you read each lesson through and then study its implications paragraph by paragraph. This is a very serious study and you will not benefit by 'scanning' or hasty assumptions. *The exercises are to be practised until results are obtained.* To try Exercise Three when you have not mastered One or Two is to achieve nullity. Patience and effort are essentials, particularly at the beginning, when you are learning to overcome the 'butterfly' thoughts and the limitations of your environmental training.

It is true to speak of this work we shall do together as 'mystico-occult', for it uses the techniques of Pythagorean Schools. The master himself learned his technique from the Egyptian and Chaldean priests and was also the great Initiator of the Grecian enquiry. Mysticism as such comes as a revelation of grace or what occultists call 'illumination', but only after certain early trainings have been done — we are all too apt to think that our Saints did not work for that nomination. Moreover there are Saints of science and philosophy whose tribulations have brought them insight. Consider and compare such men as Giordano Bruno and Einstein.

Let us then attempt this great quest together in a spirit of scientific enquiry and of reverent mysticism combined — Man's duality in practice.

Preliminaries of Exercise Work

We are starting together on a most exciting, rewarding but arduous path. Your lessons will give you theory, your exercises practice; the latter are graded so as to ensure your success, *provided* you give your quota, namely steady, daily, truthful practice. 'Truthful' because you must not delude or cheat your *'self'*.

So you have three aims: to understand the theory (philosophy if you so like to call it); to understand the exercises; and to practice them assiduously. Many beginners defeat their own object by 'leapfrogging', that is going through the exercises at incredible speed because they think the first few are comparatively unimportant—exactly the opposite is true. It is said that provided you make the first thousand the remaining thousands follow: if this is true of material wealth, it is infinitely more true about spiritual wealth.

This is a very hard study, to be compared with a university degree or the making of a great musician. Consider how a great violinist is made: (1) there are long weary hours of learning how to finger, how to control the physical instrument; (2) then comes some simple theory; (3) practising of scales follows, with all its attendant horrors and difficulties (this is the place where so many give up); (4) once the scales are reasonably played, there is some more theory and our musician starts upon simple tunes, never neglecting the scales and the fingering, which are the fundamentals of his craft; (5) ceaseless practice continues, with correcting of errors, until finally he can play a reasonably difficult piece; (6) then comes more theory; (7) but now, the first time, the higher powers start to operate (up to now he has been so immersed in getting the technique right that he has not had ability to allow his musicianship to operate); (8) and at last, *now master of his instrument,* he can express the 'I' that made him a musician, and after more theory and unending practice he can step on to the platform an acknowledged master.

There is a very good parallelism in treading the *path,* although it may well be that to tread the Path is the harder discipline of the two.

1 We learn how to control the physical instrument. This consists of simple exercises in breath control, 'sitting still'.
2 Simple theory. The duality of our study should be apparent from the beginning.
3 We begin to understand the 'Law of the seven' and to realise that like a musical scale it is an ascent to the completion of an octave. Exercises will now be used to *know* the other notes rising from the 'C' major of our ordinary life. The meaning of Rhythm will now enter. We shall define 'Consciousness', 'Prana', 'Fohat' and other terms.
4 We shall now start to combine our theoretical knowledge and our practical knowledge so that the exercises will use *both* wisdoms. We shall learn about the centres of power ('Chakras') and how they can be used to control and implement physical, mental and spiritual wellbeing and evolution. This is the stage where we can accept both

our worldly aspect of affairs (personality), and yet be motivated in all we do by the 'higher knowledge' (individuality).

5 Ceaseless practice is now producing results, as with the violinist. We are starting to produce our *own* knowledge and ability to use and *understand* our latent powers, and this growth of performance will be recognised by others.
6 This is the building of the true philosophy, the appreciation of the Ancient Wisdom, though in the most modern form (psychosynthesis, for example). It is 'stretching the *mind*' and forcing the five-sense brain to concur and become an obedient instrument for your newly acquired powers and wisdom.
7 You will now reach through the 'Oversoul' to become an 'individual': you will understand the continuity and meaning of this great concept. You have overcome fear, and death. You are approaching initiation.
8 You can enter into the temple.

Once you have blazed this trail you will understand exactly what is meant in the famous book of precepts called *The Voice of the Silence* when it says:

> You canst not travel on the Path before
> thou hast become that path itself

From the beginning of recorded time there have been those Masters who have known all the facts (and many more) that this course will put before you. This knowledge has underlain all religions. As the great Christian Master said, it was given to the few to *know* but the majority had to be taught in parables. If you enter on the Path; if you wish to be one of those who see behind the parables and appearances; then you accept the burden of *wisdom*. This at any time must to some extent isolate you from the five-senses 'common sense' people who are not yet awakened. Consider this phrase 'not yet awakened': in her magnificent work *The Secret Oral Teachings* Alexandra David-Neal has stated her Master said that to try and teach the great majority was

> Waste of time: the great majority of readers and hearers are the same all over the world. I have no doubt that the people of your country are like those I have met in China and India . . . if you speak to them of profound truths, they yawn, and if they dare, they leave you, but if you tell them absurd fables they are all eyes and ears.

At a later stage the Master returned to this subject:

> In general we distinguish three kinds of individuals: those whose intelligence is completely dull; those whose intelligence is of

average quality, able to understand some truths which are especially evident; those endowed with an intelligence better equipped for acute *perceptions,* who are fit to penetrate below the surface of the world of physical phenomena and grasp *the causes* at work there.

Another Master has said that 90 per cent of earth's present population have their spiritual eyes (and therefore their perception) blinded by the dust of earth; 7 per cent have got cracks in the dust and so get intermittent glimpses, which bring them the truth underneath the appearance; 2¾ per cent see clearly; and the remaining one quarter per cent do not need to see, they *know.*

It is essential that you realise that from the beginning of history (indeed of prehistory) there have been those who know. You are proposing to join their number—as a lowly neophyte it may be true—but *once* you begin, progress is assured; you now cannot fail to follow the path.

Please accept these remarks as vital to your attitude and approach. You cannot make any real progress without building your own philosophy and reinforcing it by your own practice. Now to method.

The Christian Master emphasised how necessary it was when attempting this communication with higher powers to 'go into your closet'. In fact this is essential—to have privacy for the periods of work is vital. The following is ideal:

1 To have a small room or enclosed portion of a room where you can work in quiet and seclusion.
2 To have in that room a straight-backed wooden chair, and a mirror on the wall with small table before it—preferably an old-fashioned lady's small boudoir fitting (these are easy to come by at secondhand sales).
3 Finally, a clean blanket on which you can lay supine on the floor.

If it is possible to keep this room *completely* private, that is excellent. It does not need excessive heating, but does need to be sufficiently warm so that you do not keep interrupting your work because you feel cold.

Obviously everyone will have their own problems and makeshifts, but please approximate as nearly as you can to the requirements named.

Exercise One

As you will learn, everything is *vibration,* and it is the power to alter our vibrations that brings us the power to alter our levels of consciousness. The human being accepts this without knowing because of his breathing, which sets up a rhythm for the whole body and for the whole of physical/etheric life. 'Breath is life'—from the first cry of the infant to the last breath of the aged, it is the important function which vitalises the body. No doubt in the early stages of man's existence on earth he breathed normally and naturally like the animals, but with the advent of 'civilisation', with its attendant pollution, poisoning and stresses, he has a much harder task. Think how many people you know who 'mouth breathe'—a dangerous and pernicious practice. Again 'shallow breathing' is a perversion, due to the stresses and haste of life, and means in fact that you are not using your lung capacity. Breathing has three distinct phases of effects upon the system; therefore our first task is to secure control over the breath. There are several occult breaths which we shall describe but it is best to make haste slowly by realising the operation of full normal breathing.

You breathe into three regions, known as the low, middle and high. It is desirable to make every breath travel this full circuit, but let us first differentiate between the regions.

Region One High breathing is the most wasteful of your energy. It is sometimes called 'collar bone' breathing because it is really 'snatching' at the air and does not utilise the lungs or the abdomen properly.

Region Two Middle breathing fills the rib cage and partially expands the chest. It is the normal breath of the average human.

Region Three Low breathing is what the physicians call 'abdominal breathing' and many medical commentaries have been written extolling this very old Yogic practice.

In fact we shall proceed to two still better forms of breathing known as the complete or *Yogic* breath and the vitalisation breath known as 'Prana' breathing. *But be sure you have done this exercise before proceeding*—not just glanced at it *but done it, thoroughly and understandingly.*

1 Lie supine and comfortable on your blanket, with no sign of strain. Relax completely—the teachers say 'study a cat' and how it relaxes (we shall return to this).
2 Put your hand on your diaphragm, just below the rib cage, so that you may feel the transit of your breathing in.
3 *Through the nose,* breathe in. Now breathing, like everything else, benefits by being done slowly and conscientiously. So take a good, slow deep breath. You will find your lungs fill.
4 As the breath enters, press upon your diaphragm so that the air enters into the chest and all three regions are filled.
5 Without strain, try to hold your breath for a few seconds (not more than four at this stage).
6 Exhale through the nose, slowly, and when the exhalation is nearly complete, draw in your abdomen.

When you feel you can do this correctly *(do not hurry but be sure)* in the supine position, stand before your window or go into the open and do exactly the same exercise.

This preliminary breathing exercise should be done for 5 minutes every morning (the Adepts say at sunrise) and every evening (the Adepts say at sunset). There is enormous power coming into you from the sun, as you will find both in later exercises and in your theoretical study. *This is why it is so important to do this exercise until you can consciously recognise the three regions.*

Instruction At the end of every breathing exercise draw one *quick* breath and exhale equally *quickly*. There is a reason for this, which you will discover in later lessons.

LESSON 2
'This Petty, Puny Age' (F. W. H. Myers)

Exercise Two   Breathing: The Complete Breath

The Greek ideal of soundness of body and mind, the Greek reverence for beauty and strength must come into their own again . . . It is in no cavilling, destructive spirit that I beg of men and women of the day to consider the human being apart from machines, to consider life apart from gold. Within the restless jangle of monstrous cogs and wheels which now turn ceaselessly and bear so called civilisation upon them, there is little leisure or quiet for the calmness or philosophic meditation out of which knowledge is born.

F. W. H. Myers / G. Cummings. *Beyond Human Personality*

A Civilisation which resigns itself wholly to materialism lives upon and consumes its moral Capital and is incapable of renewing it . . . both revealed religion and metaphysical philosophy are equally helpless before the advancing tide.   Professor McDougall

During the past thirty years, people from all the civilised countries of the earth have consulted me . . . Among all my patients in the second half of life—that is to say, over thirty five—there has not been one whose problem in the last resort was not that of finding a religious outlook on life. It is safe to say that every one of them fell ill because he had lost that which the living religions of every age have given to their followers, and none of them has been really healed who did not regain his religious outlook.

Carl Gustav Jung

These few quotations, which could be supplemented by many hundreds more, merely state what we all know. Something has gone out of life: spirit and purpose; the whole meaning of the adventure which is Man has been swamped in a permissive mess of comfort and indulgence that nonetheless fails to satisfy or to bring happiness in any true sense.

All too obviously a new 'credo' is needed. Our youth, bereft of the adventurous causes which are the heritage of adolescence, follow strange Gods. The Calf of Gold, with the approval of political leaders, is set up in the marketplace for all to worship. The sense of imperishable values, which have appealed to youth of all times, are lost in self-gratifying lusts. Our time is sick. We live in an age of outworn conventions. In 600 BC a New Age was born, and whenever that happens, its great men appear: Pythagoras and Buddha spoke for West and East. Our Christian Master brought the sword of contention to His time by opposing men and things good in their day but which men had outgrown. He brought in a New Age. *Their message is always a return to the ancient wisdom,* a plea for all men to say and mean 'I am a spiritual entity, superior to my physical body and its environment. I know this within myself—I will live by that inner knowledge'.

We are today at the beginning of a New Age. The problems of today are but the birth pangs of a new renaissance. Many of us live our daily lives in stultifying observance of common tasks and habit—routines in which we act like trained animals jumping through hoops—but most of us escape for some moments into the heights of elevated thoughts. 'There is a piece of Divinity within us that owes no homage to the Sun', said good old Sir Thomas Browne many years ago. Do we not all at times feel this to be true?

Modern life has divided mankind into two groups: (a) those who believe that all creation is 'chance' and purposeless, and (b) those who believe there is a purpose in our lives. This choice is one we all have to face. Are we 'accidents of an accident'? Is the best philosophy 'Eat, drink and be merry for tomorrow we die'? Or is the truth that this great cosmos in itself is proof of an underlying plan which permeates all existence, and to partake in which makes our lives meaningful and purposeful?

Mankind has recently passed through the 'infidel half-century', when a mechanistic philosophy ruled and Man, in his exultation at escaping the limitations of the 'All seeing *eye*' of the old religious concept, 'Threw the baby out with the bath water', to use Samuel Butler's great phrase. Mankind in its 'scientific' obsession placed all its eggs in the scientific basket: no longer was there need for a creator, since science would create for us; no longer was there need for preoccupations about eternal values, since science would create a 'New Utopia'. The phrase is that of H. G. Wells, who foisted upon his generation the image of the white-coated, bespectacled, benign, omniscient scientist working to make humanity a perfect environment, even perhaps to perfect man himself.

Wells was the popular romancer of this certainty of progress. This is exemplified by his titles: *The Food of the Gods, New Worlds for Old, The World Set Free, The Research Magnificent, Men Like Gods, The New World Order.* It is fair to say that he also wrote some excellent tales of simple folk in *Kipps, Tono Bungay,* and the superb *History of Mr Polly* but his real ability was to express, in most readable prose, the extraordinary vision of scientific power which was his, and which his fellow men wanted so much to hear.

Then came World War I. Something had gone wrong in Man's march to the New World Order. It was in the days of the war, and following the war, that Wells rose to his greatest. His *Mr Britling Sees It Through* did express the hope of many of the scientific intellectuals that *after* this holocaust it would be all right. Dimly they saw that what was needed was a fundamental 'World View'. What had happened was that the common man's background had not been sufficient. It is typical of Wells that he at once reacted. He produced, almost unaided, *The Outline of History,* which, despite its many biases, is a magnificent effort at simplification and clarity in telling Man's story. It produced fevered debate. It could only produce a sense of adventure and achievement. The years of reconstruction were his years—he was a prophet of whom every Western civilisation took notice, 'The Lonely Titan of the Western World', as one cartoon caption had it—and then came World War II.

Wells never recovered. He rethought his position. His scientific optimism fell away from him, and at the end of his great career he produced works of despairing gloom. He felt the need for a creed. He knew that there was something wrong with the glorious vision of free, mechanistic, scientific, eugenic, hygienic, evolving Man. There was something which, by its very nature, science had missed out. In his *Babes in the Darkling Wood* the young man cries out to the country Vicar for a creed:

> At the back of all there surely has to be a creed, a fundamental statement, put in language which doesn't conflict with every reality we know about the world. We don't want to be put off with serpents and fig leaves and sacrificial lambs. We want a creed in Modern English, Sir . . . and *we can't find it.*

So, through an *Anatomy of Frustration,* to the final documentation of *Mind at the End of its Tether*: 'the end of everything we call life is close at hand and cannot be evaded'. Finally his admission, his heartbreaking and heartbroken admission:

> Changes had ceased to be systematic . . . hitherto, events had been held together by a certain logical consistency . . . now it is as if the

cord had vanished and everything was driving anyhow to anywhere at a steadily increasing velocity.

This is the same man, who, in the days of Mr Polly, had believed that 'If you don't like your life you can change it'; who had strenuously searched for a creed; and who now found the whole of his grandiose conception of man 'the conqueror through science' to be an illusion, his hopes down in the dust of actual occurrence. Frustrated and defeated, he sees no hope. For him, in the last analysis, 'there is no way out or round or through'.

This famous statement of pessimistic fatalism is echoed by a declaration of that great humanist Bertrand Russell (Lord Russell), who prophesied man's future and his earth's future in these noble words:

> That man is the product of causes which had no prevision of the end they were achieving, that his origin and growth, his hopes and fears, his loves and beliefs are but the outcome of accidental collocations of atoms: that all the labour of the ages, all the devotion, all the inspiration, all the noon day brightness of human genius, are destined to extinction in the vast death of the solar system, that the whole temple of man's achievement must be inevitably buried beneath the debris of the Universe in ruins—all these things if not quite beyond dispute are yet so nearly certain that no philosophy which rejects them can hope to stand.

The author ventures to reject his concept. Note how the question is begged by such words as '*accidental* collocations of atoms'—modern science finds there is a plan in such 'collocations'—or again in the assumption that the destruction of the physical must mean the destruction of Man. There is a philosophy, an Ancient Wisdom, which denies completely Russell's dismal 'world of chance', with its ultimate destruction by 'an accident of an accident'. This is opposed by a belief that 'man shall scale to heights through the aeons of evolution which it is beyond our ability to imagine' (Teilhard de Chardin). If we consider for a moment, we all *know* that there is 'a piece of Divinity within us', and this course will plan how the 'imprisoned splendour' may escape from these gloomy materialistic forebodings.

Let us remember that science through its wisest expositors accepts that it is a continuing search for truth. It accepts that constant revision in the light of new fact must be its methodology.

Science has brought us many comforts and some illumination (also of course the atom bomb, pollution, germ warfare, destruction of the environment etc), but its dictates must never be erected as *barriers* to the advancement of the entity we call Man. True scientists know that theirs is a method of discarding forgotten so-called 'truths' and adopting new visions which may completely revolutionise past axioms: for example, in astronomy/cosmogony the Ptolemaic scheme (where the earth was the centre of the Universe) worked well for many centuries, until Copernicus brought the revolutionary teaching that the sun was the centre of the solar system and the earth revolved around it; many of his conclusions were in turn amended by Newton, and now Einstein has introduced an entirely new concept which includes the Galaxies. This will hold sway until, as Einstein has said himself, 'a new and better theory appears'. It is only the 'camp followers' of science who believe in its finality. Some years ago Professor Joad said: 'Common sense generally embodies the petrified science of fifty years ago and most of us today . . . instinctively assume that only material things are real.'

Only 50 years ago the physicists' obsession controlled the minds of men and they felt that 'material' was *the* 'fundamental'. As Professor Eddington has put it: 'As soon as men touched a piece of mechanism they felt "Here we are getting down to bedrock. This is what things ultimately resolve themselves into—this is the ultimate reality".'

It is fitting, and slightly humorous that it is the physicists themselves who have destroyed mechanistic philosophy. Eddington points out that this thinking is completely obsolete, as bad as Ptolemaic astronomy, because 'the ultimate bedrock—the red hard billiard ball of matter' has so disintegrated into other constituent parts that 'a modern physicist is obliged to think of "matter" in terms of a mathematical equation'; while another eminent physicist has said 'The next discoveries of physics and the future pronouncements may well be in terms of metaphysics'.

Most people will remember Eddington's famous explanation of his Two Tables *(Nature of the Physical World)*. He sits down at one, the familiar object of daily life, which has size, shape and colour and is considered to be real; but, says Eddington, 'I have another table'—his scientific table:

> My scientific table is mostly emptiness. Sparsely scattered in that emptiness are numerous electric charges rushing about with great speed, but their combined bulk amounts to less than a billionth of the bulk of the table itself . . .
>
> There is nothing substantial about my second table. It is nearly all empty space—space pervaded, it is true, by fields of force, but they are consigned to the category of 'influences' not of 'things'. In fact the scientific table is more like a swarm of flies. It supports objects by bombarding them with innumerable little blows from underneath. But even the minute part of the scientific table that is not empty is not 'substantial'; it consists of minute charges. Notwithstanding its strange construction, it turns out to be a thoroughly efficient table.

This view of modern physicists is basic thinking of the Ancient Wisdom (and therefore of this course), which believes that Man is very much more than the material atoms of his earth instrument—the physical body. We believe that we have powers, latent but completely within true man's nature, from which we can survey this world in all its various planes and manifestations; nay, indeed survey this Universe as a God—for a God is an entity who can control events, while a Man is an entity controlled by them!

In starting this course you must not be afraid of exalted moments, which one person finds in great poetry, another in great music, a third in great pictures, and a fourth in great literature. 'Bring me my purple robe, I have immortal longings in me' (Shakespeare), and John Masefield said 'The days that make us happy make us wise'.

Test all things for yourself. Listen to any man's philosophy, for you will learn something, but be bound by none. Erect no barriers of your own or another's, and lastly have no fear: rest confident in your real self, in your majestic 'I', which, remember, has a piece of Divinity within it; know yourself as a Son of God and therefore 'Cast out Fear'.

No coward soul is mine
No trembler in the world's storm-troubled sphere:
I see Heaven's glories shine
And faith shines equal, arming me from fear.

Oh God within my breast,
Almighty! ever present Deity!
Life—that in me has rest
As I—undying Life—have power in Thee!

Emily Brontë

Practical Work—Exercise Two

St Paul said that man was a unity composed of body, soul and spirit. The same thing was said by that great seer Pythagoras, but in geometrical terms. Pythagoras (560 BC) was trained in the Temples of Egypt, and, after esoteric adventures, settled on a site and founded what is now known as the 'School of Croton'. Every schoolboy knows he was famous for his mathematical genius, but this was but an outward symbol of his real wisdom—the wisdom of the occult. He is reputed to have said that 'all is number', and in these days, when we are beginning to understand that all is in fact 'vibration' and that such vibrations constitute the difference between materials in relation to the number of an atom's formative causes, we can easily comprehend one of his meanings.

Now we have to take the next step in correct breathing—further practice in vibratory tuning.

Exercise Two

We have learned and experienced that there are three regions—low, middle and high—which we can affect by intake of breath. We have now to create their unity in what most teachers call the 'complete breath'. Your procedure is as follows:

(a) Usual preliminaries—privacy is desirable.
(b) Stand erect (it is most important that the spine should be as straight as possible).
(c) Breathe in through the nostrils and endeavour to fill low, middle and high in one continuous inhalation. First inflate the lower part of the lungs, by using the diaphragm and then forcing the air upwards into the rib cage. Still inhaling, we now fill the higher part of the lungs, and you will find that this means a drawing in of the abdomen (all this has been experienced separately; we are now making a unity of the action).
(d) While for purposes of explanation we have spoken of three movements, this is completely untrue. *It is to be one continuous action,* and you may be helped as you breathe in if you count mentally One, Two, Three, Four.
(e) Assuming that you have been able to make the 'complete breath', now try to retain the breath filling the whole of your lungs while you count at least four.
(f) Exhale slowly.

You may find this exercise difficult for the first few times you attempt it, or you may find it easy if you have been taught correct breathing for, say, running or the art of singing. Whichever is your response, it is certain and true that within days you should be able to make the *complete breath.*

(g) Once this is achieved, make sure that you never breathe in any other way. In fact you will find that daily practice accomplishes this, and you will find an immediate betterment in health, in poise, in clarity of thought. These preliminary exercises are now commonplaces of science, but they have been used for centuries by occultists, and they have always had the hidden meaning as well as the outward benefit.

LESSON 3
Limitations of Theology

Exercise Three — Breathing—with sound use
Exercise Four — Breathing—with colour use

Not only do I leave the door open for the Christian message, but I consider it of central importance for Western Man. It needs however to be seen in a new light in accordance with changes wrought by the contemporary spirit; otherwise it stands apart from the times and has no effect upon man's wholeness.

Carl Gustav Jung. *Memories, Dreams and Reflections*

The mistake that 'orthodox' people make is to suppose that they have all the truth and that nothing more can be known.

Rev Dr W. R. Matthews, Dean of St Paul's

The measure of a man's religion is the measure of the extent to which he has been liberated from the tyranny of the small, egocentric self of everyday life.

Sri Aurobindo. *The Gita*

Children of Men! the unseen Power, whose eye
For ever doth accompany mankind
Hath looked on no religion scornfully
That men did ever find
Which has not taught weak wills how much they can?
Which has not fall'n on the dry heart like rain?
Which has not cried to sunk, self weary man
Thou must be born again.

Matthew Arnold. 'Progress'

Do you realise the number of barriers, self-made or environmental, which impede your attempts to think constructively? Everywhere there is an impetus to thrust the thinking of others upon you: the horror of the 'mass media' (what Priestley calls 'Admass') is an attempt to stop your thinking—individual thinking as opposed to mass concepts. These barriers operate from the first opening of our eyes upon the world: 'Shades of the prison-house begin to close upon the growing boy.'

The most potent of the environmental factors today are theology, science and so called 'commonsense'. All are reinforced by traditional or public relations mass-thinking. Let us consider these three limitations.

Theology

True religion is a different thing from the organisations and commentaries which compose a theology. The credos and dogmas imposed are often outside the moral and mystical principles of the religion they purport to explain.

Progress, whether material or spiritual, demands in all ages an overcoming of the barriers that previous thinking has erected. One of man's frailties is to consolidate thinking into an organisation which speedily declares that it possesses a monopoly of truth and a God-given mandate to impose it either by fear, dogmatism or, more recently, by mass publicity. The following story is told by Krishnamurti:

> . . . one day the Devil was out walking with his friend. The friend observed that a human being walking some way ahead suddenly stooped, picked something up and rose, clasping it to his breast with every sign of great elation. The friend, somewhat excited and perturbed, turned to the smiling and cynical Devil and observed: 'Look! did you see what that man picked up; he has found a piece of the *truth.*'
>
> 'Do not worry,' said his Satanic Majesty. 'I have arranged to have it organised.'

Mass organisations usually distort truth: it is the individual who finds it.

Socrates, whose nobility of character allowed him to be called a Christian before Christ, was nonetheless condemned to death for atheism. In his famous farewell speech to the jury, among many wise sayings, were these words: 'No evil can happen to a good man either in life or after death. His fortunes are not neglected by God.' Today, millions have read his parting words and know that he was no atheist, but only rebelled—in the same way as Christ rebelled—against the crudities of the organised theologies of his time.

Toynbee has pointed out that throughout history there have been periods when the crudities and dogmas of theologies, good in their day, have reached a stage at which the religious spirit has protested; and it is very necessary that we should make in this book a distinction between theologies that may be barriers to man's spiritual progress and religion, which is the everlasting light on the path of such efforts.

We live in a time in which the need to believe is acutely felt. We have previously quoted Jung's statement as to his psychiatric findings. Gordon Heidegger has stated that the meaning of anxiety, which is at the base of so much neurotic trouble today, is in fact the realisation of the self that it is not at home in a hostile and apparently purposeless world. Man has found that life has no meaning unless it has reference to a standard of purpose and of creative evolution that is the reality of the path to 'God'.

We need not be afraid to criticise our own theologies, for it is a historical fact that the great religious teachers have always been opposed to the theological dogma of their own time and to the practitioners of that dogma. This has not stopped mankind using their names in order to form organisations, and one may smile a little wryly and remember the story of Krishnamurti.

Most theological organisations, most priestcrafts, have governed by fear, ranging from the physical fears of an Inquisition to the mental fears of being outside the Establishment and its organised thinking. How very real this fear was, and how much damage it did to the cause of human enlightenment, can perhaps best be instanced by the case of Copernicus, because here was no physical hurt but only a terrible mental repression which, incidentally, might have put back human progress in the field of knowledge for many, many years.

Copernicus was a Polish scholar and Canon of a Cathedral, whose hobby was astronomy. In the course of his musings therein he came across an idea, an intuition, which was revolutionary in not only its concepts but its results. For many years the astronomy associated with the name of Ptolemy had held the field. Ptolemy had declared that the earth existed as a fixed body in the centre of the universe and that the heavens revolved round it every 24 hours. Not only did commonsense and observation apparently prove this to be true, but the Church accepted this theory, and it was a mortal sin to think anything else. Copernicus was a son of the Church, *yet* he knew in his heart that his new theory was correct, that Ptolemy and commonsense and the Church were wrong; the earth went round the sun as did the other planets.

Imagine, please, this poor shuddering son of the Church, obsessed in private with his sin against the teachings of Holy Church; fearful, in fact, of the vengeance the Church might take; and yet . . . yet so sure that he had a real insight. He wrote a book to prove his new theory; and although later ages have found it faulty in places, it was the foundation of all we call modern astronomy. For years he kept his writing secret, and only when at last he was drawing nigh to death did he dare to print it. According to hearsay, the first printed copy was placed in his hands the day he died. The Church, after a delay, forbade people to read it. It was this kind of losing battle that the Church fought against all the advances in human knowledge, and which earned the hatred of scholars until, finally, in the middle of the nineteenth century the cauldron seethed over: the men of science challenged the authority of the Church and of revealed religion, and our age went materialist.

The teachings of the Master are sometimes lost in the vast and ponderous temporal structures that have been raised in the name of Him who had no possessions.

Many of the bloodiest tragedies of history are to be laid at the feet of those in authority who claimed to speak in His name. It is a great merit of the Eastern religions that they are inclined to lay emphasis on experience rather than on authority, and do not refer, as does our Western religion, either to an infallible Book or to an infallible Pope.

The word 'infallible' is to be equated with the word 'unique' when we are talking about Christianity. The beautiful story of the Gospels, the sublime words of the Master, have been made the basis of an organised religion which has claimed completeness, although it is a historical fact that Constantine, to save his tottering Empire, incorporated many beliefs from other creeds and, indeed, from early in the history of the Church, Hellenism and Hellenistic philosophy contributed very largely to the early theology, and particularly to the interpretations of St Paul.

Because Jesus had a Jewish background, He had to accept its premise. Schweitzer says:

> The question whether Jesus thought eschatologically or not resolves itself, therefore, into the one point, whether He held Himself to be the Messiah, or not. Anyone who admits that He did so must also admit that His ideas and expectations were of the eschatological type of late Judaism. Anyone who refuses to recognise this element in His thought must also refuse to attribute to Him any consciousness of being the Messiah.

The claim of divine birth was one which He shared with such monsters as the Roman Emperor Caligula, and even His self-sacrifice as Hero-Saviour can well be paralleled in history, as Toynbee puts it in his *Study of History:*

> A very God who dies for different worlds under diverse names—for a Minoan World as Zagreus, for a Sumeric World as Tammuz, for a Hittite World as Attis, for a Scandinavian World as Balder, for a Syriac World as Adonis ('Our Lord'), for an Egyptiac World as

Osiris, for a Shi'i World as Husayn, for a Christian World as Christ.

Shaw has pointed out how the chief instrument of His torture and sacrifice, the Cross, has become a trademark for an institution of great temporal power. He had said: 'Contrasting the case with that of Socrates, one is forced to the conclusion that if Jesus had been humanely exterminated His memory would have lost ninety-nine per cent of its attraction for posterity.'

Men today are looking for a religion, but all known forms of the eleven religions (see below) have been battered out of shape for the moderns by their history and their inconstancies. The misfortune of this is that many thousands and thousands of religiously inclined young men and women turn in disgust from creeds which are guilty of such travesties as 'the resurrection of the body', and from biblical authorities which can portray God as a jealous monster and His prophets as monsters of cruelty, as in Joshua and the bears. The world still needs as avidly as ever the beautiful soul-redeeming messages of the Christ. But the superstructure raised in His name is obsolete: it shadows the beauty of His ethics and obliterates the mysteries of His teachings in favour of a creed and a dogma made in other ages for other men.

Christ lasts, as all the great teachers last, as long as one human shall draw breath. Not forever will the beauty of His work be lost in the disputations of antiquity, or the musings of men trying to prop up a falling edifice. In a New Age, crying amid the arid desert of materialism for a creed, we have to forget the institution and return to the Teacher.

THE ELEVEN LIVING RELIGIONS

Religion	*Date of Origin*	*Number of Adherents (millions)*
SHINTO	Prehistoric	17
JAINISM	Prehistoric (revised 600 BC)	1½
HINDUISM	3,000 BC	300
HEBRAISM	1,300 BC	16
CONFUCIANISM	600 BC	400
TAOISM	600 BC	impossible to estimate
ZOROASTRIANISM	600 BC	¼
BUDDHISM	600 BC	570
CHRISTIANITY	AD 30	500
ISLAM	AD 622	360
SIKHISM	AD 1420	6

All religions have taught the 'Golden Rule': consider this astounding list of quotations:

THE GOLDEN RULE

BUDDHISM Hurt not others with that which pains yourself.
Unanavarga, 5.18

CHRISTIANITY All things whatsoever ye would that men should do to you, do ye even so to them: for this is the law and the prophets.
Bible, St Matthew, 7.12

CONFUCIANISM Is there any one maxim which ought to be acted upon throughout one's whole life? Surely the maxim of loving-kindness is such. Do not unto others what you would not they should do unto you. *Analects,* 15.23

HEBRAISM What is hurtful to yourself do not to your fellow man. That is the whole of the Torah and the remainder is but commentary. Go learn it. *Talmud*

HINDUISM This is the sum of duty; do naught to others which if done to thee, would cause thee pain. *Mahabharata,* 5.1517

ISLAM No one of you is a believer until he loves for his brother what he loves for himself. *Traditions*

JAINISM In happiness and suffering, in joy and grief, we should regard all creatures as we regard our own self, and should therefore refrain from inflicting upon others such injury as would appear undesirable to us if inflicted upon ourselves. *Yogashastra,* 2.20

The Rev H. A. Williams has urged the need for revision, which might largely consist of using the words of Christ and not what men have said about them; it might also mean considering sympathetically the other ten religions, for at root their messages are the same. But it has 'paid' us as a race to feel superior to the dark skins, to adopt a 'holier than thou' attitude (consider South Africa today). The Rev Williams has said: 'Most of us have an enormous but unrealised vested interest in not recognising Christ when He comes to us in forms which our culture and civilisation disapprove. We allow ourselves to be too deafened by the music of the church organ to hear Him say "Why persecutest thou me?"'

The limitations of theology must, if one is to be honest to oneself, be recognised. We have talked so much about the narrow way that it is perhaps salutary to recognise that the Church has not necessarily followed it. To quote the Rev Williams again:

'Straight is the gate and narrow is the way', said Jesus, 'which leadeth into life, and few there be that find it'. The Churches,

> generally, preach something different: 'few there be that, having found it, have the moral courage to walk on it or remain walking on it, for it is easy enough to find, it is plain for all to see'. The ease and certainty with which the Churches point to the road, and their assumption that it is obvious to all men of goodwill, leads me to think that the road they thus recommend is not the narrow way at all but the wide gate and the broad way which leads to destruction.

The Age of Tribulation in which we live needs a religion of purpose to pit against and, in a sense, to compete with the lures of material comfort and its resultant apathy. It appears more and more probable that religion itself needs freeing from the theological shackles which impede its mission. The words of Buddha, of Lao-Tse and of Christ, contain all that mankind needs. It is a return to the sources and to a sense of underlying purpose that can be at once our balm and inspiration. Consider the noble words of Mahatma Gandhi:

> I may say that I have never been interested in an historical Jesus. I should not care if it was proved by someone that the man called Jesus never lived, and that what was narrated in the Gospels was a figment of the writer's imagination. For the Sermon on the Mount would still be true for me.

Remember that Picasso has said of his work that it is an attempt to piece together disintegration, that T. S. Eliot has written of a 'waste land', and that Jung has stated that at bottom spiritual lack is filling the beds in hospitals with nervous patients, and you will understand why an ageing theology must not limit the religious impulses of mankind in our time.

Introduction to Exercise Three

You are now in the theoretical sections, considering some of the self-made barriers of man; ponder, tolerantly, how custom, tradition, environment and the simple daily acceptance of the mass media's 'conditioning' affect the *real you.* The mind makes barriers of 'No Go' lands just as effective as the Berlin Wall, and from generation to generation is passed on the absurd idea that these barriers are static, absolute, not to be questioned. When one sees that in print, it is obviously nonsense, but perceive it in daily action and we shall realise how much it binds us, the best of us.

> The old order changeth, yielding place to new
> And God fulfils Himself in many ways,
> Lest one good custom should corrupt the world

said Tennyson, poetically stating that an outworn barrier which has been a protection can now become a hindrance. Pilate asked 'What is Truth?'

It was Heraclitus who declared, 'You cannot step twice into the same river for fresh waters are ever flowing in upon you'. This applies to every phase of life: physical (destruction of the cells every minute), mental (the upsurge of new ideas) and spiritual (evolving concepts of God's way with Man). As you study new aspects, new outlooks will conflict with your previous concepts. 'Stretch the Mind', says one great teacher. 'All is Becoming', says Buddha. All life as we know it is a constant flux; it is only to the Source that *Being* is given for 'He is That'.

Vibration is the law of all earthly happenings; vibration is everything. Every so-called solid form is a vibration (atomic construction), every thought is a vibration (think of how fear affects your body). *All* things are subject to this underlying secret.

We, as students, have to learn how to use vibrations, to raise them or to lower them to suit our own advancement and higher needs. This is why so far we have concentrated upon breathing—it is a fundamental need for vibratory control. You have no doubt by now found that complete breath is easy to use; you are, we hope, making it a habit.

We now wish to talk about movement and sound and colour, all at elementary but vital stages. *Do no exercise until you are sure the preceding one has been accomplished*—to do so is like whipping the water with a cane. So if you are ready, here is Exercise Three.

Exercise Three

1 Enter your sanctum and observe the usual preliminaries.
2 Make two or three trial complete breaths to assure you are calm and receptive.
3 Stand with your arms at your side, pointing floorwards, palms turned inwards, feet apart at an easy distance and slightly turned outwards.
4 As you start to inhale *(slowly please)*, raise your arms so that when your inhalation is finished, your arms are stretched outwards and you are in a 'cross' position with palms downwards.
5 While holding your breath, slowly turn the palms of the hands face upwards and complete the movement as you reach the end of your retention of breath period.
6 *Slowly* exhale, and as you do so gradually lower the arms back to original position, except for the reversed palms *(this is difficult)*.
7 Turn the palms back to their original position and as you do so *loudly say* either 'Aum' or 'Amen', splitting the words into two syllables and making each long-drawn-out and distinct (Hoooooooooo-Mmmmmmmmmmmm and Ahaaaaaaaaaa-Mmmmmmmmmmmmen).

These directions must be carried out exactly. They are vital for the tuning of your instrument. Think of this exercise as the tuning up of the

GLASS (MATERIAL) PRISM

WHITE LIGHT

VIOLET
INDIGO
BLUE
GREEN
YELLOW
ORANGE
RED

PLANES OF MANIFESTATION

CREATIVE CONSCIOUSNESS

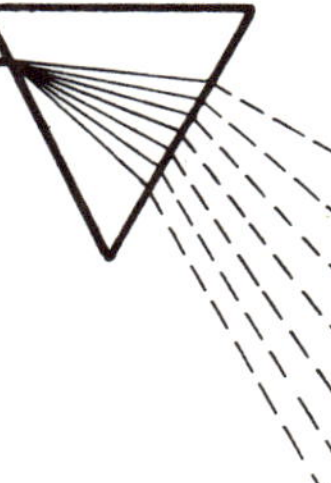

DIVINE
MONADIC
ATMIC
BUDDHIC
MENTAL
ASTRAL
PHYSICAL

VEHICLES OF MAN

PRANA-FOHAT LIFE FORCE

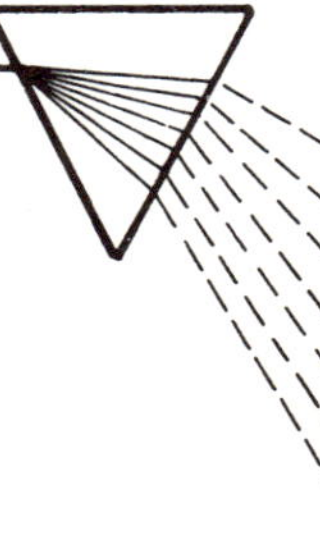

SPIRITUAL
INSPIRATION
HIGHER INTUITION
MENTAL ABSTRACT
MENTAL CONCRETE
ASTRAL
PHYSICAL

(Fig 1)

orchestra before the Musical Director appears and the overture begins. This was one of the things Walt Whitman meant when he said 'I am my own Orchestra'—he knew the value of 'tuning up'.

Exercise Four

We are now going to combine our breathing and movement with colour. Let us digress for a moment, appositely one hopes.

What is the phenomenon we call 'Colour'? It is vibration, as recognised and translated by the optic nerves. A great seer has said 'The colour is not in the rose but in ourselves'.

Try an experiment. Get a sheet of white paper, a glass prism (usually you can also do this with any cut-glass ornament) and an electric torch with a small beam (a pocket torch is best). Now shine the white light of the torch at one side of the prism and you will find it has split into seven colours—what we call the 'spectrum'—on the other side of the paper (Fig 1); a free and glorious example of this is the rainbow.

Like everything else in this world, there are some 'colours' the eye cannot 'see'—indeed everything in our experience is limited by our five-sense-brain. In this case we can use and know *but not see* the adjacent colours, and we call them 'ultra violet' and 'infra red'. This is a promise that all ESP is awaiting Man's use if he will learn it is there and how to use it. Colour vitally affects our lives, as the medical profession informs us (it was also well understood in the Egyptian Temples). We shall return to the question of colour later, but we hope you understand that we can control breath and movement and colour *as a Unity* because they are all vibrations.

Let us then proceed to the second part of our exercise. WARNING!!! It is not wise to start upon this until you are sure you can do part one (above). In this age of haste, purposeless haste, probably seven or ten days should suffice, but the writer's Masters made this a seven times a day exercise for forty-nine days before allowing any further progress in vibrations. But, again, what I then learned has lasted for sixty years.

1 Use the complete breath with movement as given in the first part of Exercise Three; practise thoroughly three such breaths from the preliminaries to the turning of the palms and the word-mantra ('Aum' or 'Amen').
2 Now again, while making a complete movement, breathe in, and as you raise your arms, visualise a flood of light, thrush-egg blue, rising around your body at the same level as your arms have reached. Some pupils find it easier to think of raising a blind of colour, some as raising a sea of colour, *but* it must keep pace with the raising of the arms, which is in complete rhythm with the raising of the breath.

3 As you hold your breath, let the colour change to purple almost like a ruff around your neck but extending further if possible. It must be a gentle, embracing pastel purple.
4 As you start to exhale, see a primrose yellow, pure but not too bright, keeping time with your breath and the downward movement of your arms.
5 When you have reached the end of the exhalation, slowly turn the palms and think of your abdomen as shrouded in a circle of gentle embracing white—this while you are mentally or vocally intoning your word-mantra, as previously described.
6 After you have accomplished this unified movement of breath and arms and colour for seven days (as many times a day as are possible), *reverse the entire process,* namely inhale to yellow, hold or retain to white, exhale to blue and clothe abdomen in purple. This exercise should also be done for a minimum of seven days.
7 When you have completed this, alternate the colours daily for eight days and complete your octave.

The reason for the exchange of colours is that all men are divided into two distinct groups—one might nominate them 'receivers' and 'senders' or, as Jung did, introverts and extroverts. Neither group is better that the other; it is that they develop (at higher levels) in different ways. The sooner you know which colours suit you the better, for you will make faster progress.

LESSON 4
Limitations of Science

Exercise Five Cleansing Breath and Rate Control

It is clear therefore, that expressions such as 'scientific truth' should be taken only in a limited sense. *There is no scientific truth in the absolute sense.*

Without the presence of man—who is the receiving set, the recording instrument and the co-ordinator—the phenomena which constitute his science do not exist as isolated phenomena.

An explanation of the evolution of life by chance alone is untenable today. Lecomte du Nouy. *Human Destiny*

. . . a science or a knowledge system which has no place for will or purpose is an obstruction to human evolution and at this particular point in history, a dangerous nuisance. Colin Wilson. *The Occult*

The principle of the conservation of energy was established as a certainty, solid as a rock . . . and yet, here was radium producing energy without acquiring it from any source. No one doubted that light and electricity were identical: they could only proceed in a straight line . . . and yet here were *'X rays'* which could go through solid objects.

The scientists who were supposed to have a monopoly of knowledge suddenly ceased to make a distinction between physics and metaphysics.

Pauwels and Bergier. *The Morning of the Magicians*

Science is the best tool of the Western mind and with it more doors can be opened than with bare hands . . . it only clouds our insight when it lays claim to being the one and only way of comprehending. It is the East that has taught us another, wider, more profound and a higher understanding, that is understanding through life.

Carl Gustav Jung

The results of the scientific method of exploration of Man and the wonders of his Universe are too well known to us both in their good (increased comfort) and bad (atom bomb) effects to need any further comment. When science deals with inanimate matter, it is truly effective: wisely educative and practically valuable.

It is very hard for people of this generation to enter into the thinking of the Victorians, who saw science coming not only as a great freeing of human drudgery, but as a great freeing of the human spirit. Today we know that materially they were right; science has offered Man freedom from the age-old curse of labour. The shoemaker of ancient Rome took five and a half days to make a pair of shoes. Every individual in the Bata Shoe Works makes ninety pairs of shoes per week. The ancient miller ground out a barrel and a half of indifferent flour in his working day. A modern flour mill in Buffalo produces 15,000 barrels per day, per man, and of better flour. Science has wrought revolutions in transport and communication which alone can make 'one world' a possibility, and it has offered, to the Western nations at any rate, a full life with ample opportunity for leisure. But we now know there is a spiritual cost, a despair and a sense of futility, which Professor Toynbee has pointed out so well, to debit against the material gain. It is completely wrong to undervalue the gifts of science or blame them for our *malaise,* but it is the attitude of material shallowness which creates the illness.

The conquest of distance, equally, is something so fantastic that it has literally caught up with the imagination of space fiction. The advent of Man upon the moon and the possibility of his travelling to the other planets of our system, and perhaps, ultimately, further, has now become a commonplace of ordinary thinking; but, most importantly perhaps for man's future, the improvement in communications, the speed with which people can get from one part of the world to another, the ability to broadcast and televise to another part of the world at the time the event happens, has resulted in a situation in which we must either accept one world, with all that means in world government and lack of national power, or we must continue to live upon the volcano which contains ever more dreaded and more powerful weapons of destruction.

The Victorian compromise produced Empiricist philosophers who took science as their fundamental, and portrayed most confidently an actual heaven of economic and material value on earth, although postulating inevitable futility in a purposeless Universe. It is when science leaves the facts of the material world and deals with the world of causation and values that she oversteps her boundaries. Not so many years ago science invented the 'Economic Man', surely the grisliest abstraction that ever emerged from the mind of the expert—a Frankenstein monster who had pockets for a heart and a bank book for a Bible. Well, that nonsense is dead, but much of the so-called 'science' dealing with life is equally foolish. T. W. N. Sullivan says in *Limitations of Science*:

> Many of the questions which seem to us to be fundamental have not been met. What, for instance, makes us regard a living organism as a whole and not as a sum of its parts? What does this notion of 'wholeness' or 'individuality' really amount to? Even if every bodily activity of the animal was explained in terms of physical and chemical changes we should feel our question was unanswered unless what appears as the purposive order of those changes was also accounted for. But 'purpose' is not yet a scientific notion.

This effort of science to deal by means of its method of classification with the uniqueness of the individual is certain to produce wrong results. As Needham says, in *The Sceptical Biologist*:

> If the scientific mind is faced with five hundred balls of all shades of grey from pure black to pure white, it will separate them into groups of grey *but these are discontinuous,* whereas from the commonsense point of view, one could not have less than five hundred groups, for *all the balls are different* by definition.

This method of classification, of the application of the methods of physics and chemistry to life, has been castigated by Professor Whitehead who says in *Science and the Modern World* that within the limits of the sciences named,

> The brilliant success of the method is admitted *but* you cannot limit a problem by reason of a method of attack. The problem is to understand the operations of an animal body. There is clear evidence that certain operations of certain animal bodies depend upon *the foresight of an end and the purpose to attain it.* The existence of the problem is not even acknowledged. Many a scientist has patiently designed experiments for the *purpose* of substantiating his belief that animal operations are motivated by no purposes . . . Scientists animated by the purpose of proving that they are purposeless constitute an interesting subject for study.

Note that science not only classifies all its data, but classifies arbitrarily. In fact it seeks to emphasise not factual differences but imposed similarities, concentrating on one aspect only, to the exclusion of all others—and those may render it unique.

Apart, however, from this method of classification, there is an arbitrary abstraction arising from it which has been summarised by Eddington, with his usual wit and grace, in his parable of an elephant sliding down a slope. Suppose a physicist wishes to give his explanation of this phenomenon. For the elephant he takes a weight, say two tons, for the sloping hillside an angle of say 60 degrees, and for the softness of the turf a coefficient of friction; so that by using these pointer readings he is able to tell us how long the elephant will be in getting to the bottom. The joy and humour of the spectacle, the glory of the hillside basking in the sun, the portentous solemnness of the sliding animal, interest him not at all. His answer is given in mechanistic terms, for *science is uninterested* in the elephant and the hillside except in such terms. Moreover, even the terms which are used are terms of the *physicist's* own mind; they are symbols of real things and do not bring us into touch with reality at any time.

Again, let us consider a musical composition. Consider how science deals with this and what it can tell us about it. The analysis can only be given in purely abstract mechanical phraseology, and the whole beauty of the music, the profound emotional and artistic significances which it creates for the listener, the communication between maker and recipient, are all for science things of no account. *But it is exactly those things which are* a piece of music. By its nature and enforced desire science cannot provide a complete picture, only a series of sections, and above all, for our human purposes, *it cannot accept any concept of aesthetic value*.

If we are prepared to accept human life as being the 'accident of an accident', this consideration will perhaps have little meaning, although it is difficult to consider any species of hedonistic life which does not include values. But if we believe, however little, that there is some sort of purpose in the vast Universe, then the mere fact that science cannot speak of values is sufficient to make us realise that it *cannot* be a final authority as to our lives. Indeed, the first people to recognise this *were* very qualified and famous exponents of the scientific method.

Science has, of course, realised this. It can only study Plato's 'shadows' on the wall of the cave with greater exactitude than does normal experience and, even then, without touching reality.

Probably the greatest single force with which applied science has done wonders is the force of electricity. Let us think for a moment of the advantages electricity has brought into our daily lives: transport, communication, light and heat. So many marvellous *uses* have been found for this force that one feels science has explored it to the 'nth' degree. *But in fact no scientist can tell us what electricity is.*

Risking repetition, please remember Eddington's famous explanation of his two tables in *The Nature of the Physical Universe.* This familiar object of daily life, which we consider to be real (there are reservations, as we shall see in the next chapter) is contrasted with the scientific table:

> It is a more recent acquaintance . . . My scientific table is mostly emptiness. Sparsely scattered in that emptiness are numerous electric charges rushing about with great speed, but the combined bulk amounts to less than a billionth of the bulk of the table itself. Notwithstanding its strange construction it turns out to be an entirely efficient table.

While there are still those eminent men who would take refuge in a materialistic explanation of life, it can be said that for the majority matter has become so inexplicable, so tenuous, so almost non-matter, that we start to think of it as a projection of consciousness. Professor Joad has said in *Guide to Modern Thought*:

> *Today the foundation for this way of thinking (mechanistic causation)* of the hard obvious simple lumps of matter has disappeared. Modern matter is something infinitely attenuated and elusive; it is a hump in space time, a 'mush' of electricity, a wave of probability undulating into nothingness: frequently it is not matter at all but a projection of the consciousness of its perceiver. So mysterious indeed has it become that the modern tendency to explain things in terms of mind is little more than a preference for explanation in terms of the less unknown rather than the more.

So this is the reversal of the position. Science, which offered to Victorian man a complete solution to all his difficulties, and a hard understandable philosophy, has itself become as incomprehensible to the ordinary layman as the visions of the mystics. Every student should read *Supernature* (Hodder and Stoughton, 1973), in which Dr Lyall Watson, a biologist, shows how, in the course of much research, he has discovered certain facts which, to quote the *Los Angeles Times,* 'accomplishes a redefinition of the frontier. Instead of the old borders, there is a kind of demilitarised zone into which occultists and scientists may go without clubbing each other into insensibility'. Dr Watson, who would think of himself as a materialist-scientist, has arrived at the conclusion that 'Science no longer holds any absolute truths' and finds that 'Supernature is nature with all its flavours intact, waiting to be tasted. I offer it as a logical extension of the present state of science'; or again, 'As man uses up the resources of the world he is going to have to rely more and more upon his own. Many of these are at present concealed in the occult — a word that simply means "secret knowledge" and is a very good description of something that we have known all along but have been hiding from ourselves.'

Let us then, while accepting with due recognition the wonders of the scientists, recognise that science, though well adapted to dealing with physical things, is not only less successful when dealing with the 'values' of life but can be positively harmful; for its method of dealing with 'parts' misses the fact that those parts are but items in a whole of infinitely greater possibility than the parts themselves. *We* must realise that there is purpose and value which are not covered by scientific method, for as J. B. Priestley has said in *Over the Long High Wall*:

> . . . let us have done with the self hypnotising notion that anything which cannot be tested in a laboratory may be ignored, its very existence denied. (The worst offenders are not the physicists nor even the biologists but the fringe men.) We should be respectful, admiring, grateful, to science when it is minding its own business. But as soon as it tries to turn itself into a dogmatic ersatz-religion, it is not minding its own business. And inevitably it behaves badly; though here I would acquit almost all the upper ranks of scientists; it is the lower ranks and all the philosophical and psychological camp followers who so often are at once arrogant and stupid.

Exercise Five

It is desirable at this stage to give you an exercise which is called the 'cleansing breath'. You will know that in many novels a character who has been under strain will utter a noise which the novelist calls 'pouf' — a breath of relief and the ordeal is over. The exercise is like that.

At the termination of many of our exercises it will help to use the cleansing breath. There are several varieties recommended by different teachers, but, liking simplicity, we recommend the following:

1 Inhale a complete breath as previously taught (do not forget preliminaries).
2 Retain as before for your allotted seconds.
3 Then, instead of exhaling as before, pucker up your lips as though you were going to whistle.
4 With force expel a little of the retained breath in a soundless whistle, then stop.
5 Repeat this 'whistle' exhaling until the breath is gone.

At first sight this appears to be somewhat trivial, but in fact it is a most important part of your armoury of psychic breaths. It will act as a refresher whenever you use it. It demands the same amount of practice as the other exercises in breathing previously given.

In this exercise you may incorporate consideration of your *rate of breathing*. The advanced student can breathe so slowly that he hardly seems to breathe at all. Normally we are told a person takes sixteen to eighteen breaths a minute. This rate is excessive if we are to make the best of every breath, and a student by the end of this course should be able to breathe at ten a minute. The results in ordinary life are excellent: 'irritability' the curse of our tension-laden time disappears, and matters are viewed more dispassionately than before. Control of breath is vital for purely physical wellbeing—consider a weightlifter, who will always pause, take a deep breath and hold it *before* he assays his lift.

So consider your breathing and try to breathe more and more slowly and regularly. It will be of enormous advantage in your quest.

LESSON 5
Limitations of Commonsense

Exercise Six Pranic Breathing

All we know is still infinitely less than that which remains unknown. The studious never think it unworthy to change their opinion if truth requires them to do so. Goethe

Whatever the humblest of men may tell me from their own experience I will listen to with attention: whatever the humblest of men may tell me from their own experiment I will adopt with attention but what the bumptious man may tell me from his opinion I disregard, for 'opinion' is a word which is used to mask prejudices and is most often in the mouths of those who have done nothing for themselves but only read, and sometimes half read, the ideas of others. Einstein

Let me exhort everyone to do their utmost to think outside and beyond our present circle of ideas.

Richard Jeffries. *Story of My Heart*

Our highest truths are but half truths, think not to settle down in any truth. Make use of it as a tent in which to pass a Summer's night. But build no house of it, or it will be your tomb. When you first have an inkling of its insufficiency and begin to descry a counter-truth looming up behind; then weep not, but give thanks. It is the Lord's voice whispering 'take up thy bed and Walk'.

Lord Balfour

The man in the street is not likely to be affected greatly by our considerations of the limitations of theology and of science, although, in practice, his everyday life is completely conditioned by them. His material comforts and material endeavours are shaped in those applications of science which surround him, while any hope of a spiritual life must be affected by the religious climate engendered by the theologians of the day.

Most of us, however, are creatures of five senses, and although we realise that, in fact, these cramp us into a preconceived pattern, we nonetheless accept them gratefully because, by so doing, we live in a familiar world, whose fundamentals we do not have to think about.

The mechanism of our five senses is awe-inspiring, surely a lasting portrayal of the purpose which created our instrument. Awe-inspiring in their action but restrictive in their use. We are like a prisoner in a tower, and our only contact with an outside world, our only knowledge of it, is obtained through five slits in our dungeon walls—the slits of our five senses. We know there is a great outside world of experience and movement and causes, but for most of us the world is winnowed down to *what we can gain* through those five slits and our interpretation of that small knowledge. Modern science has shown us through its instruments how small that actual experience is, how little a portion of true reality our five senses allow us to know. As you read this, your room or your great outside of garden or woodland is filled with music and singing and talking, of which you have no cognisance; but go to your radio or television set and switch it on and all these voices and instruments will become apparent to you. An electromagnetic instrument has seized upon the wandering waves (which were too elusive for your restricted five senses) and forced them into audible expression.

The reader will probably know that the Eastern religions distinguish between the self and the not-self, and they call all that is not-self 'maya', which may be translated 'illusion'; but for Western man this outlook appears ridiculous. For him, the five senses and things he can touch, taste, smell, see and hear, are his Universe. It was for this reason that he adopted so eagerly his misconceptions of the teachings of the Victorian scientists who, when they offered him the 'hard, red billiard balls of matter', were introducing him to something he could appreciate. When he was told that all material forms, and even life itself, could be created in a laboratory, he felt he was done with all 'airy-fairy' nonsense and had reached a commonsense viewpoint.

Tyrrell, in his *Grades of Significance,* gave an interesting analogy to assist the comprehension of his question. He pointed out that commonsense really acts towards us like our nurse or governess and, in fact, 'in every daily occupation, the more we have taken her advice, the better we have found it. So accustomed have we become to her guiding hand that it is difficult to imagine a situation in which we could call on her in vain, and yet the fact is that there is a definite limit to her trustworthiness; she is sovereign only over a limited estate and when the boundary is crossed, her guidance becomes worse than useless'. The five senses equip us to deal with the physical world only.

Like a good governess, Mrs Commonsense wants us to 'get on' in this world. Alarmingly, however, her successful charges develop neuroses; they find in practice that the rational relies upon non-rational elements. They begin to realise that Mrs Commonsense is a limited tutor whose ideas are carefully kept within her station.

In the Victorian era it looked as if commonsense was being reinforced by science, but today we know, of course, that science presents the Universe in a way so opposed to ordinary thinking that it has outdistanced the mystics, so far as the layman is concerned, for incomprehensibility of statement. Indeed, most statements in physics can only be understood by someone with a first-class knowledge of mathematics. Eddington says:

> In dissecting matter into electric charges we have travelled far from that picture of it which first gave rise to the conception of substance, and the meaning of that conception—if it ever had any—has been lost on the way. The whole trend of modern scientific views is to break down the separate categories of 'things', 'influences' and 'forms' etc., and to substitute a common background for all experience. Whether we are stating a material object, a magnetic field, a geometrical figure, or a duration of time, our scientific information is summed up in measures.

And it is noteworthy that since Eddington's writings, later discoveries have tended away even from the 'bulk' of electrons and nuclei. Professor Bohm, in his *Causality and Change in Modern Physics,* has pointed out: 'Thus, even in physics, it has been discovered that beneath the atomic level lies the level of the so-called elementary particles and, as we shall see later . . . there seems to be a new and, as yet, very barely known level even below that of these elementary particles.' At a later stage in the same book, he says:

> Thus, in the last century, only mechanical, chemical, thermal, electrical, luminous and gravitational energies were known. Now we know of nuclear energy which constitutes a much larger reservoir, but the infinite substructure of matter very probably contains energies that are as far beyond nuclear energies as nuclear energies are beyond chemical energies.

So science is now on the border line of a new set of energies, which completely destroy the material basis as it is conceived by Mrs Commonsense and her pupils. Now that the 'substantiality' of matter has been eradicated, commonsense must seek for new definitions to explain our physical surroundings, and the basis of the materialist or mechanistic Universe has vanished.

Many animals are better equipped than we are: a spider can feel tremors at the edge of his web to which our sense of touch would remain oblivious; an eagle's sight or a vulture's so far outstrips our own as to make the comparison ludicrous. In other words our senses, marvellous though they are, are *organs of limitation* allied to and only responsive to a selective brain mechanism which is the result of group and personal environment.

What really happens when you see another person? You look at another person but you never 'see' them—what happens is that an impression of vibrations caused by the refraction of light from the person at whom you are looking travels to your eyes as refracted light rays and there impinges upon the eye, activating the responses of the nerve structure in the retina. From this selective instrument impulses are passed along the nerves to the brain, which assembles them into a brain-picture which we have been taught to recognise as the other person. The same thing applies to sound. When your piano string vibrates, it causes ripples which are picked up by your ear mechanism, and once again the vibratory strengths, lengths and depths go along the respective nerve centres to the brain. Your evolutionary training teaches you to picture what the sound impulses mean in a familiar 'word', but if the person making sounds is a foreigner, you have no brain image to picture the word he is trying to convey. All our senses are instruments of limitation.

Because you are responsive to the notes of a piano, you will hear one note as being different from another—one will be higher in pitch, say. *But* a 'tone deaf' person will hear nothing different at all, for all the notes will be 'noise'; to you the succession will create a recognisable tune, but to your friend they may mean nothing whatsoever. This is not the end of the story, however. There will be sounds which are too subtle for the mechanism of our ears to handle, though a dog may hear them, and science has perfected an instrument which not only spots 'sounds' much too high for our response mechanism but can actually be used for industrial purposes.

Consider how limited is our sense of smell. For the writer, it is always a joy to read Gilbert K. Chesterton's 'The Song of Quoodle', the dog:

> They haven't got no noses,
> The fallen sons of Eve.
> Even the smell of roses
> Is not what they supposes,

But more than mind discloses,
And more than man believes.

The brilliant smell of water,
The brave smell of a stone,
The smell of dew and thunder,
The old bones buried under,
Are things in which they blunder
And err, if left alone.

The same is true of sight; the differing vibratory results of the spectrum are well known to most people and their differences and nomenclature common usage, but to some persons the vibrations do not link up with an image and we say they are 'colour blind'. Again this is not the end of the story, for science has perfected instruments which 'see' colours beyond our spectrum and so have the ability to classify and use 'ultra violet' and 'infra red'.

Our brain mechanisms are trained to receive certain vibrations *and not others:* they can accept certain stimuli and put a name to them but some remain outside the brain's classification, 'latent' octaves of vibration so far as the five-sense brain is concerned. Henri Bergson has said that the brain is *not* an instrument of action but that its function is to *limit* our mental life to what is practically useful. Tyrrell in his excellent *Grades of Significance* says:

> The world which is commonly taken to be revealed to us by our bodily senses is . . . a picture with the additions of various colours, outlines, contacts and other sensations which we receive and then there is an *interpretative* reaction on our part . . . This perceived and conceived world I have called the 'domain of Common *sense*' . . .

He then tells how science itself took the world of commonsense for granted, just as does the ordinary man, and from that viewpoint science constructed a materialistic philosophy, which we have spoken about in the first lesson, and boasted of its expected ability to construct a purely mechanistic world—the hope of the Wellsian reformers.

> Both the scientist and the plain man had been holding on unquestioningly to the hand of Commonsense while the scientist had been edging her nearer and nearer to the unsuspected frontier of her kingdom. *One day they hustled her across it* . . . and . . . thereafter slowly awoke to the truth that their long trusted friend had failed them at last.

Nowadays the physicists are announcing to a bewildered (common-sense) humanity that they find themselves in a world where 'common-sense' is almost unknown. Bernard Lovell, the eminent British scientist, has proclaimed that the next discoveries of physics may well be allied to metaphysics. Some of us think they already *are*.

Scientific man has realised the inadequacy of the five senses. He invented the telescope to survey the Universe, and the microscope to survey the drop of water. With radio and telephone he has increased the world of hearing and with TV the range of distance.

The great problem is that whatever happens to us through extra-sensory perceptions has to be assessed through the reluctant, obstructive five-sense brain, so that *all* interpretations are likely to be influenced by 'habit'. Our assessments will be the product of the original ESP vision or illumination, but our recognition of the facts will be affected and limited by the inability of the brain to image the unknown and unexpected facts. Every ESP phenomenon has to suffer this limitation, which is the result of years and years of environmentally controlled life, both among races and individuals.

Equally in this study you must be aware of the limitations of language, because all the words we use are geared to earth interpretations and every mystic, every occultist, suffers from this. Misinterpretations, misconceptions will pervert everything you are trying to say, because there are no earthly words to express super-earthly experiences. Impressions coming to the mystico-occultist are so instantaneous that it is extremely easy to rationalise them away. People will say, 'Ah well, there is a scientific explanation of that', but you will find on examination that science has *no* explanation but only a definition, a pompous technological word that does *not* explain. Remember that science cannot *explain* electricity, only use it.

In this confusion, which enables modern man to echo *Hamlet*

> The time is out of joint; O cursed spite,
> That ever I was born to set it right!

we must go back to first principles. We have to reassess reality.

Perhaps we have to go back to Plato, 'the wisest man that ever lived', and to realise that from the beginning the wisest have known intuitively that so-called reality was not reality at all. The analogy of 'The Cave' applies with even more force today than in the age for which Plato wrote. May I remind the reader that Plato imagined some prisoners were chained in a large cave in such a position that they could only look straight ahead of them. In the outer, real world, which was behind their backs, people about their daily business passed between them and a great fire, casting shadows on the wall of the cave, shadows to which the men who were chained gave names and roles and destinies. 'So', said

Plato, 'is our world. We see only the shadows of the real, and equate them with reality itself.'

Anyone who looks at a cinema screen or at a television set can experience for themselves this illusion, in which the shadows cast upon the screen seem to be discussing and talking and doing. Our senses are traitors, and, in order to actualise these 'shadows', limit our perceptions by rationalising them into a pattern of accepted thinking. Man erects his own mental barriers and stands before them immobilised by his own taboos.

All our lives are conditioned and self-limited by barriers of class or race, of upbringing or of personal habit, and we consolidate these restrictions into observances which we call 'commonsense'. This gives us a frame of reference, and selects for itself the things that are to be called real. The scientific mind abstracts and classifies in mathematical fashion, and creates its own particular reality, which often can only be expressed by a mathematical formula. The theological mind makes a frame of reference also, to which it has added the imposing but very dangerous proviso that its frame is, in fact, the only eternal truth.

In fact, as you study further, you will find all these limitations bear within them the seeds of defeat. While we must never minimise what we owe to theology, to science, even to commonsense, we must also know that there is a higher set of values which can be realised and in which we can participate by the correct approach. It is necessary, however, first of all to cleanse one's mind of previous static thinking and to realise that there are more things in heaven and earth than most of us have ever dreamed about.

One is reminded of that delightful comment from Shaw's *St Joan* when the fighting Monseigneur de la Tremouille queries the Archbishop of Rheims who says something about Pythagoras:

LA TREMOUILLE:	And who the deuce was Pythagoras?
ARCHBISHOP:	A sage who held that the world is round, and that it moves round the Sun.
LA TREMOUILLE:	What an utter fool! Couldn't he use his eyes?

All the audiences at *St Joan* laugh heartily at La Tremouille's *faux pas,* but let us remember he is arguing a very commonsense case.

Advancing knowledge will move back all Man's self-made barriers, which are the limitations of commonsense, of theology and of five-sense science.

Exercise Six

This is our last breathing exercise, but a vital one. Correct breathing is not only a preliminary to every exercise that follows, but is an essential of our transformation in daily life to one who has entered 'The Path'.

'Prana' has acquired several meanings, and Yogi Ramacharaka discusses them with authority in *Science of Breath.* The Sanscrit translation is that understood in this course, namely 'absolute energy', which, allied with its twin of 'fohat', gives the power of creation which we have called the 'Life Force'. One great teacher indeed has called Prana 'the *soul bricks* of creative energy'.

You use prana every moment of the day, for it is in the air you breathe (this is why we benefit from breathing the pure air of a mountain top); it is in your food and drink, and in the cosmic rays which permeate all nature. One may *store* prana, just as one may store electricity; indeed you will all know people who seem to have 'magnetic energy', usually because consciously or unconsciously they have stored prana. To store prana one must know how to breathe in rhythm, and how to direct the resultant energy—so read the exercise carefully and prana 'the *soul bricks* of creative energy'.

1 Lying on the floor or your bed, start breathing in rhythm. You may now have acquired your own—many use a mental count of four for inhaling, four (or up to eight) for holding and four for exhaling. Make a circuit and your unconscious will rapidly adopt it. You will 'feel' the tranquillity which comes when the circuit is working easily.
2 Now make a 'tent' of your hands with the fingertips just *not* touching (⅛in apart), fingers separated and stretching towards the ceiling.
3 While continuing the rhythmic circuit of breathing, *will* that the pranic power be localised in your tented hands. (You may feel the resultant heat, in some cases as though you held a hot tennis ball in between them.)
4 Place the 'tent' on your solar plexus (nerve centre). 'Perceive' the heat from the tent rushing into the plexus and thence all over your body.
5 Sincere practice on this exercise should, after some seven nights, result in the acceptance of the correct procedure by your unconscious (second nature).
6 When this automatic circuit has been achieved, move the locale. Now place the 'tent' over your heart; again mentally spread the prana heat all over the body, though as you now have a different point of entry you are vitalising new forces.
7 It is wise to alternate these two 'entries' for at least ten days.
8 When the unconscious has again accepted this 'instruction' (habit track), place your tented hands over your throat. *This time, however, feel the pranic force from the throat linking with the heart and solar plexus* of previous locations, and the whole acting in continuous movement as a circuit of power.
9 After each effort use the cleansing breath.

Do not try too long — ten minutes at a time is recommended — but the exercise may be beneficially done half a dozen times a day (certainly in the morning before rising and at night before going to sleep). You will feel practical physical results, but you are also storing power against future exercises and for the use of your higher vehicles.

VERY IMPORTANT — read carefully, and practise regularly and precisely.

LESSON 6
'Towards the Horizon'

Exercise Seven The Triangle

A point has arrived in twentieth century thought when a completely new impulse and direction is needed. It may well be that future generations will describe the first half of the twentieth century as 'the age of meaninglessness'. There is a general feeling that the certainties provided by religion have been lost and can never be replaced. Science by solving our practical problems, can only make the inner void more painfully obvious. It seems self evident that in the sense of purpose, of inner direction western culture has been running at a heavy loss for at least a hundred years—it is a matter of speculation how long it can go on before becoming completely bankrupt.

Colin Wilson. *The Outsider*

Let us then, avoiding fear and superstition on one hand and arid scepticism on the other, ask ourselves the questions about extra sensory happenings and, more importantly, experiment for ourselves. All true research is on the path of individual experiment.

Dennis Barden. *Research of 40 Years*

. . . It may be
Beyond that last blue mountain barred with snow
Across that angry or that glittering sea
White on a throne, or guarded in a cave
There lives a prophet who can understand

J. Elroy Flecker. 'The Golden Journey to Samarkand'

Today a New Age is here—the advent of nuclear power has offered the opportunity to men of freedom from drudgery. But the children of this age must be free from the other limitations of the old if we are to benefit. All our beliefs, though intrinsically true, must be restated in modern guise. This is being increasingly recognised, and, with possibilities unrealisable perhaps in any other age, there is a sense of wonder abroad. For the writer, this wonder is the beginning of wisdom. Man is only a machine if he merely accepts; he becomes man triumphant when his whole life is imbued with a sense of wonder and of purpose. Read again the story of those first-century Christians or, in a lower key, the first fifty years of Mahomet.

Today, through its music, its art, its poetry, the men heralding the New Age are questing—experimenting—wondering. No longer are we self-sufficient in traditional ideas of society or religion, or even of science. Today's youngsters inherit a world of ever-increasing wonder, of complexity, and probably of unity. They need a new 'world view'.

The half-empty churches, the lip service paid to creeds dishonoured in daily life, are symptoms of theology's lost grip and of the dissatisfaction felt by modern man at the limitations theology has imposed. And those who turned, eagerly turned, as did Western man in Victorian times, to the promise of science are now also disillusioned. A very optimistic person might have believed in the ultimate reaching of Utopia via scientific progress; but his illusions were dispelled by the first atomic bomb dropped on Hiroshima. Optimism after that became more difficult.

The materialism that triumphed over an obsolete theology was like a frost which bound all things. It has thawed, but we now find that the old theological and sociological boundaries have disappeared with that thaw.

The same has happened to our traditions and to our 'commonsense' view. Our commonsense world is a world of deliberate limitations, and it cannot be accepted as a criterion any longer when we are hoping to take a world view of man. Nurse Commonsense must be retired, for mankind is adolescent and nursery days are over.

Thinking man faces the ultimate choice: either we live by laws of blind chance or laws of purpose, and man will always choose a purposeful existence. Says J. B. Priestley in *Over the Long High Wall*:

> We are now living in a society that appears—outside of its propaganda and advertising—to dislike itself just as much as I dislike it. We are house guests of the Sorcerer's apprentice, who has let loose what he can't begin to control . . . In the West we are under the spell of ADMASS . . . We are supposed to be consumers, and not much else; surely the lowest view mankind has ever taken of itself. We are televised and advertised out of our senses. We exist

amongst images, not realities. And hardly anybody seems to notice that quality is disappearing, chiefly because so many small firms, which took a pride in what they were making and selling, have been taken over by large firms, which take only a pride in their dividends.

While money is more and more important, what it buys is steadily getting worse and worse . . . We have created a Society whose representative figures are politicians sold like soapflakes, and men who ask questions on television, and singers who have no voices but only a lot of hair, sweat and electronic equipment, and photographers and models. We are the supreme clever-silly people of man's history . . . The world as it shrinks sheds its diversity. The men who serve the great collectives begin to look more and more alike. Such existence as they help to create seems more and more tedious. We have allowed richness, flavour, blood and bone to be scooped out, dried and pressed to nourish nothing but an increasing monotony:

But because men must feel *something,* even when their individuality is vanishing, then there is more and more insistence upon what is raw and hot and strong—public and private violence, impersonal sex and sadistic and masochistic trimmings, idiot hate and the silencing of reason and the narrowing and blunting of imagination. Supreme masters of organisation, we are busy organising the destruction of unique experience among mankind. Why is there this talk of manufacturing robots in the near future? Our society has been hard at it for years.

In plain words, the need of man in this last quarter of the twentieth century is a religion he can understand and follow. By our inbred scientific concept it must be a religion which can be tested and criticised. It must bring a new realisation of the mysteries of the Universe. It must awaken, as the Christians awakened, a sense of such great power that one would die that it might live. And it must relate the heart and life of man to that sublime purpose—infinitely beyond our comprehension but as infinitely sustaining—that sense of purpose calling to adventure, which our young people are so much wanting today.

The writer believes that in this new age the material for building such an influence exists. 'The Kingdom of Heaven is within you', said the Master—and his universality for all ages and times could not be exemplified more pointedly than by saying this is our signpost at the crossroads of a New Age.

Within every man is that latent power—that sixth sense—by which he can find a personal philosophy whereby human life is no longer 'fragmentary' but part of a greater, nobler scheme of evolution—an evolution which is *us*. Best of all, the sixth sense does not need taking on trust — it merely asks to be developed and proved.

In 1919, in *The Undying Fire,* Wells could make Huss say of man:

> He will rob the atoms of their energy and the depths of space of their secrets. He will break his prison in space. He will step from star to star as now we step from stone to stone across a stream. Until he stands in the light of God's presence and looks his Maker and the Adversary in the face . . .

He was a good prophet — the first guess has come true; the others will follow.

Exercise Seven

All work must be preceded by the breathing exercises you have already learned, and in the seclusion of your sanctum.

For practical work there are two permissible postures. The 'asanas' (postures) may be either those of India (Yoga) or of Egypt; whichever you use, you are linking with the 'seers' of the past who trod the way you now tread.

YOGIC POSTURE: 'Tailor fashion'. The old tailor used so to sit, with the right leg under the left thigh and the left leg under the right thigh, spine erect, head poised on shoulders very slightly tilted backwards. The kneecaps should be approximately level, hands on knees, palms downwards. Now close your eyelids and you have factually and symbolically withdrawn from the five-sense body.

EGYPTIAN POSTURE: Sit on a hard straight-backed chair, preferably without arms. Your spine is erect, head very slightly tilted backwards, arms resting on knees, palms upward. Feet should be slightly apart and all the body completely relaxed. Close eyelids and you are now ready for work. Once you can forget the initial impact of the chair, this is a very good posture.

It is wise to practise both postures, as differing exercises need differing postures, but unless specifically stated use the posture which suits you the better.

Now we shall try an exercise in symbolism as a preparation.

1 Cut out a triangle with equilateral sides of about 10in. In the centre of the triangle draw a circle of 2in diameter and colour it black.
2 Sit in your selected Asana (position) and gaze first of all at the centre black spot.
3 Now consider the lines with the following comments:

BASE LINE: *Pythagoras* called this 'mathematics', because 'all is number' and the base of all material creation was number (confirmed by modern physics).

Hermetic teaching calls this *reality;* in the sense that it is what is known in the octave of vibration in which you are operating, eg usually the physical, but later when you can move into the astral that will be the reality and the physical and other planes 'shadowy'.

Alchemy was the search for the 'philosophers stone', the universal 'transmuting agent'. Underlying all things the alchemist believed in one universal substance, a fundamental as everyone knows in these days of psychic speculation. The alchemist was the mathematician and uses inductive logic.

LINE ON LEFT SIDE: *Pythagoras* called this 'Music', because it was an ascent from the fundamentals of mathematics to a high perception. It spelt out the great law of harmony, the division into thirds, fourths and fifths, until it culminated at the peak of the triangle in the octave.

Hermetic teaching called this *communication:* the ascent of the reality to a higher and culminating peak.

SCIENTIFIC RELIGION: The ascent to 'The Peak'—the 'Oversoul', the shedding of each life's personality.

LINE ON RIGHT SIDE: *Pythagoras* called this 'Metaphysics', the inspiration from higher to the earth level. It is the hidden or occult wisdom possessed by all 'Sons of God'. *Hermetic* philosophy calls this *affinity;* believing in purpose it is the pathway whereby deductive logic allows man to perceive the greater truths at lower levels—'As above so below'.

Scientific Religion, also called occultism, believes that by discipline, practice and pursuit of wisdom, latent powers are available on earth and that their acquisition expresses continuity; there is no death. *Men* are mortal Gods.

4 Gaze at each line and try to make your own concept of what it symbolises. As you finish with each line, return your gaze to the centre spot and wait—you may feel an intimation about the line you have considered that you had missed. Treat each line in order and at least once a day. This exercise cannot be done in less than thirty minutes.

LESSON 7
Creative Force

Exercise Eight Concentration Yantra

Energy is Eternal Delight.

William Blake

The most basic of all phenomena, the 'life force', owes its origin, not to some haphazardry or coincidence, but to the conscious-physical, the bio-magnetic Primary Force, the origin of which is and must be the All Pervading Universal Consciousness, which could not have been created but must be the creator.

The most important point derived from this is that the Cosmos is saturated with Consciousness.

Cyril W. Dawson. *Physics of the Primary State of Matter*

Ay! for 'twere absurd
To think that nature in the earth bred gold
Perfect i' the instant: something went before
There must be remote matter.

Ben Jonson. *The Alchemist*

I am that which began;
Out of me the years roll;
Out of me God and man;
I am equal and whole;
God changes, and man, and the form of them bodily;
I am the soul.

Swinburne. 'Hertha'

> Thus it comes that the ultimate units are not purely physical or material but point to an undifferentiated primitive world matrix which includes both the physical and thought characters of the world. J. C. Smuts. Discussion, British Association

The First Cause is, of course, beyond the capacity of man to know; all he can say must be inadequate symbology. An Indian metaphysician makes the statement that the First Cause declared that with a portion of His Self he made the Universe; *'But I remain'.* Most higher metaphysical thinking is inclined to accept this concept of a Cause which bifurcates, abstracting force from itself and leading into a manifestation. That manifestation means that all 'things and thoughts' are emanations from that sublime Unthinkable and Unknowable and that the action of such lower creations does not affect the sublime poise of *'I am'.*

In Christian thinking this has perhaps been best expressed by Meister Eckhart, who postulated a *Godhead* which was abiding and which had within itself all potentialities. It cannot be known to us, is formless and beyond thought. For Eckhart God and the Divine Trinity are 'evolved from' the Godhead and are the first fruits of its substance, being emanations from the Godhead. In his *Tractate XI* he says: 'The Father is the manifestation of the Godhead, the Son is the Image and countenance of the Father, and the Holy Ghost is the light of his countenance.' Eckhart actually contrasts the 'Deitas' with 'Deus', the Godhead with God. 'God becomes and disbecomes—High above Him stands pure Godhead.'

In Indian thought the exemplar of this thinking is Sankara. The relationship between Godhead and God for Sankara, expressed in terms of Brahman to Isvara, is so similar to the Christian thinking of Eckhart that Rudolph Otto's great classic, *Mysticism East and West,* deals almost exclusively with this thesis, emphasising the fundamental similarities.

Plotinus, as the representative of the so-called pagan thinking, postulated the 'one' or the 'Good' which was beyond the reach of human thought or language; but although it is beyond 'being', it is nonetheless the supreme 'Existent'. From this Existent proceeds the 'Nous', which is potentiality and the totality of all knowable existence—the Divine Force, the God of Eckhart's thinking. It is from 'Nous' that the 'soul/mind' of man proceeds. All individual souls are 'sparks of the divine fire', 'parts of the Universal soul'. The Christian theology borrowed largely from Plotinus, particularly St Augustine, Clement and Origen.

The *Force* of the Godhead is therefore the creative Divine urge which it uses to create the Universe (but *'I remain'.*) All other creations are derived from this original outpouring of Force. These highly abstruse speculations, portrayed in such works as Rudolph Otto's *Mysticism East and West,* Inge's *Plotinus* or Happold's *Mysticism,* is a useful starting point in that (a) we can state that the Absolute is unknowable, (b) that some portion of its power has been manifested and creates what we term the Universe, (c) that it appears probable the original force is directed by powers we call Divine and (d) that so far as we can understand, the key to such direction and potentiality is what we mean, in the widest sense, by Evolution.

This course will therefore start with the hypothesis that there is a *force* from which all that *is* is created, and that such a force is 'always becoming', ie evolving in spiritual realisation, mind apprehension and physical structure.

Such force has had many names—'Entelechy', Shaw's 'Life Force', Bergson's 'Elan Vital', among others. It is the creator of all life, and to our observation has two aspects in the formation of a Universe—the occultists call these 'prana' and 'fohat' and the scientists 'gravitation' and 'electromagnetism'. The scientific thinking is known as the 'Field' theory. It is known that every object has an electric field and this is measurable by instruments; what is not known is the *cause* of such field.

One hypothesis says that it is caused by the two named forces. *Gravitation* is a pull between two bodies. In such a pull there is an inherent tendency to increasing density; this gives each object a corresponding 'gravitational field'. An *electromagnetic* force or field pervades all space, and therefore it follows that anything passing through such a field on the way to forming matter will make a transit through ever-increasing 'layers of density'. In other words, any material earth object will have a 'gravitational field' which extends outwards from the material centre in layers of density.

We know that all vibrations, for example, have 'overtones', or as science terms them, 'secondary rhythms'. This corresponds with the theory enunciated above, and bears out well the contention that all matter has layers above its earthly density which are formed by this descent into density under a gravitation pull (prana) and through an electromagnetic field. This operation thus creates in layers (fohat). Physics tells us our solid-seeming world is made up of units of activity whose reality is in the velocity of their movement and whose aim seems to be to build increasingly dense and complex forms. For physicists matter is *not* 'solidity' but 'activity', and it follows there may be layers of activity beyond the reach of our present technological instruments. There is, however, a further analysis, which was largely the work of Albert Einstein.

The work of Albert Einstein has revolutionised many scientific concepts: he taught us that we must look to a fourth dimension in order to understand the third, the fifth to understand the fourth and possibly so on. One of the greatest contributions he made was his 'unified Field Theory'. As just stated, there are two fundamentals to our understanding of the Universe: one is the force called 'gravitation' and the other the power called 'electromagnetism'. Their different actions mean for us creation, and they have been, scientifically speaking, 'separates'; Einstein showed that in fact they were resolvable into a 'homogeneous fabric'—a single unity. Modern mass physics is proving his work, his inspiration, every new day, and we can now say that the Universe and all that is in it are the manifestations of a single fundamental stuff, a unity of 'homogeneous fabric'.

This is in accord with the teachings of the Ancient Wisdom, of Yogic Indian thought and of the divine basis of Christianity. That inspired parable men called *Genesis* indeed offers us the same thought, the individual creative ray of light. In Indian metaphysics the single creative power moulds all Maya, whether it be into the heights of intellect or the earth mechanisms of physical things. This God power of the fundamental stuff that makes all earthly things will be called by us 'Undifferentiated Consciousness'; remember that others have called it 'Life Force', 'Elan Vital', Brahma, Nous, Prana, Fohat, Prakriti and so on. Let us define our term.

UNDIFFERENTIATED CONSCIOUSNESS, the original creative power, the 'homogeneous fabric', is the basic stuff of the Universe. It is *undifferentiated* because at this stage of its creative urge it can be made into a poem or a leg. It is a 'thought of God' seeking *form* and conscious identification into what we call form, by means of 'creative evolution', which is a process of objectifying the original urge. It is *consciousness* because this 'homogeneous fabric' has a purpose and is to be thought of as God being made manifest through creation of form and individualisation of a portion of consciousness—the crystallisation of 'the spark divine'.

There is a beautiful Indian parable as to why this process occurs (obviously no man can know). The suggestion is that God is Love, but it is impossible to love oneself, so that He needed to make a Universe in order that in time it and its countless expressions of life might become worthy of His love and be advanced enough, perfected enough, to return it. 'Our Father' says the same thing in perhaps more down-to-earth terms. *Consciousness needs form.* It needs to individualise, and to do this is the purpose and search of undifferentiated consciousness, the homogeneous fabric of all creation. Omar Khayyam had this thought about the unity in his verses about the Potter:

> Once in the Market Place at break of day
> I watched the Potter fashioning his clay,
> And ever and anon, I thought I heard it say
> *'Gently my brother,* gently pray.'

That Potter and clay should be brothers is the beginning perhaps of a grand purpose, as Browning has said in his 'Rabbi Ben Ezra' (in answer to Khayyam's queries)

> Ay! note that Potter's wheel
> That metaphor and feel
> Why time spins fast, why passive lies our clay—
> Thou, to whom fools propound
> When the win makes its round
> Since life fleets, all is change: the Past Gone, seize today.
>
> All that is, at all,
> Lasts ever, past recall;
> Earth changes, but thy soul and God stand sure.
> What entered into Thee
> That was, is and shall be
> Time's wheel runs back or stops: Potter and clay endure.

'Undifferentiated consciousness' has both a scientific and an occult meaning—it is a process known to both dualities of Man, the physical and the super-physical. 'All is becoming' said the philosopher, 'All is flux', and this is again a scientific and an occult concept. For we know that all is in motion, all is in creation, all is vibration.

Professor William A. Fowler in his essay 'Origin of the Elements', while emphasising that we can only *infer* about the Universe from insufficient knowledge, bases his consideration of the elements on the 90 per cent of hydrogen in the Universe and the 7 per cent of helium. The latter it seems is in a state of permanent combustion so far as the *sun,* the centre of our solar system, the 'Life Giver' as the old sunworshippers called it, is concerned, and science reinforces this concept. We know from photographs of the sun that it has a ring called the 'photosphere', which appears to be granular in nature. The force of gravitation may well cause those 'particles' which combine with waves to cause the phenomenon of light. The sun itself, however, floats in a sea of cosmic radiation, and any rays which it passes on to earth *must* of necessity be impregnated with some of the radiation among which it floats. All rays of the sun to earth pass through a series of zones—in order the photosphere (nearest the sun), chromosphere, corona, and furthest from earth ionosphere, then mesophere, stratosphere and troposphere. The sun is subjected to immense gravitation, twenty-eight times that of earth, and therefore must concentrate the cosmic forces which are in its rays arriving on earth and carrying its own emanations, plus the cosmic radiation forces.

Professor Fowler disclaims that science can know about the underlying creation of protons, neutrons etc, but states that all the elements we know are made up of two building blocks—protons and neutrons. The simplest element is hydrogen and this consists of one of each, the make-up depending upon positive and negative electricity, which attract each other. Modern research is bringing forward ever new revaluations. For material science, exploring within the atom is a succession of ever-increasing wonders; 'so far and yet so near' might be an appropriate slogan, for the atom has only just begun to reveal its fascinating secrets. It may be said that of every branch of human discovery perhaps there is not one which has proved more difficult and more puzzling than the structure of the atom. As soon as a new discovery is made, it seems to open the door to underlying structures. And beyond all other sciences this one is taking mankind nearer and nearer to an occult interpretation of a material thing (if the atom can be called 'material').

On the occult path it has long been accepted that there is an etheric surrounding the physical—we may think of it on terms of the 'electric field', already discussed. Occultists believe that they can 'perceive' the etheric atom, which is the mould for our physical one. A Dr W. R. Kilner some years ago believed he had an apparatus which enabled him to see the etheric and thereby diagnose the disease (see his book, *The Human Aura*). There are lots of names for this etheric atom, but it is best to use the current one, 'Vitality Globule', which expresses the importance of this atom to us both in daily life and, even more, in occult seeking.

The physicist has a Table of Elements of ever-increasing complexity, and therefore of atomic weight (Elements 1 to 92); this compares with teachings of such old occult societies as the Society of the Rosy Cross or the Pythagoreans.

These Vitality Globules may be thought of as the nuclei of atoms. Annie Besant in her *Ladder of Lives* many years ago constructed a table that has had some scientific confirmation since her day.

Nature	*Conveyor of*	*Physicists' term*
ETHERIC	Ordinary current electricity and sound	Atom (the basic of earth science)
SUPER ETHERIC	Light (fohat)	Neutralised nucleus
SUB ATOMIC	Subtle forms of electricity	Positive nucleus
ATOMIC	Mind thought (Soul)	Electronic

The formation of the solar system may well be due to such forces in gaseous manifestation, and from the swirling masses of such gases modern astronomers teach us that the galaxies and their innumerable planets and stars were formed. The occultist teaches that these centres of force, vibrating beyond human measurement or comprehension, are cosmic in nature and combine the two forces 'prana' and 'fohat'. With the advent of human individualisation there is also the force of Kundalini, also a creator but with differing aspects.

The power of prana (the form creator) and fohat (the evolutionary urge) enter Man through channels of cosmic vibrations. From early Egypt and the Hindu scriptures it has been known that there are special receptacles for this force. A modern scientist calls them endocrine glands, the Indians the 'Chakras', and this course thinks of them as 'Wheels of Force'.

The scientist considers that these glands (Fig 2) coordinate the activities of the various cells which compose the physical body, and are embryologically related to the skin; they also state that temperament and physique are affected by the way in which gland secretion finds its way into the circulation. This is a restatement of the teachings of the Ancient Wisdom, for the occultist thinks of the chakras as being saucer-like depressions at the skin of *each* vehicle of Man (the fundamental difference). Within this depression there is a constant movement, which is called the 'spokes', and these control the vibratory rates of entry. When prana/fohat enters our bodies, it has been transmuted into a low rate of vibration which can be spread over the whole of the physico-etheric and thereby vitalise the bloodstream and nervous systems. *But* for occultists, as the force has entered the physico-etheric from the higher levels of Man, traces of such 'vehicles' are also present, and there are higher chakras (throat, brow and crown) which are emotionally, mentally and spiritually vitalised in our physico-etheric make-up. This means affecting temperament, as the scientist states.

One of the problems for the scientist is the pituitary gland. Kenneth Walker, Hunterian Professor to the Royal College of Surgeons, calls it in *Diagnosis of Man,* 'a tiny structure tucked under the fore part of the brain and neglected by the older anatomists. The understanding of this gland is the key to the understanding of the whole endocrine system. Although not greater than a pea it is the Master Gland.' Another gland which has an important function is the pineal, which deals with the vital action of light on our bodies. The occultist combines these two in his chakra lore and calls them either the 'Persian Saddle' or by the better known title of 'The Third Eye'.

It is possible for you here and now to learn how to control each chakra, to heighten or slow down the rate of entry and assist in dispersion of the force to required centres. While this subject is beyond the scope of an elementary course, it will be necessary to refer to the 'Wheels of Force' throughout, and students will be advised *not* to do any full chakra work until the vehicles have been properly integrated and attuned. The exercises given all help such development and integration.

The diagram on p 62 illustrates some of the points made in this

(Fig 2) GLANDS AND CHAKRAS

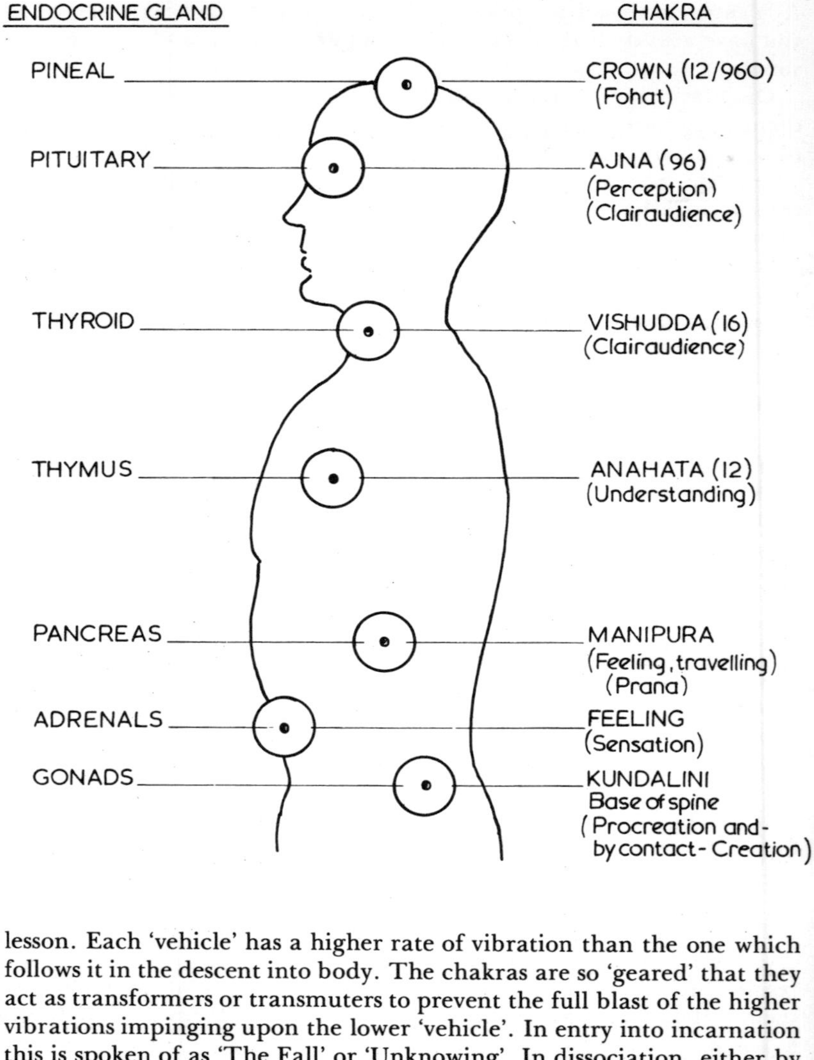

lesson. Each 'vehicle' has a higher rate of vibration than the one which follows it in the descent into body. The chakras are so 'geared' that they act as transformers or transmuters to prevent the full blast of the higher vibrations impinging upon the lower 'vehicle'. In entry into incarnation this is spoken of as 'The Fall' or 'Unknowing'. In dissociation, either by *use of latent powers development* or discarding of lower vehicle at 'Death', the alteration is made by increasing the present vehicle to a level of vibration which can bear the force of the higher vehicles' prana/fohat vibrationary octave (latent powers); or in 'death' by the return of the prana to its octave by dissolution 'Dust to Dust'.

Exercise Eight and Commentary

A 'Yantra' is an aid to concentration based upon such experiences as you have already had. These will be amplified by the work of using the yantra.

On a stiff piece of cardboard draw a circle of 6in radius (12in diameter); inside that and from the same pivot draw one of 2in radius (4in diameter); and inside that draw one of ½in radius (1in diameter). The circles are to be concentric and you may care to spend a minute considering what this word means in relation to concentration. Mentally number the circles as 1, 2 and 3 in terms of decreasing diameter.

In circle 3, the very smallest, do not at the moment put any figures or colour, but around its circumference paint a very narrow yellow rim about ¼in wide. In circle 2, and working from the outside of the yellow rim, colour the rest of the circle black. In circle 1, the largest, paint a ¼in rim around the circumference in blue.

Have a hook or drawing pin on the wall, or an object against which you can rest your yantra, about 5ft away from your chair. The use will be progressive, and the first stage to be undertaken under your usual conditions of privacy and near silence, and with light of a nightlight, only will be as follows.

Part One

1 Usual preliminaries including flooding, breathing.
2 Now take a rest with closed eyes for at least a minute.
3 On opening the eyes, gaze at the centre of your yantra (the white spot with the yellow rim). Proceed in usual fashion by staring for a few seconds and then gradually lowering the eyelids until you get to your best position.
4 Concentrate thoroughly and wait.

Different students will experience differing effects, some being fortunate enough to have a colour display of waves of colours either over the face of the yantra or in the room itself. If you experience that, then the first part has been achieved. If you do not, try the following.

First the rim colours may not be yours, so change them to what you think are your two *contrasting* colours. Try now! If there is still no result, you are probably too near the yantra. If you wear spectacles, try them without and nearer. With patience and practice results are certain to come.

When the exercise is finished, cancel it by gazing at the ceiling, where again you may have effects.

Part Two

We have now to consider the centre. We want to put in that centre some symbol or picture dear to us, perhaps a cross, an inverted triangle, a loved one's face (clear enough to be distinguished), or anything which has a special message.

Now repeat the entire process, except for gazing at the symbol or picture in circle 3 (the smallest).

The most important thing now is to *wait;* do not be impatient, for results have to come from inner distances. If the face is that of a loved one, it may help to hum their tune under your breath *while never for a moment allowing your concentration to lapse.*

If they had a special prayer or poem, say a line of it under your breath *without relaxing concentration.* Let the tune or the words be an accompaniment to concentration. Alfred, Lord Tennyson used to produce his results and his journeys into 'mystical similitudes' by repeating 'Alfred Tennyson' over and over again as he walked. This is the basic of the rosary, where repetition and concentration may lift the vibrations into the level of perception.

This yantra exercise is very important but most often needs patience and regularity before full results, or indeed any results, are obtained. But they are worth waiting for.

There are a thousand more exercises in concentration and many excellent books to point out the different paths. You have, however, all that is necessary in the exercises given to ensure the following:

1 Concentrative ability to at least three minutes.
2 That you are getting outside the five-sense world into the higher states or planes or octave vibrations.
3 You will have a sense of wonder. Although the brain will rationalise all your experiences, you will know that they were real in a sense that earth sight and hearing are not.

You are at the door, do not be afraid to go through. It was Eugène Ionesco who said: 'There is no such thing as unreality, there are only various forms of reality.'

LESSON 8
Octaves and Vibrations

Exercise Nine Concentration Watch

. . . a rate of vibration can best be conceived as an oscillatory movement which can impart an impulse to the surrounding air and thence to the 'Matter of its octave'.

Modern mass physics uses five dimensions and has to postulate some other carrier than air as this term is understood of earth atmosphere. Whilst it is experimentally unproven it appears that 'air' (which a decade or so ago was called aether) may have effects which we know as 'Cosmic variations'.

Professor F. A. Lindman.
Indeterminacy and the Modern Quantum

Vibrations like electrons are only known by their results. The vibration is a measurement of which we can only know the results in that they affect the surrounding air in 'earth' conditions and the postulated 'Aether' in cosmic conditions. Human beings are responsive to some of these results but more from the technological research and its instruments.

Article on Mass Physics in *Modern Science Encyclopaedia*

O world invisible, we view thee,
O world intangible, we touch thee,
O world unknowable, we know thee,
Inapprehensible, we clutch thee!

Francis Thompson. 'The Kingdom of God'

The Law of the Octave (Vibrations and Octaves)

Like all words which today are used as labels, the word 'vibration' has become so common that we do not try to understand its meaning. Vibration is a facet of energy or force and, indeed, energy as vibration can be seen in such effects as the ripples of waves which travel on a smooth lake. It is equally a commonplace of observation that if there is a constant impact on the water—for example, something moving up and down in the centre of the lake instead of an occasional stone thrown in—the ripples will be much closer together, and it is this frequency of rippling, or vibratory ring, that we must try to understand.

The dictionary defines 'vibrate' as 'to cause to shake, to move to and fro, to measure by moving to and fro'. Let us try a more practical illustration. When I throw a stone into a pond, I produce what we call 'ripples'—movements of vibration which disturb the face of the water and which bear an intimate relation to the *mass* of the stone and the *force* of the throw. Again we are dealing with Einstein's scientific concepts. We can, however, prove this potency of vibration and its astounding results for ourselves. Please go to your piano and take off the front; note the mechanism of the keys, which causes a hammer to strike a string that then vibrates to produce sound. Let us strike middle 'C' and then, moving up the keyboard, strike the 'C' which we associate with the third space on the stave. The resultant vibrations, of course, impinge upon our ear, and we shall notice a similarity between them; in fact the two sets of vibrations bear a specific relation to each other which we call the 'interval'. Let us now strike the 'F' (first space on the stave) and follow this by striking the higher 'F' (fifth line on the stave). Again our ear will distinguish a similarity, again there is an interval or specific relation between the two sets of vibrations.

The wonderful thing is that for the whole of the keyboard of the piano, and probably for all earthly things, *the interval remains constant* and we speak of this constancy as *'The law of the octave'*. In music every octave consists of an initial note, a climb of seven notes to the completion of the octave, and the last note, which is itself the beginning of a new octave. The Law of the Octaves was known to modern chemistry in the middle of the nineteenth century, when it was promulgated by Newlands. He suggested that elements were related to one another, and measuring the relative masses of many of the elements made it apparent that they fell *into groups* and that the properties of such groups were similar. *Moreover,* if the elements were arranged in the order of their atomic weights, it was found that the properties of the eighth were similar to those of the first, those of the ninth to those of the second and so on. In other words, there was a repetition of these properties *in every eighth element.* The Russian scientist Mendeleef devised a complete chart, which was known as the Periodic Table.

This research of course continues, but the law has spread far beyond the original concepts of music and chemistry and now is a basis for several branches of human knowledge. This is in accord with what the great Master, Pythagoras, taught in his school at Croton 2500 years ago. He stated that there were three branches of study which could elevate human thinking: they were Mathematics (the study of earthly symbols and relations), Music (the study of universal harmonies, the language of the Gods), and Metaphysics (the unification of the true wisdom).

We people of earth can only appreciate a small range of vibrations, namely between 34,000 and 64,000 waves to the inch or from 400 to 750 billion waves to the second. The whole of the rest of the enormous scale of vibrations is closed to our five senses.

There are some known seventy octaves of vibration (Fig 3), and of these seventy Man can perceive only octaves 5-16, which are audible sound, and octave '49', which is visible light. Of course, through his

(Fig 3) MAN'S SENSE PERCEPTIONS AND THE 'UNKNOWN OCTAVES'

	OCTAVE	SENSE	TECHNOLOGY	UNKNOWN
	?			
	70			
	65		GAMMA RAYS	
	60		X RAYS	
	55		52 ULTRA-VIOLET	
	50	49 VISIBLE LIGHT	46 INFRA-RED	EXCEPT FOR OCTAVES SHOWN, OTHER POWERS ARE UNKNOWN
ETHER	45		42 HEAT	
	40			
	35		31 SHORT E-M	
	30		28 RADIO	
	25		LONG ELECTROMAGNETIC	
	20		18 ULTRA SOUND	
	15			
AIR	10	AUDIBLE 5-16 SOUND		
	5			
	1			

instruments Man has greatly increased his knowledge of the 'blank' octaves. We know that the regions of what we call 'ultra sound' are only just beyond our sensory apparatus. So real are these unseen vibrations that not only do some animals hear them, but Man can use them to boil water, to clean machine parts, to drill glass and teeth, and to kill bacteria. We all also know that there are wavelengths used for television and for wireless, but so 'accommodating' is our sensory apparatus that we do not usually think what this means. In the air around us, unknown to our senses—so unknown, indeed, that only a few years ago the statement would have sounded insane—voices, sounds and sights are permeating our vibratory life, though we can only perceive them by means of an apparatus. Equally, of course, there are those who have claimed to see such 'unseen' sights or heard such 'soundless' voices throughout the ages—the seers and the prophets. *Please* consider this everyday fact most carefully. Here is a whole realm of appearance that was dead to our forefathers because their sensory apparatus was not able to accept the vibrations, which were not in the scale applicable to our human feeling.

The facts demand repetition. Out of some twenty octaves of waves normally transmitted through the air, eleven are registered by our sense of hearing; while out of fifty or more known octaves of electromagnetic waves, only one octave—visible light—is known to us.

It is a known scientific fact that the composition of matter can be expressed in terms of vibration. What is the difference between a piece of glass cut like a diamond and a real diamond? As far as some qualities are concerned, such as transparency, both seem to be like glass, but a diamond, as we know, has a hardness and a brilliancy which glass cannot have, and the secret of this difference is that the matter composing the one is matter of a different frequency from the matter composing the other. It was this knowledge which was at the base of the old search for the transmutation of metals.

Therefore, it is scientifically true that the number of vibrations per second is not only what makes the thing we call 'matter', but it is the basis of the difference between one kind of matter and another. Now this difference of vibration can be expressed and understood in terms that theologians have used, such as 'higher' and 'lower' or 'above' and 'below'; and these terms can be a simple expression of the mystery known as 'frequency of vibrations'.

As has been pointed out, vibrations unknown and unrecognised are all around us, and it is by no means difficult to understand that matter of much greater vibration than we know can be present with us and, indeed, moving through us. To the occultist this is the vibration of spirit, and he believes that, like the various layers of an onion, so man is a composite entity with different vibrations. The lowest of these vehicles, the 'hardest' as it were of the vibrations, is the physical, and it is probable that man is also responsive to the very highest vibrations beyond our known frequencies.

Our consciousness depends upon our perception of vibrations, and it is accepted that our five-sense perceptions are extremely limited, and that even those limited perceptions are grossly liable to error. What, then, if we could extend the various rates of vibration around us? We can easily see what the results might be—the air filled with sound waves carrying popular music, and plays and pictures on screen are all around us—but until the right selective medium is used, either of radio or of television set, they cannot be perceived. Our ability to tap this vast concatenation of sound is limited by the fallible instruments of our perceptive senses.

May it not equally be, then, that there are vehicles and sights around us which are not to be perceived unless we have the necessary organ of perception? Now occultists who are clairvoyant, and mediums who claim to be sensitive, tell us that this is, indeed, true; and that there are numerous entities in every room with us when we are alone. The writer believes that he has proof of this, and that on occasion he is susceptible to this sixth sense of perception. He sees nothing supernatural about this, though it may be, if one wishes, supernormal; many occultists believe that every human being has these latent powers, and that the New Age will see them developed.

The Law of the Octave is used by science and by occultism (which is mystic science). Occultism teaches that Man (who is a 'God i' the germ') has to obtain complete control of the earth octave, and this means the ability to use to its highest power each note or function of his earthly life. He is called an integrated man by psychologists when he has reached this complete control.

Carl Gustav Jung divided our functions into four: (a) *sensation,* (b) *feeling (emotion),* (c) *thinking* and (d) *inspiration.* The occultist has for centuries had these divisions, but expands them into the seven notes of earth's octave (Fig 4), as follows:

1 SENSATION: Physical commitment without other than sustenance needs, eg *Neanderthal* man in his cave.
2 LOWER FEELING: (OR EMOTIONS): Those concerned with the survival of oneself, a completely selfish approach: lusts, hates, fears, envy, the whole gamut.
3 EMOTION PROPER: The expansion from purely selfish motivation into recognition and care for others: sympathy, love of another to one's own self sacrifice (a mother for her child), devotion to a 'cause'.
4 CONCRETE THINKING: Thought concerned with personal matters and aggrandisement—fame, 'keeping up with the Joneses'—leading at its best to practical technology.

5 ABSTRACT THINKING: The thought that is selfless absorption in the non-material: the dedication of the pure scientist (of theory) as opposed to technology, the absorption of the musician, the constructs of the pure mathematician, the problems of the philosopher.
6 LOWER INSPIRATION: The thoughts that enter into our heads from where we know not but which have a relation to our intuitive faculties—precognition, 'hunches', instinctive reactions.
7 HIGHER INSPIRATION: Socrates and his 'daemon', communication of the mystic or the initiate with higher octaves, the approach and near finalisation of man's integration.

Occultism further divides these seven factors into two groups: 1, 2, 3 and 4 (because we think of sensation and lower feeling as being inextricably bound) make the *lower triad,* the person of man as an earth creature, a 'selfish' entity; and 5, 6 and 7 the *higher triad,* because all these attributes, which go to make the integrated man, have little or nothing to do with 'selfish' preoccupations and seek only to serve.

This break up into 'seven' has many scientific correlations. Consider the diagram on p 31, which shows the break-up of a ray of white light directed through a prism. With a sheet of white paper, a torch and a glass prism, you can perform this rewarding experiment for yourself. You will see that the entry ray of pure white light is split into seven colours, ranging from red to violet. This is because the vibrations vary according to the angle of departure. A very simple example is a rainbow, whose arc of concentric bands in the colours of the spectrum is due to the refraction and reflection of sunlight.

The same diagram also shows as a comparison the break-up of the creative ray into the various manifestations of earth. 'As above so below' is a very old and important occult maxim; here you have a concrete example of how the break-up of light symbolises the break-up of man and his earth forms or bodies. *Please consider this very very carefully.* It is the basis of much future exploration.

Thus the Law of the *Seven,* which has an age-old acceptance, leads us to the important eighth note, and this is always a duality. As on a piano, it is the culmination of an octave and at the same time the start of a new one.

The Law of the Octaves has another important usage. We believe with Religion that man has three 'bodies' (vehicles, expressions)—*body, soul and spirit.*

Occultism believes man is a threefold entity, comprising the *physical* (material earth form), the *mind* (the superconsciousness, which controls the five-sense-brain mechanism) and the *spiritual* (the highest group of Man's powers before he becomes a higher entity. We reserve *spirit* for that higher ascent).

Just as on your piano you can run three octaves that are linked in the

(Fig 4) EARTH OCTAVE EVOLUTION OF FORM

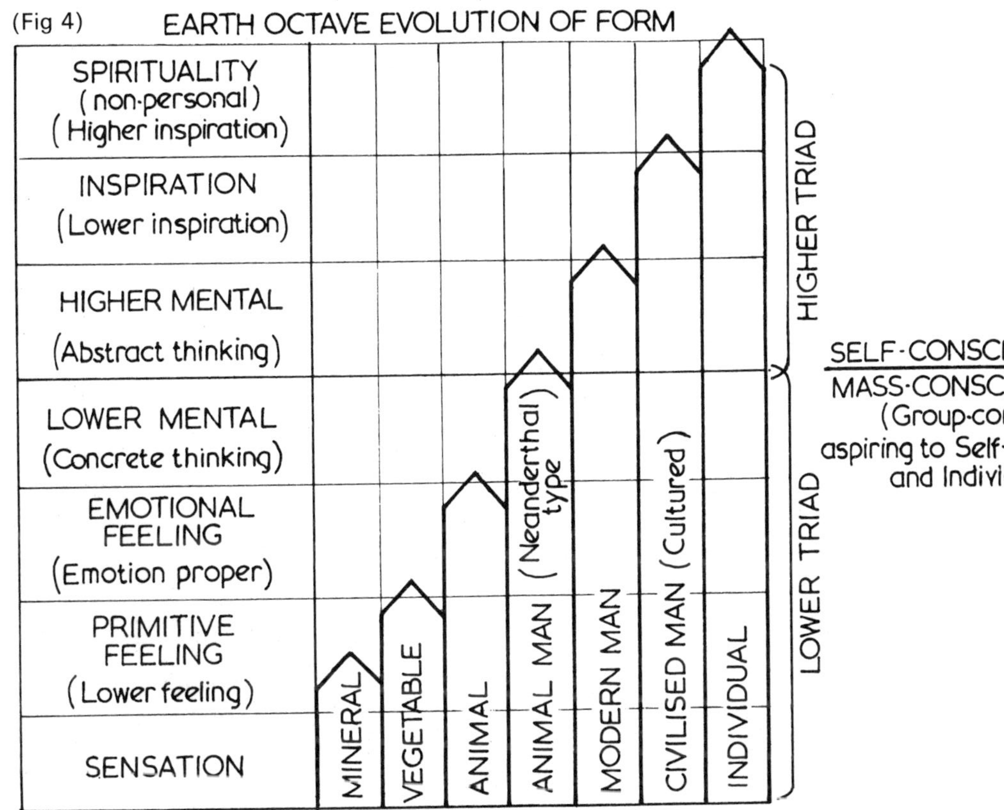

scale because the eighth note is both culmination and beginning, so we believe that it is possible for an integrated man, while still on earth, to experience each of the three octaves—what Tennyson called 'states of mystical similitude'. So it is very important for your *practical work upon yourself* to understand this theoretical background.

Introduction to Exercise Nine

Anyone can learn to concentrate, but few people realise that this is a tremendous study not to be achieved by most of us without mind labour. The writer once had a lady in a beginners' class who returned after one or two lessons flushed with success, happily stating that she had concentrated for twenty minutes. Asked how she knew this, she replied, 'Oh, I kept on looking away from the candle to my watch to see how I was doing.' Obviously she had not concentrated at all!

Concentration for us means one-pointedness—the burning glass which focuses the sun's rays and sets the leaves alight. It is the art of bringing one's whole attention, of sharpening one's mental power to a single point, a single thing, whether that be tangible or intangible. The philosophy of phenomenology, and notably Husserl, have found this answer.

It is in the writer's opinion wrong to confuse concentration with 'visualisation' or meditation. While they are allied, and the last two flow out of the use of the first, their final aims are different. Concentration is the art of controlling butterfly thinking and being 'one-pointed'.

Before you start on the exercises, you must be warned you will be your own greatest barrier. Your brain, being coerced along unfamiliar paths, will react: it will try to force your mind work into daily symbols of earth life, in other words rationalise. It will raise all sorts of doubts and objections and you will find

(a) The illusions of everyday life will press upon you. The physical and emotional sides of your self will demand undivided attention. The brain will deride all knowledge which does not come within its five-sense purview.
(b) The emotional barrier will obtrude: when you secure the first results you will suffer the pressure of fear, because you are entering unknown territory.
(c) Silence and privacy are essential. Discuss matters with no one but your tutor; do not tell others of the experiences you have achieved. You will find great temptation to do so.

So know that you have to break down your own barriers, which are constructed for you from your first days in the cradle. You have to think for yourself, individually.

Before you start these all-important exercises, remember the following:

1 *Never* go on to the next exercise until you have mastered the present one. That is like the lady who always turned to the last page of her thriller to know 'who done it'.
2 Do not read too many books at the beginning of your work. You can only walk along one path, serve one Master. Later it is valuable to read avidly, to compare—when you already know.
3 You are to think of sharpening your attention at one point. To take a familiar analogy, if you try to pierce a sheet of cardboard with a blunt iron or even wooden stake, you will merely buckle the cardboard; *but* if your stake is sharpened to a point, you will go through the obstructing material.

Exercise Nine

After about a fortnight of 'colour', you will probably have found your 'right' one. *Do not move on to this exercise until you have found your colour.*

1 Usual prepared room, nightlight and mirror.
2 Perform *all* usual preliminaries.
3 Flood the room with your colour.
4 Take your watch, or have a clock with a second hand and place it in a position where it may easily be observed without disturbing your 'asana'.
5 Decide to concentrate on the tip of the second hand only; watch it move around, regardless of the figures of the hours or the other hands.
6 The moment you find your attention has wandered, STOP! Now, if you note down the minute you started and begin with the second hand upright, you will easily time how long you really concentrated. *You must be truthful with yourself.* You will find thirty seconds quite good to begin with, and you will probably work up to at least a minute. Some systems consider it necessary to proceed no further until you can concentrate for three minutes. The writer believes that if you can concentrate for one minute you are ready for further exercises.

These are admittedly 'baby exercises'. But your mother wisely taught you first to crawl, then to totter, then to walk and then to run. This is a sound regimen in all things.

Concentration is the key to all the 'mysteries'. Match yourself against the betrayals and pitfalls of the senses, and when you can keep the brain shadow-show at bay for one minute, you are ready to take still further control.

LESSON 9
Evolution

Exercise Ten Concentration Colour Cards

God only acts and is in existing beings chiefly Men.
Therefore God becomes as we are that we may be as He is.
William Blake

Man is an animal who is trying to evolve into a God—many of his problems are the result of this struggle . . . 'My Mind to me a Kingdom is' said Sir Edward Dyer—and when Man realises that his mind is a kingdom in a most literal sense, a great unexplored country, he has crossed the borderline that divides the animal from the God . . . He would explore the countries of the Mind as Livingstone and Stanley explored Africa. He would discover that he had many 'selves' and that his higher selves are what his ancestors would have called Gods.

Colin Wilson. *The Mind Parasites*

A fire and a planet
A crystal and a cell
A jellyfish and a saurian
And caves where cavemen dwell
Then a sense of Love and Duty
And a face turned from the clod
Some call it evolution
And others call it God.

W. H. Carruth

When one uses the key word 'Evolution', most people would equate it with the work done by Charles Darwin and Alfred Russell Wallace and their successors, which has provided us with a concept of supreme importance. Everyone is familiar with the well known story. The 'Record of the Rocks', to use Wells's phrase, has told us of the long cooling process which solidified into our recognisable world; and the aeons during which life crept through various bodies, from the early protoplasmic substances through all the forms of the sea until, finally, it came to land. Of how form became ever and ever greater until vast creatures roamed the earth, creatures which might use Kings Cross Station as a kennel, but which had a brain the size of a peahen.

Then Man appears upon the scene. What a small insignificant creature he must have been among the vast animal creation, and yet he bore within him the power to outstrip them all! *And it is important to note that that power* was not a material one; it was a mental one, it was a creative one. From the first moment we know of Man, he has a different symbol from the rest of creation. It is as though the path of evolution proceeded as far as it could in vast bodily forms, found that mere mass was insufficient, and then decided to evolve upon another plane—the mental and the creative one. From the first, Man is a creative artist. It has always seemed to me that Chesterton's illustration from *The Everlasting Man* gives a valuable clue to Man's real evolution. Readers may remember how he envisages a normal boy finding the pictures in the cave, which are perhaps our first documents of artist Man.

> What would be for him the simplest lesson of that strange stone picture book? After all, it would come to this: that he had dug very deep and found the place where a man had drawn a picture of a reindeer. But he would dig a great deal deeper before he found a place where a reindeer had drawn a picture of man. That sounds like a truism, but in this connection it is really a very *tremendous truth* . . . This is the simplest lesson to learn in the cavern of the coloured pictures: only it is too simple to be learnt. It is the simple truth that Man does differ from the brutes in kind and not in degree, and the proof of it is here; that it sounds like a truism to say that the most primitive man drew a picture of a monkey, and that it sounds like a joke to say that the most intelligent monkey has drawn a picture of man. Something of division has appeared: and it is unique. Art is the signature of the man.

The word 'art' must be liberally construed: not only in music and literature, painting and sculpture, but in the highest scientific visions, the abstruse rapt expression of religious myth, the philosophies and perhaps, at its highest, in mystical ecstasy, does Man prove his uniqueness on his world—a uniqueness that displays itself in individual mental creativeness. So we must apprehend more than mere physical in the concept of evolution. It is a part of 'the materialist fantasy', which for a time stole the minds of men to think of evolution only in terms of bodily creation; but as a matter of historical fact the idea of evolution was first proposed by Empedocles, who, speaking of the four known types of vibration—which he called Earth (solid), Water (material in fluid form), Air (material in gaseous form) and Fire (material in spiritual form)—taught that all forms of life arise from these four, which in themselves arise from the one creative spirit. Other important 'evolutionists' are Linnaeus, Goethe, St Hilaire, Lorenz Oken, Lamarck (a notable figure, whose *Creative Evolution* is now starting to oust, as a pure philosophic concept, the more limited 'accident of an accident' of Charles Darwin), Schopenhauer, Erasmus, Darwin (of course) and Alfred Russell Wallace (who unselfishly entitled his completed book *Darwinism*).

Oken, in particular, seems to have played a part similar to that of Teilhard in our own time. He combined his religion with his scientific skill, defining all natural change and growth as 'the science of the everlasting transmutations of the Holy Spirit in the world', and postulating a creative substance, which he called 'Urschleim' (we call it protoplasm), from which came all the various forms of known nature.

Darwin merely (and this word undervalues his wonderful work) pointed out that in fact evolution could (repeat 'could') proceed without 'the transmutations of the Holy Spirit', to use Oken's phrase, simply by the survival of the fittest. The neck of the giraffe as an illustration stretched, as Shaw has said, 'across the whole Heavens and made men believe that what they saw there was a gloaming of the gods'—this because the giraffe's amusing neck could be due to the fact that the longer your neck the nearer your food. But it *could* be caused, as Lamarck said, simply by Will (Schopenhauer's thesis). 'The will to live' which primarily 'grew' the longer neck is discounted in Darwinism. (We have used the preface to Shaw's remarkable *Back to Methuselah* in the above analysis.)

To all occultists there is no doubt that evolution far surpasses its mere physical meaning, for we see it as a fundamental law of the creative power which applies 'as above so below'.

The mechanistic philosophy which sprang out of Darwinism is dead. Even forty years ago Professor Joad could write in his *Guide to Modern Thought*:

> From a number of quarters evidence is accumulating to suggest that the mode of behaviour of a living organism is *fundamentally* different from that of a machine and can never be explained in terms of it. Life, it seems, is fundamental, moreover it is creative

and uses the moulds, the forms of living organisms *as instruments* to further its purposes and serve its end.

In those intervening forty years the advent of Einstein, of modern mass physics, has reinforced Joad's dictum to such an extent that physicists are now using metaphysical expressions to elucidate their concept of 'matter', which otherwise would remain as an expressed mathematical equation.

So, in thinking about Man's evolution, we have to accept that the law operates on other than a purely physical plane; indeed, would it not be a strange thing if this evolution dealt with all the beasts of the lower animal kingdom, with all the plants that beautify our earth, and omitted altogether to have any contact with the mind or spirit of Man? Surely such a thing is so illogical as to be unthinkable, but once we accept the evolution of individual mind and, therefore, presumably spirit, a true religious prospect opens out.

It is true, of course, that in their first zeal the early Darwinian disciples asked too much from the theory, and it was easy for satirists like George Bernard Shaw to pour scorn upon some of their work; also it was natural that an intelligent man like Butler, who foresaw the spiritual dangers implicit in the theory, should urge that it had 'banished mind from the universe'. But it is in mind and its power that we should consider Man's true evolution.

It is very strange how the concept of evolution, which has altered for ever Man's thinking, is so often overlooked when we are considering Man himself. The materialistic outlook has biased us to think in terms of the body, and, as all know, at one time even thought itself was assessed as body reactions. Our error has been to equate the word 'progress' with material gains and their ancillaries. *That kind of progress cannot any longer carry the hopes of mankind.* We realise that no definition of progress can be true which does not include the *whole* man, and that in our preoccupation with material values we have left out the most important part of Man.

From a physical viewpoint Man has not evolved for many, many centuries. Edward Carpenter, in his *Civilisation—Its Cause and Cure,* has inundated us with examples to show that, in the physical sense at any rate, civilised man has deteriorated, not evolved, over the centuries; but in a spiritual sense (and one is thinking of such things as cruelty, of scorn for the lame and the crippled, of intolerance) and in the mental sense, men today are evolving giants. It is true to say that, in the case of mankind, evolution means the evolution of mind.

Professor Lester Ward, in his *Pure Sociology,* gave us a botanical analogy—monopodial and sympodial development—which he applied to the growth of human societies. He pointed out how, in the case of such plants as the cacti, the nerve cells, having reached a certain place, rushed as a whole down the new branch, which virtually became the trunk. In due course this secondary branch, which now contained the bulk of the fibro-vascular cell bundles, was sacrificed in the same manner as the original stem. This development is called 'sympodial'. The ordinary branching, similar to that in a tree, is called 'monopodial'. Professor Ward suggested that, as far as human beings were concerned, it was possible that our evolution was sympodial in its nature. Man, having reached the end of physiological change, and having perhaps now neared the frontiers of pure intellectual achievement, is perhaps turning to spiritual growth in his next phase.

This concept has found in our own time a great exponent in Teilhard de Chardin. It is not too much to say that this Jesuit priest and outstanding scientist (a remarkable combination) has illuminated modern concepts of evolution. What was the message of this great seer for our work? Here are some of his views.

Firstly, he believed there was a great creative force which operated on different *planes,* and he called this force 'radial energy'. He further postulated that it had much similarity to the scientists' 'fields of force', but stressed that it enters into and vitalises all the various planes. He said:

> If there is one thing that has been clearly brought out by the latest advances of physics, it is that in our experience there are different orders of 'spheres' or 'levels' in the unity of nature, each of them distinguished by the dominance of certain factors which are imperceptible or negligible in a neighbouring sphere or on an adjacent level.

The student will recognise this thinking and its differentiation between physical, emotional, mental etc.

Secondly, Teilhard saw *consciousness* as the force which creates everything and thought that this factor had been ignored by science because it was too difficult (compare Whitehead). It is the supreme fact that consciousness is always seeking form of expression and evolutionary valuation. He said: 'Consciousness necessitates consideration of new aspects: new dimensions in the stuff (make-up) of the Universe. We shrink from the attempt to discover the *universal hidden behind the manifestations'.* The last sentence is an admirable definition of the quest of the occultist and his purpose.

Thirdly Teilhard recognised duality in all our becoming, but also knew the underlying unity. Without the slightest doubt there is a something which material and spiritual energy hold together, and they are complementary. In the last analysis somehow or other there must be a *single energy* operating in the world. Compare Einstein's 'homogeneity', and the Indian 'Prana/Fohat' uniting in 'Prakriti'.

Teilhard also realised that in some way this unity lay both within and without our organism:

> Since the inner face of the world is manifest at the very base of our human understanding, and there reflects upon itself, it would seem that we have only got to look into ourselves in order to understand the dynamic relationships existing between the *within* and the *without* of things. In fact so to do is one of the most difficult of all things . . . What makes the crux—and an irritating one at that—of the problem of spiritual energy for our reason, is the heightened sense that we bear within ourselves that our action seems to depend on, *and yet be independent* of material forces.

Fourthly, he was the prophet of wider evolution.

> *Evolution* is not merely a branch of biological science: it is the method, the way, indeed the hope of God's manifestation.
>
> Everything from a speck of dust to the vastness of the expanding Universe is subject to God's law of evolution.
>
> *Evolution is the light that illuminates all facts.*

So he arrived at the conclusion that Man's physical evolution was completed and he must now start to evolve primarily at a higher level. Present life is limited by the biosphere; he foresaw the next stage as a mental-spiritual stage, which he called 'Noosphere' (fuller communication with the 'I'—latent powers used by everyone) and he also had visions of still higher levels of humanity's climb to divinity, culminating in 'Christogenesis'—the place where all men shall be aware of their divinity, Sons of God. He summarised the evolutionary concept in two laws (as stated by Bernard Towers): (1) throughout time there has been a tendency for evolution in matter to become increasingly complex in its organisation, and (2) with increase in material complexity there is a corresponding rise in the consciousness of the organism.

The first postulate states concisely and accurately our previously explained idea that when 'prana' enters into each octave group, it starts to create 'forms'. For us on earth this begins with the mineral; as the whirling mass of gases which later became an earth cooled, various stresses ensued and different combinations of structure formed. By mere chemical processing these became 'solids' of different densities, but all in mineral forms. The progression then was into ever more and more complexity of form—vegetable, animal, until we reach the wonderful structure called Man (not as some materialistic mechanics will tell us 'perfect', but still a marvel of engineering and adaptive structural skill).

Occultists find that many of Teilhard's statements are verifications of the Ancient Wisdom. For example:

> Evolution is a light illuminating all facts; a curve that all lines must follow . . .

> What makes and classifies a 'modern man' (and a whole host of our contemporaries are not yet 'modern') is having become capable of seeing in terms not of space and time alone, but also of duration, or—and it comes to the same thing—of *biological* space time: and above all having become incapable of seeing anything otherwise—anything—not even himself.

The second quotation is a magnificent paraphrase of the occult 'I' sense (4th and higher dimensions) opposed to the five-sense brain of our three-dimensional world.

For us, however, his most important hypothesis is his conclusion that all that exists from the first particle formed on our earth to the highest development of Man is the result of energy (Life Force), and that this manifests itself in what he calls a *tangential* force (we call it 'prana') and a *radial* force (we call it 'fohat'). The former force creates form and thereby creates our environment; the latter works on the inner reality of an entity. This duality creates not only complexity of form but, as Teilhard's Law states, an ever-increasing comprehension of consciousness which marches with (perhaps even sometimes leads) the form. He further believes that the inner radial energy carries with it an imperative, that of order. In other words, as the occultist has always taught, life grows through mineral, vegetable, animal stages to Man, and as the forms alter (see the analogy of Lester Ward's sympodial development) so does consciousness increase from the mere sensory of the mineral to the sensory/emotional of the vegetable (students should compare Rudolph Steiner's work with plants), then through the sensation/feelings/lower thinking of the animal to the creature that is 'different in degree' (to quote Chesterton), because Man has added to the other functions that of non-selfish thinking and of response to inspiration, and the prerequisite of this development is *purpose*.

This view of creative purposeful evolution means that every entity has two aspects: an outer or material one which science can study and an inner radial aspect which is the ever-improving and increasing consciousness of 'understanding more about more things', and which para-philosophy and occultism study. These evolutions proceed together, and each is necessary to the other; but the pull is always to the higher—to use a religious phrase, 'a return to the Creator'. All life is subject to the push in the back from the past and the pull to the fore of the future. All aspects of evolution proceed together. Gerald Heard has said in *Pain, Sex and Time*:

> Physical evolution is paralleled by, is the invariable concomitant of a *psychical* evolution. There is a mind/body complex present from the beginning of life . . . The organism increased in awareness by a

series of steps, each indicated by a corresponding alteration of physique.

It may be said, in summary, that our occult research accepts with little qualification the *physical* concept of evolution as seen by Darwin and his successors, but like Butler believes that in the first access of zeal the Darwinians threw the baby out with the bath water. They 'banished mind from the universe', and so to do is to banish purpose and meaning. Mind/soul, which phrase is used to correct the casual use of the word 'mind', is in fact the reason, the force which makes for evolution. Teilhard has suggested that the *physical* form of man is now fully evolved; if Man is therefore to continue to evolve it must of necessity be in the sphere of *mind*. Just as we breathe in the atmosphere, and have an organic envelope of life which we call the biosphere, so he asserts we must now live in a sphere of mental activity which he calls the Noosphere. For the writer this concept was admirably stated by Gerald Heard in the book already quoted:

> Now that evolution takes a further turn and is stepped up to a high intensity, his (Man's) mental evolution (which through the pre-historic periods was certainly sub-conscious and which through the historic periods has still in the main been unintentional and unapprehended) *must henceforth become conscious*. If we are to advance to the achievement and mastery of new faculties, we must do so deliberately—and by a scientific technique understand how to enlarge our apprehension.

With Heard's conclusion, this course completely agrees; it has been the attempt of mysto-occultism throughout the ages.

Please notice too the conclusion that the technique must be scientific. That is why each lesson gives not only a theoretical explanation in simple terms (best suited to the writer) but *practical experiment,* which can enable you to prove those 'new faculties' for yourself.

In this way you as individuals may daily evolve.

Exercise Ten

Before starting, you need six postcards; on three of them draw an inverted triangle on the other three draw a circle. Now colour wash the forms as follows:

Triangle first day—pale red.
Circle second day—pale orange.
Triangle third day—pale green.
Circle fourth day—pale blue.
Triangle fifth day—pale yellow.
Circle sixth day—pale violet.

On the seventh day you merely need a white card to look at until a colour comes. All the above should be stiff enough to stand some weeks of work, and the colouring should be done in quite pale pastel shades.

In your silence room have only a nightlight in a saucer of water. The Greeks taught the four elements of earth, water, fire and air, and by using a nightlight you are following that Ancient Wisdom and also ensuring that you have sufficient but not too much light.

Regularity in time of work is most desirable—the old teachers taught sunrise and sunset, but in our hurly-burly life we must make our own time as near as possible to those hours.

1 *Usual preliminaries.* We repeat that these are essential.
2 Place your postcard at eye level according to your use of the Indian or Egyptian positions.
3 Gaze only at the figure; give it all your attention and refuse to allow any other thought. If you really concentrate, you will find the colour will come out to surround you. With practice you can fill the room with the colour of the card.
4 Use the different cards in the order named and on succeeding nights. You will find one colour has a definite affinity with you; it will 'flood' more easily than any other. As in all other matters, do not be misled by preconceived ideas—'Oh, I know my colour is . . .' You do not, for our purpose. Try until you find your colour; you may have two but no more, and these will have a feeling of 'rightness'.
5 After about one month of work discard all colours but your own main one and a secondary if you have one. The writer's colours are thrush-egg blue and primrose yellow. He uses the blue for occult meditation and the yellow for 'orders' or latent powers.

You will find as you progress that you can do this exercise anywhere. Flood your bus, your office or your canteen with your 'right' colour, and watch for the results of others. Blue is always a good colour to send round for health reasons. Green is secure group harmony.

LESSON 10
A Glimpse at Cosmology

Exercise Eleven Concentration The Candle

The Universe shows evidence of a designing or controlling power that has something in common with our individual minds.

The Universe can best be pictured as consisting of thought—if the Universe is a Universe of thought then its creation must also have been an act of thought.

Sir James Jeans. *The Mysterious Universe*

Go take thy glass, astronomer, and all the girth survey
Of sphere harmonious linked to sphere in endless bright array.
All that far-reaching Science there can measure with her rod,
All powers, all laws are but the fair embodied Thoughts of God.

John Blackie. 'All Things are Full of God'

Gone is the picture, held for the greater part of man's history, of a Universe with our earth as its centre, round which the fixed stars rotated. Gone, too that of a Universe of fixed stars, with our solar system as its centre. Gone too that held by astronomers within the life time of some living today in which the sun was regarded as the centre of a stellar system of millions of stars distributed through an extent of space which would take twenty thousand light years to traverse. Now we are bidden by modern astronomers to envisage a Universe so vast that the human mind faints in its attempts to grasp its immensity.

F. C. Happold. *Mysticism*

> To expect us to feel 'humble' in the presence of astronomical dimensions merely because they are big is a kind of cosmic snobbery . . . what is significant is mind.
>
> Lord Samuel. *Belief and Action*

Advanced occultists study cosmology with such concepts as the progression of the globes, but this course will not do more than take a hasty glance at this advanced subject. Cosmology is as old as the records of Man, and certainly was a key feature of the thinking of the Chaldeans and the Egyptian priestcraft. Both had complete systems, which worked remarkably well. For them astronomy and astrology were sister subjects and part of the whole. With the advent of the seventeenth century and the telescope, astronomy came to the fore.

The advent of Einstein's Theory of General Relativity has brought cosmology as such back into prominence. The dictionary definition is 'the Universe viewed as a whole'. Professor George Gamow expands this into 'the study of the Universe in space and time. Since the only forces at work between the galaxies that make up the material Universe are closely associated with the modern version of gravitation as presented by Albert Einstein—this has presented us with a picture of an evolving Universe'.

Gamow conceives that at first the Universe was only radiant energy (compare with the occult teachings), and indeed the relative densities of matter and radiation have been charted: matter is apparently created by the 'cooling' of radiant energy which has evolved a gaseous structure and the foundation of 'matter' may well be the 'ashes' of the vast masses of burning helium, a by-product of hydrogen, which Hoyle thinks is being constantly renewed. Four million tons of hydrogen are transformed every second in this way.

Some of the findings of modern astronomy may be worth our glancing at. The starry heavens above us, which so excited Kant's wonder, give an entirely wrong impression to our mortal eyes. The first fact is the fantastic *emptiness* of space. Jeans has used as an analogy a picture of six specks of dust in an otherwise empty Waterloo Station. In such a case the station would be more *crowded* with dust than is space with stars. Allied to this emptiness, one then has to visualise the enormous number of stars. This can again be stated by analogy: if grains of sand to the depth of 6ft were spread to a width of ⅛ mile, it would take 6 million miles of such a packed beach for the number of grains of sand to equal the number of stars. Such 'homely' similies help us to realise the truth of the statement of the famous savant (and occultist) Francis Bacon (1561-1626) who said: 'The Universe is not to be narrowed down to the limit of our understanding but our understanding must be stretched and enlarged to take in the image of the Universe as it is discovered.' Since his time the advent of the modern telescope has so vastly enlarged the picture that he would stand amazed; although his proposition remains true.

As has been said, many occult students have done much work on this subject, but we must eschew these paths and adhere to our own more limited course. What is necessary is for us to realise the comparison between the Ancient Wisdom and its teachings and the 'discoveries' of modern science.

The vast masses which our scientists observe and which are spoken of as 'galaxies' are the seven veils of our Ancient Wisdom. Such galaxies as are observed by our telescopes are thousands among the billions which probably exist, so that our minds are bewildered by such immensities. The galaxies are created by the cooling process, and there are three main types:

1 The *irregular,* which show no recognisable form or order and make up possibly 2 per cent of the whole.
2 The *spiral,* which are possibly the next stage in a galaxy's evolution. These are the majority, probably 80 per cent. They have a spheroid centre body which is surrounded by a disc-like elliptical shape of less dense matter, which revolves around that centre core.
3 The *spherical,* which are, as it were, the culmination of galaxy evolution. These also have the centre core, and are densely packed with stars near to that core; but the starry objects appear to thin out towards the outer edges.

Hubble thought that our galaxy lay between the spiral and the spherical, probably at the end of the spiral classification. He said that 'the history of astronomy is a history of receding horizons'. It is essential here to remember the statement that two things cause wonder: the vastness of the 'immensities of the starry heavens' and 'the mind of man which can measure them'.

Our own solar system belongs to the Milky Way galaxy, and the most remote galaxy from our own is thousands of million light years away (light moves at 186,000 miles a second or 6 million million miles a year). The sun is 26,000 light years distant from the centre of our own galaxy.

The solar system consists of our sun, with nine planets, including the earth, their satellites and hundreds of asteroids. The sun itself is assessed at a diameter of 865,360 miles, and its vastness is such that a million earths could be packed within it. The distances even in the solar system itself still stagger our imaginations. Accepting the sun as a ball of 1¼cm (3in), then Pluto is 32m (105ft) away.

In the whole of this vast sea of force and radiation swims our little globe, whose orbit is controlled by the sun. Our earth is constantly bombarded by cosmic influences and by the direct rays of the sun. Rays from the sun (Fig 5) pass to us through seven belts: the photosphere (nearest the sun and of granular composition, according to

THE '7' AND THE SUN

(Fig 5)

Cosmic radiation

1 2 3 4 5 6 7 SUN

1 Troposphere
2 Stratosphere
3 Mesosphere
4 Ionosphere

5 Corona
6 Chromosphere
7 Photosphere

EARTH

Between each sphere there is a 'PAUSE'

MOON

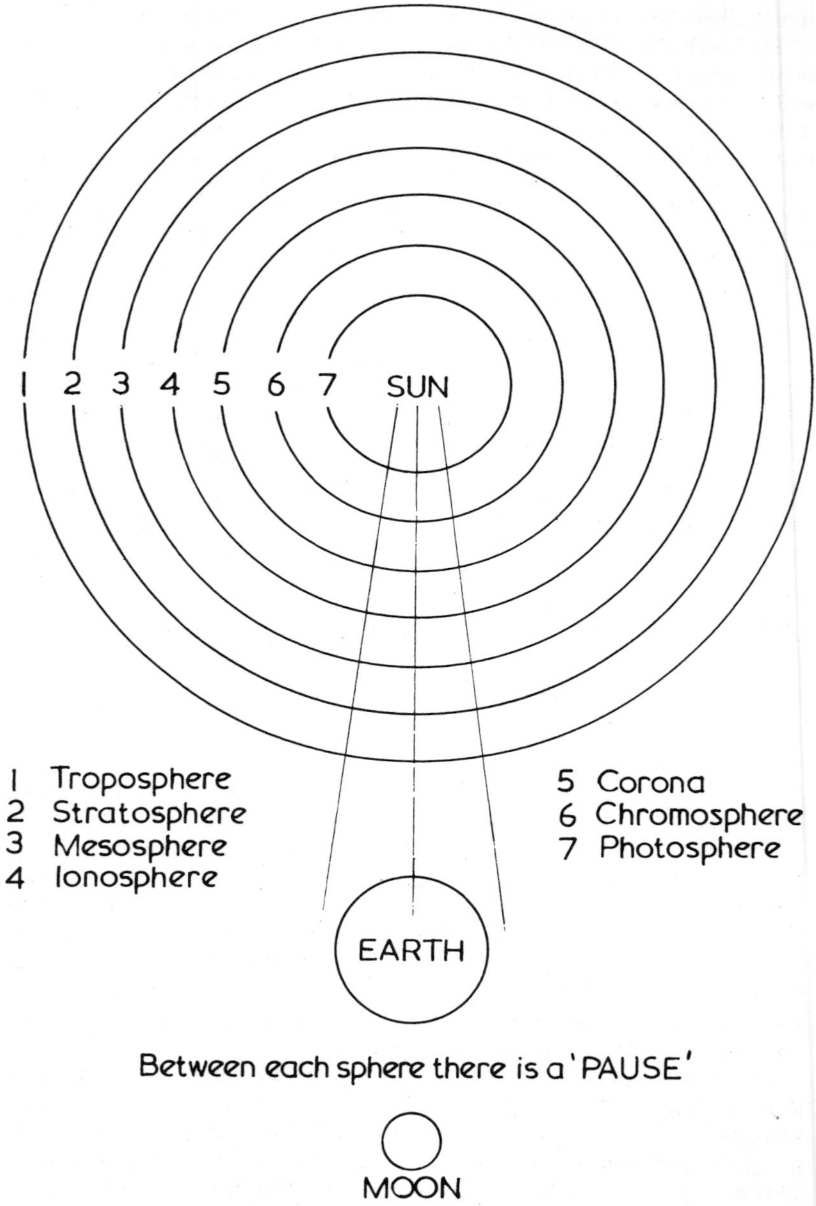

photographs), the chromosphere (the belt of colour/vibrations), the corona and then, after a gap, our own earth's ionosphere, mesosphere, stratosphere and troposphere.

The occultist believes that these seven layers are comparable to transformers insulating our earth and its creatures from the high 'forces' which otherwise would 'blast' life. The planes are created by the original 'Life Force' or 'homogeneous unity', and represent the passing through transformations into form and density (prana) and the electromagnetic force (fohat). As the force passes downwards, it forms into octave groups measurable by vibrations per second. It is wise here to remember the old maxim 'As above so below', and that all creations of higher planes are mirrored in form shape at lower levels.

This rule applies throughout, despite the relative sizes: the diameter of the sun is over 8,000,000 miles and the atom's 1 million-millionth of a centimetre, and yet, in both cases, we have the *hard* core of matter and densities that can be measured in terms of the rotary magnetic forces which surround that core. Moreover the atom swims in a sea of galaxy-vibration matter and is responsive to cosmic rays, as is the sun itself.

It will be seen how *size* as such is apparently immaterial to this universal law, which Pythagoras called the law of number. Jeans has said that the Universe could be imagined as a thought in the mind of a mathematical thinker, which concept adequately supports the sage of 2,500 years ago.

Let us pay tribute to the scientific thinkers and their technologists, who are forever widening man's concepts, and in so doing forever approaching the time when metaphysics shall become a guiding light of man's thinking and evolution. We quote James Jeans again:

> Travelling as far back in time as we can, brings not to the creation of the picture but to its edge: the creation of the picture lies as much outside the picture as the artist is outside his canvas. On this view discussing the creation of the Universe in terms of time and space is like trying to discover the artist and the action of painting by going to the edge of the picture. *This brings us very near to those philosophical systems which regard the Universe as a thought in the mind of its creator.*

Introduction to Exercise Eleven

You are now to take a step which, despite its simplicity, is nonetheless the beginning of 'illumination'. We are going to use your nightlight in a saucer of water in order to impose will upon light. Every student should learn something of the mysteries of light and realise its power. 'Let there be light' is a creative command, and Einstein's relativity is based upon his great understanding of light in time-space.

When you use your saucer, water and nightlight, it is partly symbology, for Egyptian priests in their temples used a small lamp in the training of their neophytes. Empedocles stated that there were four elements—earth, water, fire and air— and fire was recognised by the ancients as the great power of man, as is evident in the legend of Prometheus, who stole the secret of fire from the Gods and brought it to Man. It is notable that many mystics, notably Pascal, have experienced the sense of being bathed in fire. Their visions raised the pitch of their vibrations of perception to such a height that they seemed to be bathed in fire. R. M. Bucke, in *Cosmic Consciousness,* said: 'All at once without any warning he found himself wrapped around as it were, by a flame coloured cloud. For an instant he thought of fire—some sudden conflagration in the great city. The next instant he knew the light was within himself.'

Fire is the mystic symbol. So when you light your nightlight, remember this symbology; it links you with the savants of the ages.

Exercise Eleven

1 Usual preliminaries (never forget).
2 Flood room with colour (we shall in future consider this flooding as part of the preliminaries—it is always useful to slough off the daily strains and to attain poise).
3 Stand your nightlight at a level about 4ft distant from your eyes when seated on your chair (which is the best posture for this exercise).
4 Look at the flame. It is wise in all these exercises to start the visual concentration by staring for a few seconds only. Then very slowly and very gently close the eyelids until there is only a slit left for normal vision. At some time during this procedure you will find the 'right' place, where the flame seems brighter. This stage is the correct veiling of the eyes for you. Keep to it.
5 Within a few moments of gently held concentration the rays from the flame will be seen; they will go off in all directions from the flame.
6 When the rays are quite clear to your sight, *will,* deliberately will, that they converge and shine towards you.
7 They will either shine directly to your heart, your throat or your nose root. This is because those are the focal points for the development of your special latent powers. They are known in the East as 'Chakras' and in our terminology as 'Wheels of Force'. Let the rays come, or most of them, because, unless you are very strong in will, there will be 'rogue rays' which escape. Let the rays come then to the place which you find natural for you. Some students will have an immediate following experience but these will be very few—it will not be until the mirror work that most of us will 'perceive'.
8 Practise until the rays direct themselves to the correct chakra without your active willing.

LESSON 11
'The Fall'

Exercise Twelve   Concentration   Candle and Mirror

Our birth is but a sleep and a forgetting:
The Soul that rises with us, our Life's Star,
Hath had elsewhere its setting,
And cometh from afar:
Not in entire forgetfulness,
And not in utter nakedness,
But trailing clouds of glory do we come
From God, who is our home.
William Wordsworth. 'Intimations of Immortality'

Give reverence, O Man, to mystery
Keep your soul patient and with closed eye hear.
Know that the Good is in all things
Being by Him pervaded and upheld.
He is the Will, the thwarting circumstance
The two opposing forces equal both
Birth, Death are one.
William Bell Scott. 'The Year of the World'

He fixed thee midst this dance
Of plastic circumstance
This Present, though, forsooth, wouldst fain arrest:
Machinery just meant
To give thy soul its bent
Try thee and turn thee forth, sufficiently impressed.
Robert Browning. 'Rabbi Ben Ezra'

The Cosmic to Man

Occultism believes that Man passes through seven planes in his progress towards incarnation on earth. When we speak of planes we must remember that these are in fact *octave groups* of vibrations and that the matter of each plane is responsive *only* to instruments using its range of vibrations. The four planes that concern us are the following:

BUDDHIC or Spiritual (as distinguished from 'Spirit', the divine spark of Man): Few men attain consciousness at this height. It can affect the great men among us, however, in the form of inspirations, of 'mystical similitudes', but of it little can be said. Through this plane the Oversoul is in direct touch with the lasting 'individual'; the Oversoul is able to function in any of the lower planes and is therefore, in earth terms, multi-dimensional.

MENTAL: This is divided into two main states: (a) the concrete mind, which deals with man as an earth entity, self-centred although not necessarily in a derogatory sense, and (b) the abstract mind, which deals with all thought which is not self-centred. This is the vehicle which man most needs to develop by using other than the five-sense mechanism alone. It is probably five-dimensional and timeless.

EMOTIONAL (Astral): This deals with the feelings of Man, and is again dual, the lower level recording 'personal' interests and the higher 'selflessness'. This growth evolves from the hates and lusts of the primitive, through increasing perceptions of fears and hopes and 'selfness', to the higher emotional groups, where the 'Self' finds unselfish emotions and dedication to a cause. This state is four-dimensional and in 'Now' time (with memory of past events).

PHYSICAL/ETHERIC: Again this is dual. The physical, which is the instrument Man dons for earth experience in matter composed of chemical constituents, is combined with the etheric, which is the vitaliser. The physical affects the five-sense-brain mechanism, and the brain records all sensory impressions and tabulates them into an environmental concept. The etheric acts between the higher planes, carrying down the impulses from those planes and trying to get their messages through the five-sense mechanism and affording a channel of ESP communication. This is the 'L-Field' of Burr.

The etheric dies with the physical death and dissolution, although some have taught that it outlasts the physical for some small period.

Again let us emphasise that each plane is responsive to its own octave group, but, as the planes interpenetrate to some extent, there are linkages. The table of vibrations (Fig 6) will give some concept as to the incredible speeds which we can already apprehend either through our instruments or five-sense brain. For example, consider the rate of

VIBRATIONS			
OCTAVE	*NUMBER A SECOND*	*5 senses effect*	
1 to 5	2 to 64		SOLIDS
6 to 16	128 to 33, 768	SOUND	
7 to 25	33 T to 33 M		Unknown
26	1,000 M		Electricity
27 to 46	34 M to 70 B		Unknown
47	200 B		HEAT
48	281 B		Unknown
49	500 B	LIGHT	
50	1,125 B		Cosmic Rays
51 to 59	2 T B to 576 T B		Unknown
59	1M B		X Rays
59 to 62	4 M B		Unknown

(Fig 6)

vibrations of the X-ray machine, which, as you know, sees through flesh. See also Fig 5 (p 86), which shows the seven planes from the Cosmic (through the sun) to earth.

Man's Ancestry

The attributes, powers and potentialities of Man have an affinity with the seven planes through which he has passed to incarnation. As the descent into earth matter continues, the Life Force makes its vehicles of expression on each plane, created by the prana force of that 'plane' and activated or awakened by the 'fohat' force which accompanies the 'prana'.

Einstein stated the relation between mass and energy in the famous equation ($E=mc^2$), where 'E' is energy or the quantity of radiation which appears as 'm' grammes of matter disappear, and 'c^2' is the velocity of light squared. This energy is 'crystallised' or made into a body vehicle, and these instruments are on all planes.

This process of crystallisation can be traced throughout earth history. When the gases first started to cool, there must have been enormous pressures of heat and cold. These created densities, and thereby different atomic forms or chemical elements.

On earth this would lead first of all to the creation of minerals. The mineral would be subject only to 'sensation'—it would not have emotion or thought in itself. Many years ago Sir Chundra Bose, a great pioneer, made experiments which showed how minerals experienced sensation, and modern researchers have of course amplified his analysis—'fatigue' for example, is now well known and a measurable factor in technological work.

We must now remember the facts of sympodial development and

realise that evolution proceeds not in steady growth from manifestation to manifestation but in 'leaps' similar to the cactus leaves. The next 'leap' was into the vegetable kingdom, and this added the function of 'feeling'. While in no way affecting the permanence of the mineral form, the vegetable added this new feeling function, and gave greater validity to the mineral in that the vegetable 'fed' upon the mineral. The earliest forms of vegetation were possibly lichen and mosses, but every gardener knows how dependent our vegetable kingdom is upon the mineral in the shape of soil and chemicals. The new forms of the vegetable kingdom started perhaps in lowly fashion, but led to the forest giants we all admire. The vegetable kingdom prepared the way for another form, in that they gave off the vital oxygen gas and extracted the deadly gases from our atmosphere. Moreover plants can be responsive to 'feeling'—the sensitive plant is an outstanding example. One of the basic beliefs of the Anthroposophists, as enunciated by their founder, Rudolph Steiner, has to do with this response to 'feeling' mechanism in the vegetable.

The next development was now prepared, and in due course the animal appeared. In function this added a higher emotion, the rudiments of thought, and, in the physical, movement. The animal used sensation—it used feeling, touching, 'higher emotion' in mother love. The long evolution of the animal is the subject of Darwinian evolution, and the advent of domesticated animals brings in the first glimmerings of thought through emotional pressure.

At last man appears. Physically of animal origin, his sign manual is that of mental creation (remember Chesterton and the cave). The true animal man had perhaps little contact with what we think of as thought; he took over from the animal the sensation, the lower emotions, but also touches of higher emotions and 'glimmerings' of thought. His thoughts would all be of a self-centred nature, limited by the cave, but gradually the tribe would emerge, and to fears of physical ills would be added fears of abstract forces such as the 'voice' of the thunder. We may speculate that the millennial ascent of Man will stretch far past our own time into the aeon when he will use the *whole* of the earth octave, and become a mind entity who has shed mere self-centred preoccupations and is starting to reach out from the footstool of earth to the stars. His ascent will allow him to use all the gamut of sensation, feeling and thought, and he will enter into his spiritual faculty and realise the meaning of 'individuality'. *This is his birthright as a spark of the divine.*

Man has been 'born' of the seven 'planes', and is at our stage affected every minute by the lower four—spiritual, mental, astral and physical etheric. In fact he is affected beyond the etheric. Because each individual man has passed through these planes, he has a vibratory 'vehicle' or body which is his instrument of functioning on the appropriate plane. But also, because we have passed through those planes, the physico-etheric has vibratory impulses within it which are in accord with those higher planes. Indeed one of the purposes of earth life is that those higher-plane vehicles could not be fully evolved without the experiences of earth life.

The law of attention now applies: we can usually *only* think of the thing in which we are immersed at the moment, so as our lives are spent largely in worldly affairs of home, earning and competition, we shall be acting and thinking in the physical body. But in doing this we shall be using powers of the personality which affect and are affected by the plane of their special manifestation. If we are thinking of any philosophy or music, it is very easy 'to lose ourselves' and to forget all other surroundings, in other words to live for that moment of time *on* the plane to which our physical/etheric instrument is momentarily attuned. 'How' will be explained later.

It will be found that there is always this 'two-way traffic', the higher inspiring the lower but in turn the lower feeding data to the higher, which it can use for expansion.

> Let us not always say
> 'Spite of this flesh today
> I strove, made head, gained ground upon the whole
> As the bird wings and sings
> Let us cry all good things
> Are ours, *nor soul helps flesh more,* no, *than flesh helps soul.*
>
> Robert Browning. 'Rabbi Ben Ezra'

This two-way traffic means that every act of every day should lift up the physical man to the purer level, and evolve the higher vehicle to include experience that only earth life can give.

So we can now return to Teilhard's Law and understand how complexity of form, the making of a suitable instrument (the diver's suit) has proceeded. We can also understand how with complexity of form comes the growing expansion of consciousness, allowing man in the physical to become less self-centred and more and more the master of his earth vibrations—his earth octaves—and yet, and at the same time, to feed into his higher vehicles of expression earth experiences and thereby *increase consciousness.*

We shall now find that this increase of consciousness is what really matters to Man: we have mentioned Jeans and his 'mathematical thinker'. It was another great Englishman, Sir Arthur Eddington, who said: 'Recognising that this physical world is entirely abstract from its linkage to consciousness we restore *consciousness* to its fundamental position: instead of regarding it as an inessential complication, as the Victorian scientists tended to do.'

Exercise Twelve

In preparation for this very important exercise you will need two nightlights or candles in front of a mirror. Space the lights so that their reflections come at the sides of the mirror when you are seated (Egyptian position) 4-5ft from the mirror. You must complete all preparatory exercises, particularly breathing, before sitting down. Then rest for a few moments.

1 Gaze directly into the eyes reflected in the mirror. At first stare with absolute intensity (making sure the candles or nightlights are reflected in the mirror).
2 After a short while start to lower your eyelids very slowly (*slowly*) until you are just seeing through the slits and *wait*.
3 Many different things happen to many different people:
   (a) Your reflection may disappear altogether; if so, *wait*. It is possible that *your* Master may appear. *(Do not dramatise* and be truthful to yourself. It is possible such appearance may be behind your shoulder at first and only later in the mirror.)
   (b) Your reflection may change in appearance; this is known as transfiguration and has many meanings—try to work them out for yourself, but if you cannot, and have no suitable exponent in you district, you may write to the author (see notice at end of book).
   (c) You may experience waves of colour, such as those in Disney's *Fantasia,* Bach fugue episode.
   Variations of (a), (b) and (c) are possible.

This exercise is of primary importance. It should not be attempted until you can bend the rays, and only after proper preparatory work (Exercise Eleven).

There is absolutely nothing to fear. It will put you in contact with your own higher self and this is your aim.

Experience of fifty years enables me to assure you that there is absolutely nothing to fear.

LESSON 12
What is Man? The Vital Question

Exercise Thirteen Concentration The Tulip

What a piece of work is a man! How noble in reason! how infinite in faculty! in form, in moving, how express and admirable! in action how like an angel! in apprehension how like a god.

William Shakespeare. *Hamlet*

We will have to subject our conception of man and of the Universe to a thorough going revision. It does not mean that we shall have to reject 'in toto' the findings of modern science though we may well find that some of them will have to be revised much as Einstein revised the findings of Newton. We shall, however, have to widen considerably the field to which science now limits itself.

Douglas Hunt. *Exploring the Occult*

Know then thyself, presume not God to scan,
The proper study of mankind is man.
Placed on this isthmus of a middle state,
A being darkly wise, and rudely great:
With too much knowledge for the sceptic side,
With too much weakness for the stoic's pride,
He hangs between; in doubt to act, or rest;
In doubt to deem himself a God, or beast;
In doubt his mind or body to prefer;
Born but to die, and reas'ning but to err;
Sole judge of truth, in endless error hurled;
The glory, jest and riddle of the world!

Alexander Pope. 'An Essay on Man'

Truth is within ourselves, it takes no rise
From outward things whate'er you may believe.
There is an inmost centre in us all
Where truth abides in fullness, and around
Wall upon wall the gross flesh hems it in,
This perfect clear *perception* which is truth.
A baffling and perverting carnal mesh
Binds it and makes all error: and to know
Rather consists of opening out a way
Whence the imprisoned splendour may escape
Than in effecting entry for a light
Supposed to be without.

Robert Browning. 'Paracelsus'

The quotations on the previous pages typify the bewilderment with which the savants have faced the great question—*What is Man?* In a scientific age this was almost the last question asked. The resultant science of psychology (some call it a pseudo-science), initiated by that great man Sigmund Freud, has unravelled many mysterious facets of Man—as the Upanishads had done 3,000 years ago.

In the materialistic boom of the late Victorian age each science had to have 'laws' supposed to have the same provable certainty as those, say, of pure mathematics. The creation of an 'economic man', a creature without heart and only pockets, was an example of this curious craze. Today we realise that these pseudo-sciences cannot have the same 'laws' as those we call concrete sciences. Economics, psychology and sociology are subject to the variation of the individual, and must deal with general (or aggregate) laws. Psychology has suffered from this Victorian desire for concrete laws in its application to individuals; in fact, today, psychologists would be the first to admit the foolishness of the pretension. Professor O. L. Zangwill has recently said: 'The traditional idea of psychology as the science of the mind is today in process of revolution.' Nearly a century has elapsed since psychology first took shape, and, during that time, it 'has produced many facts, a few generalisations, and even an occasional law, but it has, so far, failed to produce anything resembling a coherent and generally accepted body of scientific theory'.

Behaviourism, even the work of Pavlov, has failed, may one suggest, because the Behaviourists have been trying to describe Man merely in terms of body. They have fallen between the old difficulty that Johannes Scotus Erigena long ago exposed. They have taken Man to be the visible, and forgotten that most of what we know as 'man' is, in fact, invisible. His thoughts, his moods, his emotions, are much more important than his physical shape or physical brain.

The world owes a great debt to Carl Gustav Jung for his work and research. Born in 1875, he grew up to take a medical degree, and then his enquiring mind quickly took him into the regions of psychiatry. He had been greatly influenced by Freud and championed the latter's work; they met in 1907 and became friends, and for many years fruitfully worked together; but Jung was dissatisfied with what he thought were the limitations of Freud, and gave up his association with him in order to be able to devote his time to his own scientific research.

The odyssey of Jung is extremely interesting and revealing. His work *Psychological Types* gained immediate notice because of his invention of the terms 'extrovert' and 'introvert'. It is true that the facts were by no means new: indeed, historically, they were exemplified in such contrasts as Plato and Aristotle, both great leaders of human thought, whose approach differed fundamentally. The two 'types' are subjects of everyday observation, although few people, if any, are wholly one or the other.

Another concept was the *four functions*—the four main ways in which we experience phenomena. Again one goes back to Plato, with his 'four mental states'. Jung divided his four functions into thinking, sensation, feeling and intuition. One is reminded that Gurdjieff calls these 'functions' or motivations 'centres', and adds to the four of Jung the 'sex centre' (which Jung, with Freud, places in the subconscious). The occultist terms this centre Kundalini.

We assess our world through the means (or vehicles) of thought, feeling, sensation or intuition. Thought and feeling are *rational* processes with basic forms of evaluation—in thought by the 'true/false' judgement, and in feeling by the 'agreeable/disagreeable' judgement—and 'these two fundamental forms of reaction are *mutually exclusive* as practical determinants of behaviour'. If we 'give way to feeling', we think not at all or vaguely. If we consider a problem, the 'purity' of that consideration depends upon how unmixed it is with any emotion. Either thought or feeling *must* be predominant although, naturally, they intermingle. In *Modern Man in Search of a Soul* Jung says: 'When we think, it is in order to judge or to reach a conclusion; and when we feel it is in order to attach a proper value to something.'

The 'irrational functions', in Jung's phrase, are those of sensation and intuition, and they are mutually exclusive. Sensation is a physical perception without evaluation or interpretation. Intuition is conversely a perception from an inner (or 'super') basis, equally without evaluation *or* interpretation. 'Whenever strange conditions have to be dealt with, or situations met where established values and concepts do not work, then intuition must be brought into play.'

It is very important to realise that every man, according to his own make-up, tends to adjust himself to reality through one of these means, and that this orientation usually results in an *increasing* bias. In Jung's words, 'it becomes the dominant function for adjustment, it gives the conscious attitude its direction and quality'. Gurdjieff probably meant this when he spoke of the dominant 'I' centre which determines a man's type of mechanicalness.

But no man is exclusively a thinker or an emotionalist. He has a secondary function, possibly, say, as a sensationalist.

If all four functions could be raised to equal consciousness, the whole circle of man would be in light, ie in conscious manifestation. If a man could do this he would cast off mortal fallibility; he would become a Master of life. He would be a complete octave, an individual. Jung says:

> If one has all four functions at one's disposal in sufficient measure—which would be the above mentioned ideal state—one could, for example, comprehend an object cognitively, track out by means of intuition its inner concealed potentialities, then, touch it all round by means of sensation and, finally, by evaluing its agreeableness or disagreeableness, *feel* about it.

Such a complete view of an event, or cause, or effect, would obviously re-orient human life, and that is the aim of the occultist teaching.

To understand our functional type, to 'self realise', is a primary need, for then we can learn to deal with inferior functions which disturb our 'I' by breaking in from the unconscious. Of such inferior functions Jung has said: 'Not you have *it* in hand, but *it* has *you*'. He goes on:

> The two pairs of oppositions (thought/feeling—sensation/intuition) must however stand in compensatory relation to each other. In case of over exaggeration of one function in a person (eg who *lives* only intellectually) the complementary function feeling will strive to compensate of itself and will work in its inferior form. This intellectual will then be overcome quite unexpectedly by altogether infantile bursts of emotion (very often 'sex' related).

Now this inequality results in the individuality, the construction of a concept, a 'persona', a personality with which to front the world and to attempt to come to terms with it. *But* this personality is *never* the individuality, the true self which is to be remembered. In *Psychological Types* Jung says: 'The "persona" is a "function complex" which has come into existence for reasons of adaptation or necessary convenience, but by *no means* is it identical with the individuality'.

It is, in Jung's opinion, of the premier importance to find out our own psychological tendencies, a real assessment of weaknesses and strengths. It is to be remembered that we shall have a 'dominant' function and a supporting, but weaker, function, but that the two opposite functions are largely our *terra incognita,* and much of our work of integration, therefore, consists of exploration. This territory is the land of the 'shadow'. This difficult complex—in its true sense of something twisted together—may usurp the 'dominants' in certain extreme cases, and everyone has read of cases of possession, which usually arise in such a way. They are the 'rubbish heap of repressions', and personalise very often in dreams or trances.

It is essential for 'wholeness' that this dark 'shadow' side of our personality be faced and integrated. It is the first 'dweller on the threshold', which all occultism teaches we must meet. As Eliot says:

> Between the idea
> And the reality
> Between the motion
> And the act,
> Falls the Shadow.
>
> Between the conception
> And the creation,
> Between the emotion
> And the response,
> Falls the Shadow.

This is what Jung means when he says: 'The shadow is a moral problem which challenges the whole.'

Jung preaches the need for humility: he believes that if the ego can relinquish some of the belief in its own omnipotence then 'supreme oneness' is achieved. When this happens, then the rapt all-comprehension of the mystic occurs—a universal 'oneness' in which all is perceived instantaneously and known lastingly. Jung, master of clear exposition, faltered at this point; indeed, many have found this knowledge beyond words. The Blessed Angelice of Foligno said: 'All that is to say of this (her vision) seems to me to be nothing. I feel as though I offended in speaking of it.' Jung said of this supreme achievement in *The Secret of the Golden Flower:* 'It is as if the leadership of the affairs of life had gone over to an invisible centre.'

The path to the self, the reality behind 'wholeness', is the method of integration. Jung realised this quest for integration would not be easy: 'Integration is a favour that must be paid for dearly' he said, and again: 'The man who wishes to follow the way of individualisation must, above all, be loyal to his own fate; there can be no retreat from self.'

He has traced unerringly the repressions found in the subconscious and their effect upon our daily life. He has laboured to let people know that, indeed, we cannot assess our motives and our actions in terms of the physical consciousness only; we have to accept the different selves which appear, each self a group of traits fairly consistent within its own range, but different from—indeed, often opposing—the other selves in the same person.

Jung has tracked the conflicts of our multiple selves, which are often bitter, like that between 'Doctor Jekyll and Mr Hyde'. The resultant disunity is the cause of war in the individuality.

Jung's later teaching developed strongly along the lines of Eastern thought.

Dream analysis became the keystone of his constructive process, which aimed at integration and the discovery of the self. A dream is a manifestation of psychic activity, and in a later section we shall discuss some ideas held by occultists about this universal phenomenon. The study of dreams led Jung, like the occultists before him, into a study of symbols.

This symbolism is the language of occultists; it is, as it were, the mathematical figures of their reckonings. Such figures as the cross in its varied forms, the circles, the serpent swallowing its own tail and the triangle all have positive meanings.

Jung spoke of such symbols as 'Mandalas', a Sanskrit word which translates roughly as 'magic circle'. Jung found such symbols recurred constantly in the dreams of his patients. In *Development of Personality* he shows how the reconciliation of opposites through meditation may bring illumination: 'It is as if a river that had run to waste in sluggish side streams and marshes suddenly found its way back to its proper bed, or as if a stone lying on a germinating seed were lifted away so that the shoot could begin its natural growth'.

The death of Jung not only deprived the world of a great scientific pioneer, but of one of the few Western men who was able to apprehend the wisdom of the East in terms of the West.

We have dealt at length with the work of Jung because he gave a new direction to his science and pointed the way, particularly in his later works to the real Wisdom. Readers interested must be referred to books on the history of psychology as from his day. The names of Alfred Adler and Otto Rank (fellow students of Jung), Karen Horney, Smuts (of Holism), Allport, Maslow, and Murphy, to mention but a few, spring to mind for their brilliant contributions. There has, however, been the fundamental division between those who started from the body and its responses and those who thought there was more in Man than body mechanism and sought for 'psi' faculties. So we get such thinking as Watson's behaviourism and the experiments of Pavlov, the more or less intermediate work of Sperry and the Chicago School, and at the other end the work of Rhine, Soal and many others, an increasing number, who by experiment are endeavouring to establish the 'psi' ability as a scientific fact. They are having some success: Rhine himself has said 'on the issue between the two "centrisms" on the nature of man . . . a creeping recognition is manifest that man is more than body and bodily responses'.

There are now many brands, one of the most fruitful being depth psychology, which is probing further into the meanings of dreams and visions as messages or intimations from the deeper levels. Psychosynthesis, formulated by Dr Roberto Assagioli, includes tenets which may be claimed to be pure occultism. For example:

1 The method of starting from within.
2 The concept that each individual is growing successively in latent possibilities.
3 The central importance of meaning and of values.
4 The emphasis on the future and its linkage with the present.
5 The recognition of the uniqueness of every individual.

The fact of the duality of man (at the least) has been forced upon the scientists, and the search is now for modes of *integration,* which has been a basic of occult thinking for the last 3000 years, notably in Egypt and Greece.

Let us consider the question of what is integration.

> There was an old sailor my grandfather knew
> Who had so many things that he wanted to do,
> That whenever he found he was ready to begin
> He couldn't because of the state he was in.

This piece of doggerel emphasises the fact that we are creatures of a number of impulses, pulled this way and that by conflicting emotions, rational ideas, entreaties and suggestions, and it is the purpose of all psychology—as it is the purpose of all occultism—to integrate these 'I's' into one person. 'I think, therefore I am', said Descartes. But what, or who, am 'I'? In a general sense, everyone knows, but, to be particular, very few people have found the 'I'.

Once Schopenhauer was walking along the street absorbed in meditation and cannoned into another person, who berated him with fervour. At the end of the tirade, the injured party exclaimed: 'And who are you, anyhow?' 'Who am I?' said Schopenhauer, 'Don't I wish I knew!'

In this materialistic age, as perhaps one must still call it (although in fact the popular conception of physics as materialistic lags fifty years behind the modern conception), most people might equate the 'I' with the physical body. If, in so doing, they wish to be logical, they must also adopt the brave scepticism of a Bertrand Russell and accept that after seventy years more or less of sorrow and joy, of effort and sloth, of aspiration and despair, they must pass away. In fact, according to their philosophy, life is a journey to the manure heap.

Except for the rash of scientific exuberance which attacked us in the nineteenth century (a rash that has subsided, leaving a great many of the greatest scientists as near to metaphysicians as makes no matter), it would be true to say that mankind has always accepted the idea that

Man was more than his physical body. So when we are called upon to define what we mean by the word 'I', we immediately run into difficulties. This difficulty of defining the self is mixed up with the difficulty of deciding what we mean by the things which, in the phraseology of Indian philosophy, are *'not-self'*.

We have said that Man is a compound of various impulses which may be physical, emotional, mental or intuitional. It is most dangerous for the whole man if any one set of impulses gains control. Sound physical health is a blessing, but such people as Charles Darwin, who was 'almost continually unwell'; Robert Louis Stevenson, who was a victim of tuberculosis; and Hellen Keller, who was blind and deaf; remind us that the body is only one of Man's possessions. Equally, emotions cannot beneficially be allowed to control the whole. The little boy who was scared by a barking dog and, on being asked if he was frightened, replied, 'No, I am not afraid, but my stomach is', had discovered a great truth. Today, we consider most emotional upsets under glandular headings, and this allies itself to the old Eastern idea of the chakra. A man or a woman whose whole is controlled by their emotions is likely to live an irregular and unfortunate life.

Nor must the mind be allowed to govern the entity. How often do we find in life examples of men of knowledge who are not men of wisdom? If, in the category of great demagogues, we might cite Hitler as a person who ruled by, and was ruled by, emotions, so, equally, we might cite Napoleon as one who ruled by, and was ruled by, calculating intellect, but both of them found their own St Helena.

When we are complete, 'whole', real 'doing' can begin; this is what the psychologist calls integration and the occultist the entry into the inner court. It is this climb towards integration, this effort to truly finish oneself, to achieve a high degree of unity, which is the purpose of occult initiation, for unless this is achieved, the rest cannot be added.

One observer has said of Einstein that the outstanding characteristic with which he impressed others was the fact that he seems to be 'all of a piece. He has gathered himself into wholeness and coherence.' It is probable that our path leads from reflexes to habits, from habits to traits, from traits to multiple selves, from multiplicity towards integration, and from integration to initiation, so that the seeker on this path must recognise the vital importance of becoming a unity, of being above the passions of the moment, or of what old Carlyle called 'logic chopping'. He has to become an integrated self, surveying his needs and wants, his urges, his hopes and his despairs, as dispassionately as if they were those of another person. This formula of perfection is not as unachievable as it may sound; it is, indeed, the basis of the system of Guru and Chela. It is the purpose of the old monastic system, and has been beautifully expressed at work in such books as *The Clouds of Unknowing* and Hilton's *Ladder of Perfection*. Those who know anything of the trials of a novice in such retreats as a Zen Monastery will realise that these trials are aids—often unpalatable aids—to integration. Jung himself has said that no man can find integration except at the cost of great personal effort and even pain.

We have spoken then of integration, but this in itself is not wholeness (haleness). A person cannot be a man of integrity without integration, but integration does not necessarily mean integrity. Napoleon, whom someone called 'organised victory', and who was undoubtedly a very strong integrated personality, was not a 'good' man despite his integration. It appears to the writer that one of the great mistakes that has been made in our age is to forget the moral standards necessary for wholeness, and to seek for psychiatric treatments which tranquillise but do not integrate.

The real self must face loneliness; in Matthew Arnold's phrase, 'we mortal millions live alone'. The high disciplines of the lonely vigils, and of the view from the mountain, are essentials for the evolving man. If the world beneath, when viewed from the mountain, appears only as a toy for the advanced soul to use, then that soul's achievement has been in vain. Unless the tempter can be put behind and repulsed, as the Master reproved and overcame temptation on the mountain, and unless Divine charity can also be called into play, the integration may well lead to a 'black magic' outlook instead of one of service and evolution. Therefore, in searching for integration our quest must go hand in hand with humility and with tolerance, and if these two strands can be woven into a whole cloth (and again we have the memories of the discipline of the monastery before us), then the integrated Man may stand as master of this physical plane and as a perfected, responsive instrument to that great 'Over Self', that archetype, of which he is the expression in physical terms.

All religions know this, and Whitehead has said: 'There are two all important prayers for the loneliness of the soul: "Thy will, not mine, be done", and "Be quiet and know that I am God". Only in that solitude of complete renunciation can the voice of the silence speak to us.'

We must fully appreciate what a difficult task this 'integration' is—we have so vivid a conception of our own 'persona' and rarely see ourselves whole that we unknowingly mistake our selves. Our conception of our false personality (which we use to excuse our errors and to rationalise our habits), is an 'I' quite different from the real 'I' which speaks to us intuitionally and through the conscience.

It has been well said that we judge others by their actions and ourselves by our intentions. It is the purpose of our false personality to give us a picture of ourselves and of our good intentions which excuses all our faults or treats them kindly, which rationalises our laziness, our voluntary or involuntary lying, and which, indeed, presents us to ourselves as a 'hell of a fine fellow'.

It is a mistake to think that we are always one and the same. We are continually changing; we are swayed by the mood of the moment. The sudden rages, the sudden hates, the sudden falsenesses, are all part of this constant changing, which shows the 'false' personality wearing first one mask and then another a moment later. ('Persona', the root word of personality, means mask.) We assess ourselves in a certain character and change the mask to assume another.

This flux of 'I's' we may rationalise, but there is always a true 'I' which cannot, will not, accept such rationalisation. Gurdjieff, the purveyor of a very fine psychological, mystic system, which aims at integration, has taught:

> One of man's important mistakes—one which must be remembered—is his illusion in regard to his 'I'.
>
> Man such as we know him, the 'man-machine', the man who cannot 'do', and with whom and through whom everything 'happens', cannot have a permanent and single 'I'. His 'I' changes as quickly as his thoughts, feelings, and moods, and he makes a profound mistake in considering himself always one and the same person; in reality he is always a different person, not the one he was a moment ago.
>
> Man has no permanent and unchangeable 'I'. Every thought, every mood, every desire, every sensation, says 'I'. And in each case it seems to be taken for granted that this 'I' belongs to the Whole, to the whole man, and that a thought, a desire, or an aversion is expressed by this Whole. In actual fact there is no foundation whatever for this assumption. Man's every thought and desire appears and lives quite separately and independently of the Whole, only physically as a thing, and Man has no individual 'I'. But there are, instead, hundreds and thousands of separate small 'I's', very often entirely unknown to one another, never coming into contact or, on the contrary, hostile to each other, mutually exclusive and incompatible. Each minute, each moment, man is saying or thinking 'I'. And each time his 'I' is different. Just now it was a thought, now it is a desire, now a sensation, now another thought, and so on, endlessly. Man is a plurality. Man's name is legion.

The esoteric and very difficult system of occult thought propounded by Gurdjieff is built upon this fundamental and the need of man to subdue these claimant 'I's' into an integrated and real 'I'. The likeness of the 'man-machine' of Gurdjieff and of the behaviourist is to be noted.

The following words from a well known doctor and psychiatrist who was also, at one time, a minister of religion, are worth studying:

> In confronting this task, man's situation is altogether 'sui generis'.

He is the only creature that can consciously help to create itself. The fulfilment of the possibilities of its species may be the primary function of a seedling tree, but the tree is unaware of that fact and cannot deliberately cooperate. Man alone consciously assists in the fulfilment of his nature.

We are not simply creatures, we are self-creators. As Wordsworth put it: 'So build we up the Being that we are.' Professor William Ernest Hocking writes:

> Of all animals, it is man in whom heredity counts for least, and conscious building forces for most. Consider that his infancy is longest, his instincts least fixed, his brain most unfinished at birth, his powers of habit-making and habit-changing most marked, his susceptibility to social impressions keenest—and it becomes clear that in every way nature, as a prescriptive power, has provided in him for her own displacement . . . Other creatures nature could largely finish; the human creature must finish himself.

So by the scientific paths and by the path of philosophy our questionings have now reached the place where we can give an occult answer to the question 'What is Man?' Let us start by considering what you mean when you say 'I'. What do your friends and associates mean by your 'self'. They mean your personality, and they will always wrongfully assess you. Do you remember that little story from an almost forgotten book by Oliver Wendell Holmes, *The Autocrat of the Breakfast Table,* in which he points out that in any conversation between two people in fact six people are conversing: there is Tom's idea of John, John's idea of John and the *real John;* and there is John's idea of Tom, Tom's idea of Tom and the *real Tom.* What we have to do is to define the real 'John'—in effect the real 'I'.

Ramana Maharishi, the great Indian sage who died comparatively recently, taught that one of the great paths was 'Enquiry into the Self', and he wrote a treatise for his students (preferring not to speak) titled in those words. It asks the question 'Who am "I"?'

Am 'I' the body? Only a very little enquiry will show us that we are more than our bodies. Of two identical twins lying on slabs before us, assume one is dead and the other alive. We could have little doubt that *the 'I' belonged to the living.* The one is a hulk of flesh with organs similar in every way to the living twin *except that it has no 'self', no life.* The animating principle we call life has departed and with that departure also the 'I' has fled, for the remaining tissues and organs will comparatively soon resolve themselves into their original elements. As Longfellow said:

Dust thou art, to dust returnest,
Was not spoken of the soul.

'I' consciousness is absent from the physical in sleep or trance. Shakespeare's 'Sleep that knits up the ravell'd sleeve of care' is that state of rest where physical brain, five-sense mechanism, is in abeyance because the high force we call *mind* and the still higher 'I' are no longer operating through the brain mechanism; they have entered into their own higher states.

Dreams are usually of three kinds: the highest is the dream of warning or illumination that comes from the height of the 'Oversoul'; the middle is the product of the *mind* and will usually be a dream of prevision or retrocognition; while the most common is a jumble of emotional five-sense-brain recollections linked with a message from the mind level. *All* these dreams have to come through our five-sense-brain mechanism on waking, and this is why they are so often jumbled and hazy. Later we shall talk about the nature of dreams, the work of such men as Dunne, Carrington, Jung and Martin, and the meaning dreams have for our development.

The body as such is only a physical instrument for functioning in the physical world. The 'I' is another entity, and we really acknowledge that fact every time we say '*My* body', '*My* idea' and so on. There is an observer, a self, an 'I' which is *not* the body.

Emotions. Is the 'I' the emotions? Are the hates, the loves, the fears, the angers, the lusts, the various emotions which sway us—are these the 'I'? No one would like to think so and indeed we know even in the midst of our anger that it is not really our 'true selves' who have given way to this tempestuous rage. Most of us have moments of poise and calm when we are not subjected to emotional stresses of any kind—this calm detachment is carried to its heights in such people as Teresa of Avila or the Sage of Arunachala. The changeable gamut of the emotions are merely ripples on the sea of our real self—the unchanging, continuous, calm, poised 'I'.

Intellect. The separateness of the 'self' from either body or emotion is easy to understand and achieve, but it becomes more difficult when we deal with our intellect, because the sign manual of man on his earth is *just* that ability to think and reason and, even more significantly, to indulge in abstract cogitation where the personal enters not at all. Our thoughts can be divided into two groups: those which deal with personality, our daily affairs and home life, our local and national environment, thoughts about 'concrete' things; and, secondly, those which can best be designated 'abstract', as when we become 'immersed' in music, say a symphonic performance, or enlifted by a noble poem.

Our personality thoughts change daily, hourly; they do not represent the continuity which is the essence of the 'I'. Indeed very often in moments of contemplation we can almost feel the 'I' which is watching us. Blessed is the man or woman who can laugh at themselves as personalities, as a result of that contemplation.

Bergson some years ago in *Mind and Memory* pointed out that our brain is really a selective instrument which conditions or habituates our thinking to a preconceived set of traditions and ideas, which are the result of our natal environment, the impact of race and the growing-up period of our subsequent lives. ('Shades of the prison-house begin to close upon the growing boy', said Wordsworth.) Think of this for a moment; it is vital for our self-analysis. The brain deals with all our thinking but it *selects* a pattern which falls within our normal earthly experience; it 'rationalises' if you prefer the word. *But in all this process there is a knowledge that some higher self,* some observer, is calmly assessing our personality actions, our personality emotions, our personality thinking, and yet remaining uncontaminated by our daily routine of personality/brain processes. The real 'I' is above all such manifestations. In the words of Thomas Traherne:

> Oh Joy! Oh wonder and delight
> Oh sacred mystery.
> My Self a spirit infinite
> An image of the Deity
> A pure substantial light.

Or Alfred Noyes:

> This outer world is but the pictured scroll
> Of worlds within the soul.
> A coloured chart, a blazoned missal-book
> Wherein who rightly look
> May spell the splendours with their mortal eyes
> And steer to Paradise.

It is the belief of this course that the poet in those words has uttered a grand truth: that here, on this earth, you and I may recognise our true stature; achieve powers of intellectual and spiritual worth which will indeed 'steer us to Paradise'.

In this lesson the main propositions are (a) we are more than body, emotion or thought, we are a divine inspired 'I'; and (b) that there are practical scientific steps whereby that realisation and its attendant powers can be found during this lifetime. It helps if we again define the grand quaternion that is *man.*

INDIVIDUAL: The completion of the octave. That which can use all the seven octave groups of development and, standing on the eighth, is also standing at the start of a new octave, freed from and master of the earth and from lives in the octaves of Man form.

OVERSOUL: The 'higher' self. It has been called by a thousand names but Soul/Mind is the one we prefer. It is the continuant entity and stores the experiences of all Man's several lives. It can observe and control the personality and the person.

PERSONALITY: The commonsense five-sense brain which produces censored versions of phenomena. This personality derives from our sensations, feelings and thinking about our earthly environment and our daily place in it, including those aspirations which sometimes urge us onwards. 'Persona', the Latin word from which our English one is derived, simply means 'a mask', and this course believes that personality is one of the masks individuality wears in its ascent to higher worlds of experience.

PERSON: The actual physical presentation of daily life—not the Full Personality. The visible thing we can touch and photograph.

It is very important to recognise that *you* are these different levels: that the person does the daily things; the personality creates the habit tracks which arise from your daily life, whether good or bad; and that your oversoul stores them, selects the beneficial results and 'burns the dross' (a kind of purgatorial expunging of impure habit impulses.) Our need is to let the 'Individual', the real self, inspire the Oversoul (as Brunton called it: Personality No 2 as Jung called it) and lastly direct our daily life.

There is an old story, said to be Persian, which is worth consideration. Outside the door of a mansion stands a superb carriage carefully built after years of experience and trial and error (our evolved physical body); to it are harnessed two horses, one black and one white (they are our emotions). The horses are controlled by reins which are sufficiently connected with bits to restrain them (these are our five senses), and the reins are held by the coachman on his box (our personality brain). The equipage is ready to proceed, but it can make no fruitful journey until the *Master* (our true 'I') comes out of the house and gives the appropriate directions. For many people the Master does not enter into their daily lives, and the coachman and his carriage dash hither and thither purposelessly. Think how many times you have heard people say, 'It's just the same old dreary round over and over every day'; think how folk try to lose their boredom in so-called pleasures which too often merely mean subsequent pain. *But the directed individual* will know no boredom, no frustration, but a daily sense of achievement and slow but certain evolution and poise.

This has been a long lesson, but its importance is beyond measurement.

Exercise Thirteen

You have learned how to concentrate, how to put the beam of attention on some object. You have now to take the important step of using your 'ruby laser'. The name of this power is 'visualisation'.

Before starting your exercise, provide yourself with a vase similar to those in which you grow tulips or hyacinths in water. Light blue is an excellent colour, but so long as it is harmonious, it does not matter what colour. Fill the vase with water to within an inch of the top.

Please follow the instructions carefully; stop if you find the exercise too difficult and try later.

1 Usual preliminaries. *Never omit these,* they are essential. It is good to have your nightlight, candle or red lamp behind you, for, while the vase should be seen clearly, you do not want conflicting shadows.
2 First concentrate on the vase itself. You will know that what you are doing is to some extent magnetising the object, particularly the water. You are bringing the object into harmony with your mental power.
3 When you feel you are *en rapport,* place a tulip bulb in the vase. *It does not matter whether it is a material tulip or a thought form.* The writer always uses the latter.
4 Examine the bulb; note the different colorations of the skin, perhaps where it has peeled away in one place. *See* the tulip; when you can do so, gently close the eyes and perceive it through the closed eyes; it will probably seem nearer than when it is on the table. When you have done so, *open your eyes and stare at the tulip.*
5 Visualise the growth. Perceive how, from the bottom of the bulb, small tender white tendrils appear almost like little worms drawn by the power of the water and its magnetism. If you watch, they will reasonably quickly touch the water, and you may 'perceive' the small vibrations.
6 Once the roots are in the water, you will see a small green shoot come up from the top of the bulb. It will grow under your fascinated 'sight' until finally, proud and erect, the flower shoot and bud will emerge. For some this will actually burst into flower, and if it does so, *note* the colour—it will have a later meaning to you.

This exercise is of course culled from the celebrated Tibetan 'Tigle seed'. (See *Tibetan Yoga* by W. Evans-Wentz.) It will take time to accomplish, but when you have done it, you will have allied your concentration to visualisation, and many powers will lie in your ability.

LESSON 13
The Vehicles of 'Man' — Physical

Exercise Fourteen Moving Consciousness

It is tolerably evident that if we are to believe in any conscious entities of beings whatsoever in the Universe whether of a Cosmic or more limited nature which have their existence apart, independent of physical matter or physical bodies . . . such entities must have a substantial vehicle or body in or through which Life and Consciousness subsist, function and manifest objectively.

William Kingsland. *National Mysticism*

Our normal waking consciousness, rational consciousness as we call it, is but one special type of consciousness whilst all about it, parted from it by the flimsiest of screens, there lie potential forms of consciousness entirely different.

William James. *Varieties of Religious Experience*

I think the chief characteristic of my life, the one in which it differs most markedly from the lives of other people, is the fact that I have been continually aware of three levels of life and consciousness.

Minnie Theobald. *Three Levels of Consciousness*

The spectrum of light is composed as follows: on the left a wide band of Hertzian or infra-red waves; in the centre a narrow band of visible light; on the right, an infinite band ranging from ultra violet X and Gamma Rays to the unknown.

And what if there were a comparable spectrum of intelligence, of human light? On the left the infra, or subconscious; in the centre the narrow band of consciousness; and on the right the infinite band of the ultra-conscious. Until now only the unconscious and the conscious have been studied. The vast domain of the ultra-conscious seems to have been explored only by mystics and magicians. Pauwels and Bergier. *Morning of the Magicians*

Man can be conscious on all the 'planes' which have been enumerated. But to act or cognise on each plane, he needs a 'vehicle' on that plane, and a response system in his earthly instrument suitable for the reception of that plane's frequencies (Fig 7).

Although we correctly term the bodies or vehicles of 'Man', we must not think or be bound by the concepts of the purely physical frame, which is indeed the 'hard core'. It is a good analogy to think back to the make-up of a 'spherical galaxy', and remember that at the core of such a galaxy there is a 'hard core', the densest matter of the galaxy. The remainder of the galaxy is an elliptical whirl of gases, energy potentiality which surges round that hard core and grows ever less dense as it moves to the outer confines. This is largely a picture of man and his vehicles.

The vehicles are formed as we have suggested by involution, the outpouring of the divine impulse and the gradation into various octave groups. This descent is the province of advanced occultism, and we shall take up the story from where the divine force reaches its lowest point of density manifestation, namely physical matter, and how in turn mineral, vegetable and animal are energised, and how they proceed to help the evolution of the faculties of sensation and feeling, and prepare for the advent of Man and the thinking faculty in use.

It is from the earth plane that our type of evolution begins its ascent The object is to develop consciousness in all man's vehicles to the fullest extent, and to reach towards the individual who has control over all the planes of Man's evolution. This ascent is twofold in its action, as already stated: (1) it purifies and causes Man to evolve as a physical being and (2) it helps the higher-plane vehicles of the individual to evolve, by his passing through experiences and impulses which could only be gained at the lower level. This continues through all planes.

Obviously it is best for the individual to start with earth matter, densities and vibrations, because such matter is the coarsest, largest and easiest to control, 'to handle'. This is why Man is first of all an 'animal man', conscious only in his physical body or with very slight impulses from his higher powers. But from the moment Man appears, all the four functions are available, and he rapidly adds to those he has inherited from his animal-evolved consciousness the higher abilities which have hitherto not been awakened on earth plane.

Before we can grasp this Law of Evolution working in consciousness we must have some concept of the various 'vehicles' of the Man on

(Fig 7) MAN AND HIS VEHICLES

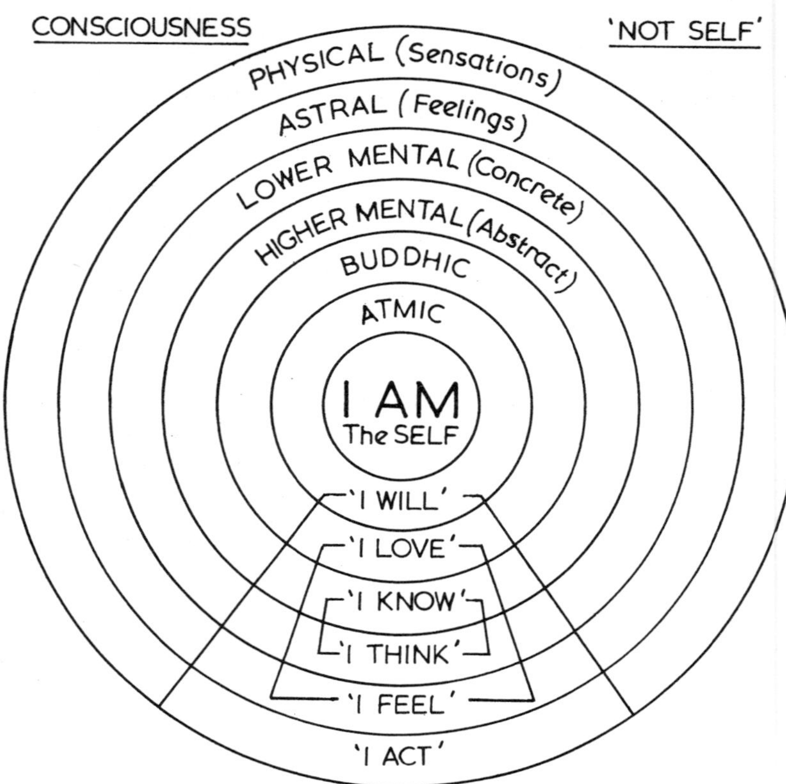

'I am the Self seated in the Heart of All Being' (Krishna)
'I and the Father are One' (Jesus Christ)
'In the heart of All being I AM' (Zoroaster)
'The way, the path and TAO are one' (Lao-Tse)
(Tao is the unity of all)

higher planes than that of the earth octave group. Let us therefore consider the various vehicles.

The Physical Vehicle

To quote Robert Browning:

> For thence: a Paradox
> Which comforts while it mocks—
>   Shall life succeed in that it seems to fail?
> What I aspired to be,
> And was not, comforts me:
>   A brute I might have been, but would not sink i' the scale.
>
> What is he but a brute
> Whose flesh has soul to suit
>   Whose spirit works lest arms and legs want play.
> To man—propose this test—
> Thy body at its best
>   How far can that project thy soul on its lone way?

Although St Paul declared that we had a spiritual as well as a physical body, and although our official religion considers Man as a trinity of body, soul and spirit, it is remarkable to what an extent even believers accept the tyranny of the senses and equate 'I' with the physical body. The idea that the body is only the instrument the 'I' uses to manipulate and cognise physical matter seems very strange. After all, 'Here is my body', and one can bang away at it with one's hands. It is obvious, direct—something of mass that can cast a shadow, a nice solid object on which to base our conclusions.

But is it so obvious? What is this physical body? It is, first of all, an aggregation of chemicals. A rather whimsical list has expressed it as follows:

> SUGAR enough to sweeten a hundred cups of coffee,
> LIME enough to whitewash a small henhouse,
> IRON enough for a one inch nail,
> MAGNESIUM enough for half a dozen flash pictures,
> POTASSIUM enough to explode a toy cannon,
> SULPHUR enough to rid a dog of fleas,
> PHOSPHORUS enough to make twenty boxes of matches,
> FAT enough to make a dozen bars of soap,
> COPPER enough to make a halfpenny,
> WATER enough for a child's bath.

So our body is a motley chemical collection of sixteen elements of little monetary worth.

Actually there is not one physical body, but several. There is a bone body, a muscle body, a nerve body, a blood-circulatory body, a lymphatic body and a tubular body—all enclosed in a skin body, and all making a special contribution to the physical vehicle.

However, let us suppose all these separate systems to be correctly assembled, the chemicals suitably mixed and fashioned in the shape of a man—head, arms, trunk and legs. Is this, then, a man? We know that it is not. A television set suitably constructed is valueless unless, and until, it is vitalised by suitable vibratory currents carried by electricity. So, too, is this physical body a hulk which can only proceed to decay unless it is vitalised. In other words, the physical vehicle is only an instrument and awaits its vital current. It may be that, before that current can pass into it, there must be a transformer for the vital energy. That transformer/conductor is the Etheric, to be considered in Lesson Fourteen.

Further consideration proves the assertion that 'here in the physical body is the *man*' is untrue; for, according to our senses, it is obvious that the physical body has a permanence which remains the same from day to day, except that as the years go by a slow change and decay creeps over it. This is an obvious fact, and like the obvious facts that the world is flat, that the sun rises every day in the East and sets in the West, making a journey round the earth, and that matter is hard and solid, it is completely untrue.

Far from being a permanency, our physical vehicle changes with every passing moment: the countless millions of cells of which it is composed change with bewildering frequency and, indeed, the scientists tell us that the physical body of today *has nothing in it which was there* only seven years ago. (Yet we have that sense of 'I'-ness from youth to age, but of that more anon.) Huxley likened the body of a man to a fountain which retains its form, its recognisable shape and apparent solidity, though the parts are not the same even for a second. The fountain, like our physical body, is a continuously changing mass. *But* if this is so, how can we possibly be our physical body? What of these cells of which our body is composed, these tiny minute lives which give to our structure the aspect of permanence? We know that they die comparatively quickly, but what are their powers? In other words, are they the man, an 'I' (which they *must* be if 'I' is solely physical)? The answer is 'No, they are not'. Their attributes are at a different level from the man as we understand that word (yet with similarities—'As above so below').

Let us set out the powers in tabular form.

	The cell can	*The man can*
1	Absorb oxygen	Absorb experience
2	Build protoplasm from food	Build wisdom from experience
3	Make physical changes in its environment	Make changes in his social environment through mental decisions
4	Build increasingly more complex forms by coordinating activity with other cells	Build social organisations and procedures by mental effort with other men and, later, by spiritual endeavour

In other words, the component parts of our bodies, the cells, are dealing with physical *matter,* but the man deals with *mind.*

There is still another confusion to consider—the solidity of man's physical frame. The animal beating on its chest does not doubt the solidity of that form, but if we remember what the scientist told us about solids, we shall also remember that solidity is an illusion. Eddington spoke on this subject in *The Nature of the Physical World:* 'If we eliminated all the unfilled space in a man's body and collected his protons and electrons into one mass, the man would be reduced to a speck *just visible* with a magnifying glass.'

This, then, is the scientific finding about our physical vehicle. It cannot *live* until it is vitalised in some way. If it is not, it stands like the television set that has not been switched on, unable to perform. *What is it that animates this chemical vehicle?* Is it something separate from what we think of as the physical body? It was once held that the brain produced thought as the liver produced bile; this idea is, today, beyond the pale even in psychological thinking (and psychology was born in, and clings desperately to, a mechanistic explanation wherever possible). It seems certain that body, as such, is a vehicle for mind. That the 'I' is *not* the physical body seems an inescapable conclusion.

Let us take a few more examples which support this statement.

If the body is really 'I', then where do 'I' go in the hours of sleep; if the body was the real self, then surely consciousness would be persistent for every hour of the day, but all men spend at least a third of their lives in sleep, when the awareness of the body and of the physical senses is blanked out. Of course, one may point to dreams, but we are all aware that a dream which may occupy so long in its apparent action, in its timeless state (of this more anon), does in fact act upon the body for only a second of time—*such a second of time* as one would expect to intervene if the 'I' was returning to, or leaving, its physical instrument. But in deep sleep 'I' becomes absolutely unconscious of the body. *Consider this please* and you will see it is a proof of the fact that 'I' is something more than the physical instrument.

In somewhat gruesome vein, consider those poor mutilated victims either of tyrannous regimes of the past, or of the horrible wars of the present, who have lost limbs, eyesight, hearing, even in some cases taste, but who still are definite and complete 'I's'. Anyone who has been in a hospital, or known the exhaustion of the battlefield, will know how the sufferers can forget their most horrible physical agony in an exhausted sleep. Where, then, is their 'I'—in the mutilated body? But then there could be no rest.

In the East there are fakirs who can hibernate like a frog and who can enter into a death-like trance in which all the organs of the physical are in a state of suspended animation, and yet, when they return to their earthly bodies, their sense of 'I', of continuing personality, is completely unaffected. These facts considered can only lead us to the definite conclusion that man, that 'I', is something additional to the physical.

Finally, if the physical is the 'I', then so long as there is a body, the phenomenon we call 'death' could not intervene. If 'I' am the body, 'I' should go on as long as the body did not disintegrate. It is something being withdrawn from the body that means the extinction of that part of the real 'I'.

It is, therefore, true to say that 'death' can logically be used to prove the fact that the 'I' is *not* the physical, which is left when 'death' occurs and lies there with only the animating spirit withdrawn (but what an 'only').

If we are honest, we will realise that we have always found it easiest to think of the physical as 'I'. Just so did the men of old find it easiest to think of the world as the centre of a universe which revolved around it. It was, to them, a fact obvious from appearances, even as it was true from appearances that the earth was flat. It is later research that has shown us that those 'facts' were untruths derived from appearance.

Today not only is our earth removed from its position as the centre of our solar system, but our solar system has become but one out of thousands in a galaxy in an expanding space. It was easier to think of the earth as the centre. It was obvious to think so when the sun rose and, quite obviously, traversed the heavens. But it was not true.

Just as for generations man was the only important thing on the only important planet in the Universe, so Man has thought of his physical body as the only important vehicle of consciousness, and the world observed by its senses the only important world.

It is easier so to think—but it is equally untrue.

The physical vehicle is the Oversoul's medium in this state of vibration, and when the time comes to leave it, the true self will take off the physical as a man takes off his overcoat when he comes home.

Introduction to Exercise Fourteen

One of the tyrannies of our physical body is that it limits our possibilities and viewpoint. We all automatically assume that hearing, sight and the rest of the five senses can *only* be used through the brain-response mechanisms we associate with the functions concerned. But a little thought will tell us that this is untrue. Consciousness and the mind are far too marvellous to be limited in this way. Do you not know someone who is deaf and yet can take part in an animated conversation by means of lip reading? This is a substitution of one sense by another, in other words mind consciousness overcoming five-sense limitations.

Max Carrados, Bramah's blind detective, was more than compensated for the loss of his eyes by his development of other faculties, and although this is fiction, do you not know some blind person who 'is marvellous the way he gets about'? The writer knows of one such person who not only gets about his house, but tends and plants a most adequate garden, knows most of the flowers by name, owing to his sense of smell, and crosses street junctions with apparent certainty (*not* main roads).

There are many case histories but we shall only mention three. *Mollie Francher* lived in the same house in a state of chronic invalidism for fifty years, thirty of which she spent in her bed with her limbs twisted beneath her and in a state of permanent blindness. She lived 'for years without sustenance enough to feed a baby'. Although she was blind, she crocheted and knitted, and was competent in other such handicrafts, judging the shade of the material she was using by putting it to the back of her head; Judge Dailey says 'she distinguished even the most delicate shades'. By way of variety she read letters from her forehead and with much greater rapidity than one could do from normal sight. This case is accredited by doctors, newspapers, judges and other sources.

The whole phenomena was brought to the television screen when we had the experience of seeing one of those remarkable blind readers tell the interviewer colours without a mistake. The book that deals with such abilities is *Eyeless Sight* by Jules Romain; and the Russians gave full details in *Soviet News* of the work of Rosa Keleshova, who had this faculty.

Many deaf people can 'hear'. From our viewpoint this is a species of telepathy, but excluding the well known phenomena of lip reading, there are a number of deaf folk who can sense what you are saying to them. Padre Pio, it is stated, often reminded his penitents of things they had 'forgotten' when confessing. Indeed this humble man of peasant origin must confound all materialistic explanations. Not only did he have the stigmata of the hands, like St Francis and others, but also his feet were pierced, and an open wound in his side never healed and always afflicted him. Apart from being an expert telepathist, he could dissociate and be in two places at once, as was accredited by high authority. He was a potent healer and had abnormal scent perception. His life story is well worth reading.

What does all this amount to? It means that the body is an instrument of consciousness which, although geared to five senses with appropriate organs of response, is yet a tool of consciousness that is greater than the organs, so that we can 'perceive' through other means.

When one tries to practise this, there are great difficulties of usage and tradition to overcome. Many people learn to write with both hands, but they find it extremely hard at first so to do, and if they are over thirty, it is near impossible, so geared are we to thinking of writing as being a process of *one* of our hands. Yet all of us know many people who use the other hand or both. So because you are accustomed to five-sense usage of consciousness, there is a traditionally great barrier to overcome when you try to diffuse consciousness over the whole of your body. Yet the writer assures you this can be done. Obviously you have to fight tradition, usage and your own incredulity, but after trying the exercise below, you may appreciate the possibilities of these new powers.

Exercise Fourteen

Usual sanctum with yantra on wall, small light (one nightlight) and hard-backed chair. Adopt Egyptian position. As a first exercise in the spreading of consciousness we are going to 'perceive' through several points which coincide with chakras or glands.

1 Preparatory exercises.
2 Gaze at yantra, full stare, normal, and slowly close eyes.
3 As you close your eyes, try to retain yantra centre (not essential).
4 Realise you have been seeing through the eyes; now let us move consciousness to another point. Feel you are 'seeing' through the root of the nose. Do not consider this command as idiotic; it is not. If you succeed in moving consciousness, you will find a slight pain at the root of the nose. This is the pineal gland, of which the dictionary says it is 'a vestigial optical organ: thought by Descartes to be the seat of the soul'. We, as occultists, know it as the third eye.

   If the vibration at the root of the nose does not appear, then, with your eyes still closed, focus your physical eyes to the root of the nose—in other words 'squint'. This is purely an action to assist the movement.
5 Now that you have felt the slight pain, *move the consciousness* downwards, first to the tip of the nose (many Eastern Societies use this as the 'squint to the entry gate'. See W. Y. Evans-Wentz. *Tibetan Yoga*). Rest awhile at this point.
6 Continue the path downwards over the *closed* lips and to the throat. Many will here get their strongest impressions. Rest awhile.
7 Travel downwards until you reach the physical shoulder bones. If you are right-handed, go left; if you are left-handed, go right; and proceed to the location of your physical heart. Rest awhile.
8 Now take the opposite side and go upwards to the shoulder, thus making an inverted triangle from the shoulders, with heart as apex.

9 Now go back to root of nose, retracing former path but not resting, and on arrival slowly open eyes and gaze intently at the yantra.

This is of course only a beginner's exercise in moving consciousness, but it is very valuable; apart from anything else it will locate your main chakra—either pineal, throat or heart. Once you know this, much has been achieved. This is a good exercise to practise, and when you reach a sufficient degree of concentration, it can be done anywhere by visualising the yantra.

As in all these works, practice makes perfect.

LESSON 14
The Vehicles of 'Man' — Etheric

Exercises Fifteen, Sixteen and Seventeen
Perceiving the Etheric

Today the scientist describes a world of unseen energy frequencies and patterns which can be registered and identified by various scientific instruments. In the middle of the nineteenth century a Kashmiri Sage predicted that one day the astronomers would hear the stars before they saw them. Today radio-astronomy has discovered many stars because of their radio broadcasting before they have been able to locate them with the telescope. Our instruments pick up radio waves and cosmic rays and many other types of energy frequencies unknown to us even a few decades ago. The energy fields and patterns which the sensitives see have not yet been verified by instrumentation. However, part of the adventure of research in this field is the challenge to find instrumentation.

Many of the more intelligent and integrated sensitives with whom I have worked describe interpenetration fields of energy around the human being. One of these is the vital field or energy body closely related to the physical. Much of my experimental work so far has dealt with this field, extending a foot to eighteen inches beyond the body, and the mental field extending an average of two feet or more beyond the periphery of the body, which are part of the unified field surrounding the human body. To the sensitives these different fields are clearly discernible. They are able to observe an effect on any one field or on all the fields. The experiments so far carried out involving the emotional or mental field or both have yielded some thought provoking data.

Dr Safica Karagulla, MD, MRCPE, DPM.
Breakthrough to Creativity

The body is not bounded by its skin;
Its effluence, like a gentle cloud of scent
Is wide into the air diffused and blent,
With elements unseen, its way doth win
To ether frontiers, wheretake origin
Far subtler systems, nobler regions meant
To be the area and the instrument
Of operations ever to begin
Anew and never end.

John Charles Earle. 'Bodily Extension'

It is not easy to describe the vehicles man uses on the different states of consciousness without giving a sense of separateness; but this concept is untrue, for all the vehicles interpenetrate. A classic analogy, which is apposite but not quite true, is an imaginary bowl of water in which is placed a sponge; the sponge represents the physical interpenetrated by the more liquid form of matter and contained in the bowl of the Oversoul.

Of all man's vehicles, the greatest interdependence is perhaps that between the physical and the etheric. The etheric is sometimes called the 'electric matrix' in which the cells—those myriad separate existences which combine to make our physical body—are contained and given form.

Remember the analogy of the television set, complete with valves and wires, tubes and screen, and all the many attributes which go to make up its entity. So our physical body is composed of nerves, sinews and tubes, all chemically and structurally complete. *But until either set or body receive a vitalising current* they are inert pieces of matter and fulfil no purpose but that of decay. When they receive a vivifying current, all their several parts are brought into play. When the 'Life Force' (which, equally with electricity, we can appreciate but not define) enters into the physical body, that body starts to operate and becomes a man-machine.

Let us note something else. This vitalising current does more than merely create a unity, it motivates functions which are vital to the machine itself—the functions of digestion, of breathing, of excretion, of blood circulation—all of which are carried on the moment this current is switched on and finish the moment the current is switched off in death. So it seems sensible and logical to postulate some form of current, personal to the 'I', which animates the man instrument and turns it into the man-machine, able to use the senses—to move, to breathe—and which makes the chemical body into the organism we usually think of when we use the phrase 'physical body'. In fact the body is not only the various physical parts bound into the skin, but also this vital energising current which the East calls 'Pranamayakosha' or the 'vehicle of prana'.

The etheric body can be seen by a great number of people, and such perception can be awakened by the exercises of our course. To the writer it looks like a blue haze varying in distance from half an inch to two inches from the body. Often such perception can be awakened by the following method. When the sun is strong, turn your back upon it and gaze at the sky with steady but not forced gaze. You will probably see sunspots, which are in fact vitality globules. If you do not, maintain your steady gaze and slowly close your eyelids until they *just* allow physical sight; then wait for a moment and just as steadily open the eyes. At some stage you will perceive the sunspots, and when you do, turn the gaze towards some object—a person or a distinctive post, or something similar (a person much the best). At first the perception of the etheric may well be minimal, but practice will evoke steady perception. Sunny conditions help the beginner.

It is possible that you may also see the colours of the etheric, because, in our School's teachings, the etheric itself is in near contact with the astral (a colour vehicle); it is taught also that the deeper colour of the 'misty grey blue' is nearest the physical body but that the outer etheric may show signs of other colours. It is again necessary to stress that the etheric is *not* a separate 'vehicle' of a plane, as is, say, the astral, but is the 'field' of the physical and acts upon and in conjunction with the physical. Its dual purpose has been mentioned already: first, it is the means whereby vitality can be brought through certain channels and distributed into and over the physical frame and organs; and secondly, it is the bridge between the physical and the five-sense brain and the higher planes of manifestation, particularly the astral. It can receive messages and impulses from such higher planes, and the development of extra-sensory perception largely consists of learning how to accept and how to return such 'messages' and powers to our higher planes of prowess.

Dr W. J. Kilner wrote a book called originally the *Human Atmosphere* and later expanded and retitled as the *Human Aura.* He was a physician and admits to having been interested in Swedenborg's saying that 'there is a spiritual sphere surrounding everyone'. He made experiments with and investigations by means of coloured screens containing dicyania dyes in alcohol. The operator looks through this dark screen at a light for a little while, and then gazes at the patient. He will then perceive the etheric. Kilner dealt with hundreds of cases, and the book is largely a recapitulation of the case histories.

He emphasised that for him this was a medical investigation, but of course he did also recognise that from the most ancient times this etheric perception has operated. Unfortunately the work was opposed to the thinking of the materialistic age, and the advent of the two world wars broke off to a large degree his pioneer work.

Scientific confirmation of Kilner's work has been achieved by Harold S. Burr, an Emeritus Professor of Yale School of Medicine. In his *Blue Print for Immortality,* which Neville Spearman described as a 'breakthrough book', and whose contents were described as 'one of the most important scientific discoveries of this century' by reviewers, he details how by the use of modern technology he has *proved* that all living things, from mice to men, from seeds to trees, are controlled by 'electro dynamic "fields"', which can be mapped and measured with standard voltometers.

This scientist, who would still perhaps call himself a materialist, states: 'The Universe is an ordered system, the human organism is an ordered component—in short the Universe has meaning, and so have we.' And again: 'The Universe in which we find ourselves and from which we cannot be separated is a place of Law and Order. It is not accident or chaos, it is organised and controlled by an electric dynamic field capable of determining the position and movement of all charged particles.'

He has called the fields of manifestation which can be perceived *outside* the confines of the physical body 'L Fields'. He emphasises that they can be measured with precision, and that they are like the fields already known to physics in that they are part of the organisation of the Universe. They are influenced by the vast forces of space and, again like the simpler fields of physics, can produce an effect across a gap or space *without any visible intervening means.*

This scientific confirmation of the Ancient Wisdom, which has taught the same facts for 7,000 years, should be considered when studying all the vehicles of man, but it is particularly important to the student for perception of the etheric and the auric. The student of latent powers needs no instruments—he can himself perceive, as you will discover.

At the death of the physical, that is when the etheric ceases to energise, there is a separation and the 'golden bowl is broken', 'the silver cord snapped'. The cells struggle to separate, to decompose, while the etheric stays near its physical, usually in a dreamy state of consciousness. In turn, the vehicles of higher states now leave the etheric, and this withdrawal ultimately means the disintegration of the etheric, which is now valueless to the withdrawing self.

The relationship while in earth vibrations is made through force centres, called 'chakras' by Eastern thought and endocrine glands by Western medicine. This will be the subject of a later lesson.

Exercise Fifteen

This is an exercise of great importance—it may be termed entry into extra-sensory perception. It endeavours to facilitate cooperation between soul/mind and physical/etheric at a lower level—the Etheric.

As always the *preliminaries are vital.* Do not start any of the exercises which follow without the full regimen of breath and tranquillity, silence and privacy. You are hoping to make your first contact with the etheric, and it is essential to be in the 'right frame of *mind*'.

1 Preliminaries.
2 Lie face upwards on a suitably folded blanket. (This exercise is always performed by the writer in the privacy of his bedroom, in either light pyjamas or without clothing (preferable), and in subdued light (one distant nightlight is excellent).
3 Place your feet 20in apart and turn them outwards until each foot is relaxing on the blanket; let your toes and ankles also be supine. Head is supported by a cushion or pillow so that you can just 'squint' down your form.
4 Place hands palms upwards about 10in apart from the body on either side.
5 Make sure your shoulders are 'flat' and that all your body is *relaxed.* (Think of a cat, how it lazily enters into complete relaxation.)
6 Hold that feeling of complete comfort, and while so doing, let your weight seem to sink into the floor or bed. Let everything seem to become more heavy and more relaxed, so that legs, arms and body all seem to be too 'heavy', too relaxed, to move at all. *This is very important.*
7 Now let your mind consciousness take over; you have severed from your body sensation, and it is lying comfortably comatose. Now mentally go down to your toes and feel every portion of them—picture the big toe, feel it glowing with health, feel it so intensely that you can visualise the bones, the muscles, the coursing blood, until it is really glowing.
8 *Then slowly, slowly raise your leg so that* the big toe is just visible. Can you now 'see' the haze around that big toe, which was glowing in your thinking? This is the etheric.

As in all things, do not expect immediate results. Practise with both legs in turn. Once you have 'seen', the slightest success will become prolonged success. You will have more advanced work as the exercises proceed.

Exercise Sixteen

1 As a variation and after the same preliminaries, instead of raising the leg make a tent of your hands (see Exercise 6).

2 In this exercise let the fingertips just touch, the fingers wide apart and stretching.
3 As soon as you feel they are in comfortable union, just slightly break the contact. This will cause the etheric which you have vitalised in the 'tent' to jump between the fingers (like a 'spark' in the plug); this can be seen in dim light, preferably when you have a black cloth or similar background.

Exercise Seventeen

1 Perform the usual preliminaries, which should include the gripping of the thumbs and making a 'tent' (when in fact you feel the heat between the tented hands).
2 While this is happening, *stare* at a black cloth on the table in front of you and wait for the heat to come.
3 Then put the hand on the place at which you have been staring, with open fingers stretched to capacity. You will then, with practice, see the etheric around the hand.

LESSON 15
The Vehicles of 'Man'—Astral

Exercise Eighteen 'Seeing'

The word 'astral' which means 'starry' is used in different ways by occult societies. For some it is the whole realm which lies beyond the physical: for some it is confused with the etheric: for others it is a separate instrument. For the Tao Yogist the latter applies.
F. H. Lowson. *Commentary of 'Tao'*

The psychic body, fully emancipated, obtains all its nourishment from the Cosmic—it becomes transparent to light and porous to air. It is then that those delicate centres which are called Chakras in the East are given space to expand and fulfil their functions, of which not the least is the ability to unite the consciousness with other worlds. Margaret Livingston. *The Future of Mr Purdew*

That is the road we all have to take—over the Bridge of Sighs into eternity. W. H. Auden. *Kierkegaard Anthology*

For though he voyages further than the flight
of Earthly day and night,
Traversing to the sky's remotest ends
A world that he transcends.
Safe he shall hear the hidden breakers roar
Against the mystic shore.
Alfred Noyes. 'The Two Worlds'

Jung's function of 'feeling', meaning particularly the feeling and emotion which arrives at a sense of values or is dictated by them, is thought of as a separate function of the whole man. The emotional vehicle—or astral body, as it is usually called in psychic literature—must then be considered separately. When the physical instrument ceases to operate, the lowest consciousness which the continuing 'I' will be using will be that of the feeling—emotional or astral—so that the student should now consider the possibility of consciousness moving from the physical organism to an organism which has experienced emotions and known values. For most of us, after the sensations of the physical, the feelings of the emotional world have been the most prevalent. To repeat, when the physical is dissolved and its cells go back into their own separateness, and when the etheric has ceased to shepherd our cells into form and, in its turn, disintegrates, Man passes into the next stage of consciousness, the realm of emotion, feeling.

It is essential to remember the great law of *interpenetration*. Just as our physical bodies are, at this moment, penetrated by waves of sight and sound of which they are all unaware but of which a medium, called a television set, can make our dull physical senses aware—so do all bodies interpenetrate.

The chemico-spatial earth body is penetrated by the etheric or electrical field body which performs the unconscious functions of living, binding the independent cells together, and together they make what we call the physical body—an apparently independent entity. *But* that entity is only *conscious* and communicable when it is penetrated by mind stuff and feeling; these are the hallmarks of the man. Consider how you can be swayed by a feeling which momentarily, at any rate, dismisses all thought processes except those concerned with giving that feeling control.

The feeling-emotions are perhaps the hardest thing to understand about Man. At their lowest we share them with the animals, in, for example, the quest for warmth and the purr of contentment when it is found; at their highest men become angelic, in the selfless love that can die for another, and which transcends all thought and reason in a sublime act of surrender. 'He who would save his life must lose it.' Yet it is easy to mistake abounding emotion for spirituality and forget that the one (emotion) rises up from our physical planes to the higher ones, while a true spiritual intuition, or inspiration, comes downward from higher states of consciousness to our physical one.

When considering the emotions, the psychologist uses the analogy of our primitive savage ancestor; but it is very doubtful if we know what our early ancestor was like. Books have been written describing his life and character, but to mistake them for scientific *fact* is quite wrong. They are hypotheses, and quite possibly untrue. Chesterton issued a timely word of warning on this head in *The Everlasting Man:*

> [The scientist] found in Java a part of a skull, seeming by its contour to be smaller than the human. Somewhere near it he found an upright thigh bone and in the same scattered fashion some teeth that were not human. If they all form part of the same creature, which is doubtful, our conception of the creature would be almost equally doubtful. But the effect on popular science was to produce a complete and even complex figure, finished down to the last details of hair and habits . . . A . . . detailed drawing was reproduced, carefully shaded, to show that the very hairs of his head were all numbered. No uninformed person looking at its carefully lined face and wistful eyes would imagine for a moment that this was the portrait of a thigh bone: or of a few teeth and a fragment of a cranium.

Our knowledge of the ancestral savage is based upon what we know of modern savage tribes. Nonetheless, it does seem probable that the first men were little removed from the animals, and that therefore a man's chief preoccupations would be the providing of food, relations with woman, the preservation of his safety and, perhaps arising therefrom, preservation of communal safety.

Most possibly his village was his world. Most certainly his thoughts could not envisage the world we know. The heavens must have been mysterious, as mysterious as they still are, despite our facile air of explanation. Indeed, to digress, one may almost say that modern astronomical explanation has succeeded in making the heavens and our expanding universe *more* mysterious than they probably were to our ancestors.

However, enough has been said to suggest that in his infancy Man would find his chief non-physical self in his emotions. Love and hate, courage and fear, warmth and cold, enthusiasm and despair, these would have been his preoccupations. For the moment let us leave the orthodox psychologist and assess, so far as we can, *how* much his life would have been one of emotion and how much one of thought. While it is quite easy for us to see that *thought* is different in *kind* (not degree) from *emotion,* there is yet a very strange interpenetration.

As has been said, some emotions are almost entirely evoked by physical wellbeing, as when we stretch our bodies cat-like to the grateful heat of a fire. Some emotions are so great that they transcend even the limits of thought: zealots, for the sake of an emotion truly felt, can suffer even the crucifixion of the physical, almost with joy (let us please remember that this applies not only to the Great Exemplar but to many thousands who for His sake and an emotional belief transcending ordinary thought also were martyred).

Under the stress of a great emotion, Man seems to have periods when he is above reason and above physical pain. A notable example is surely that of Cranmer. This Archbishop, a very fallible human being, fearing pain and death, and appalled by the burnings of Latimer and Ridley, signed a document which he felt to be untrue. When his conscience finally prevailed, he allowed his hand to burn off, as it was the member which had offended. This ability of mind and feeling to transcend ordinary human physical pain points unswervingly to the fact of a higher vehicle—to the fact that man is more than physical.

The Astral—the vehicle of emotion—is the reservoir of all the happenings which has affected Man's 'feelings' and emotional character.

One significant thing is that people who have been near to death tell how their lives flashed in front of them; this means, of course, that for that moment at any rate, in the expectation of physical ending, they had left 'now time' and gone into 'duration'. It is probable that ideas of hell and of torment arise from mystical knowledge of this happening, and one can imagine that emotional needs, stimulated perhaps by late physical desires, could make a very real torment before they were overcome. It is obvious that mere cravings derived from the physical, such as the need for alcoholic liquor or cigarettes, will rapidly die away, but there are other lusts and thoughts of the human body which will not go so quickly. A mind habituated to avarice and money-grubbing, for example, will not cure its passion so easily. J. B. Priestley's magnificent play *Johnson over Jordan* portrayed the unconscious in Johnson's new freedom after physical death in acts mixing up all the different life experiences. In the scene of earth-bound desires we were shown two old men entirely obsessed and controlled by the needs to make money, and therefore bound to earth routine. The occultists believe that the refinement of our experiences on earth comes through the winnowing away of the bad things which we have in our unconscious 'feeling' selves, and the passing of the good things from our unconscious to our higher state of mind, which we call the superconscious. The superconscious is that state still connected with our earthly and individual experiences in which all creative thought has been garnered. In cases where emotional thinking has been motivated by pure love, this good strata of the unconscious reinforces all the reading and thinking that the individual, in his lifetime, has done about that wonderful word, 'love'.

The emotional effect of music is allied to its intellectual content and illumines the superconscious. Likewise, the sway and surge of great poetry fuels our intellectual consciousness.

It is erroneous to think of all vehicles as separate; they are interpenetrating—vehicles of a true consciousness. Emotions can be—and are, indeed—daily affected by physical sensations, and as we have just pointed out, they are equally affected daily by intellectual (or thinking) content. On the whole, however, the consciousness at the astral stage will examine feelings of all kinds: love and hate, repression and blossoming, jealousy and disinterested affection. All these constitute the matter for consciousness in the astral world.

We have already stated that we must not allow the form of the physical to cause us to expect like make-up in the higher bodies. In fact the *Astral* is an ovoid shape and an ever-flowing mass. It swirls under each new impulse, and sensation and feelings are not localised but affect the entire egg. To clairvoyant perception these impulses show as colours, and of course we know that colour is a question of vibration. Clairvoyant perception can be awakened by awakening fully the corresponding band in the earth vibrations. This can be done voluntarily by exercises so designed, and very often also comes involuntarily. The writer remembers one of his students who was most unconvinced by the teachings. One day, however, when she was alone in the house, to her knowledge, and doing her exercises, she heard a slight noise and turned and saw someone in the room. She said: 'I had such a shock and for a moment I did not seem to be able to see the person at all but only a large egg glowing with colour and a dull centre. This lasted only for a second I presume, when I saw it was my daughter whom I had thought was out but in fact was dozing in her room. I still find it hard to understand but I have no doubt for I saw the egg.'

Notice the emotional shock which temporarily increased the rate of vibration and therefore gave perception.

The ovoid will change colour rapidly if various emotions are being experienced at earth level. An often-felt emotion—fear, love, anger—will form a background of the respective colour, and this will come ever more rapidly to the forefront every time the emotion is felt; this is the 'emotion habit track' of the psychologist.

At death we are taught that the Astral naturally realises its source of information is passing, for the physical is ceasing to feed it emotions; consequently the Astral rushes about and sends all its coarsest matter to the outer shell, as it were, of the egg in order to protect its own entity. After the shock of dissolution, this shell gradually wears out, but because of this action, Man has to pass through his worst emotions to arrive at the inner of the astral. This is purgation at astral stage.

An old Eastern analogy, though a poor one, speaks of Man as a psychic onion. As he discards one layer, another awaits, impregnated with the outer layer but in turn to be discarded. The next layer that man has to deal with is the important one of the mental, man's sign manual on earth.

Once again science by its use of technological measurement is confirming the effects of the emotional body. Dr Leonard J. Ravitz, who worked in a group with Burr, has measured voltage rises of strong emotion to as high as 15-20 millivolts. These rises affect the whole organism, which possesses local fields (we term them vehicles) that represent the organism's component parts and are linked in a chain of authority, Ravitz calls them 'L fields'. This term, as previously explained, is but the scientific name for the Ancient Wisdom's 'vehicles of Man'.

Exercise Eighteen

Lowson's quotation (p 126) makes a valid point: it is confusing for neophytes to read books and find that the writers use the words 'Etheric' and 'Astral' in different ways. Dr Kilner in his famous work *The Human Aura* is really speaking about the etheric (with perhaps glimpses of the astral aura). The Hon Ralph Shirley (*The Mystery of the Human Double*) discusses this point at some length but finishes up by talking about 'astral projection', although his chapter is headed 'The Nature of the Etheric'.

For this course, as for most occult schools, there is little doubt about the need to differentiate. The *etheric* is the vitaliser of the physical body; without its presence the physical is dead. The etheric pervades the physical and vitalises the whole, although, as you have probably seen, it does stick out (as science's 'electric field') 1in to 4in from the physical. The *astral* (a word wished on to us by the old alchemists and meaning 'starry') is the higher 'vehicle', above the physico-etheric, and is, as this lesson has taught, the emotional body for Man.

Between each vehicle there is a gap (like the one in the human brain, to use a physical analogy), and this is a 'dark space' (say the clairvoyants) in which, for occult students, the 'Cosmic Shield' exists. These gaps (or this shield) may be paralleled by electricity. The power of the force generated at source would 'fuse' an electric light, for example, so that the technician 'steps' down the force by transformers. Equally the cosmic shields working through the chakras (the means of communication between one body and another) act as 'step down transformers'. As in the electrical analogy, the 'stepping up' method can be used. *This is why there is no fear:* you cannot experience vibrations higher than your stage of acquirement. When St Paul saw the Lord he was blinded for three days *by the enormous output of that unshielded celestial body*.

Obviously you have now reached the stage where you must perform exercises without ever forgetting the preliminaries of breathing (very important) and colour flooding.

1 We shall now combine the mirror exercises (12) with the etheric (15, 16 and 17).
2 *Full* preliminaries. (If you have a friend at the same stage, he or she may be in the room; otherwise please be alone.)
3 Perform mirror exercise *until you get some result.* As previously explained, this cannot be foretold. Taking a common result—for

example, the disappearance of the reflection: when this happens, stretch out your physical arms with extended fingers as though trying to reach the walls opposite and at right-angles.

4 While the vitalising of fingertips proceeds, move your consciousness to the root of the nose and 'perceive' through that locale.

5 You will now experience some happening; usually the mirror will show a ring of colour or colours and probably a face or a symbol will appear in the centre of the ring (probably only momentarily).

6 In addition, if there are two of you in the room, both at the same level of development, then instead of looking at the mirror, look at the other person, who should be seated some 6-7ft away. Naturally take Exercise Eighteen in turns, preferably on alternate nights.

The author tells you as fact that after some months, but more probably after years of practice, you will see auras of others in ordinary daylight in the street. Like all powers (nuclear) it is two-edged, and that is why your moral development, your philosophic outlook, *must* proceed slightly ahead of your search for powers (which after all are only crutches).

LESSON 16
The Vehicles of 'Man'—Mental

Exercise Nineteen Perceiving the 'Egg'

And though, my mind, aspire to higher things;
Grow rich in that which never taketh rust.
Sir Philip Sidney. 'Astrophel and Stella'

An average man's mind is filled with a thousand thoughts and therefore each one is extremely weak but when instead the man can bring his mind to one-pointedness then that *one* thought is of great power. Ramana Maharishi. *Collected Works*

In the faith that looks through death
In years that bring the philosophic mind.
Wordsworth. 'Intimations of Immortality'

No lesser study than self is worthy of the highest powers of man's mind. For he could not perceive the world outside him and he could not register his impressions of it through his five senses did his 'SELF' not exist to receive these perceptions and those impressions. In short the world would not exist did he himself not exist first. Scientists already know, through the experiments of hypnotism that the real 'seeing' agent is not the physical organ of the eye but rather the mind that uses that organ . . . they have yet to discover what it is that works the mind and when they do they will come into contact with the real self of man, the being out of whom both mind and body derive their existence and maintain their lives.
Paul Brunton. *A Message from Arunachala*

According to the hypothesis we have adopted, all Man's activities create for themselves a separate 'vehicle' of matter vibrating at such a rate as can respond to the activity concerned. The mental vehicle must have fine and responsive 'matter'—do we not say 'as quick as thought'—and on our hypothesis uses the physical brain as an instrument. Among the philosophers this suggestion has been fully explored by Bergson, who pointed out with a great number of instances that the brain was merely a selective instrument whose task was to allow *only* those perceptions which relate to the physical world to enter Man's consciousness. This business of rationalising our world and adapting ourselves to a physical environment is a commonplace of child psychology.

It is not difficult to see that if we can think of man, the spiritual being, as functioning through different vehicles of consciousness (different intensities of consciousness), then these could have attributes which would gather 'physical' experience (sensation), 'emotion-feeling' experience (the astral), and 'thinking' consciousness—although we must realise to what an enormous extent the vehicles interpenetrate. If, at the moment, in our physical body we have stomach trouble, this will result in deadened feelings and lethargic thinking; just so, when we suffer an emotional shock, the physical body reacts and we experience cold or numbness, although the shock is purely emotional. Equally, there is a great correspondence between feelings and thinking. We have really to define what we mean by 'thought' before we can understand this to be true. Payne and Bendit, in the book called *The Psychic Self,* write of the power of thought to create images as follows:

> As we know only too well, few people are really capable of clear thought, partly because most thinking runs concurrently with an emotional—or feeling—train, and partly because so few people are able to conceive a clear idea of anything. Looked at from the thought world, the man in the street's idea of a house would probably evoke immediate condemnation from the Borough Surveyor, because the roof might be askew, the walls shaky and the back of the house unthought of and therefore non-existent. The same often applies to one's political and religious views.

The world of psychology has had to accept the *fact* of telepathy, much as the world of medicine has had to accept the fact of hypnosis, after having called its protagonists by every name from cheat and liar to self-deluded hypocrites. One of the most interesting reports given to us about telepathy is that written under the names of Soal and Bowden—*The Mind Readers.* Told with humour and the charm of complete integrity, it is the story of two Welsh cousins, Glyn and Ieuan Jones, who possessed to the full not only the impishness of boyish natures but the telepathic faculty. On occasions, using 'animal cards' (sets of twenty-five cards with five pictures of five animals in each pack), the boys actually 'guessed' twenty-five cards correctly, which represents such fantastic odds against chance as to be conclusive. These experiments were, on occasions, conducted in the open air at distances of 150ft. They were checked not only by the distinguished academic authors but by a skilled and sceptical expert, who vouched for the authenticity of the communication. Among others who vouched for the ESP nature of the tests were F. Bateman, MSc, G. W. Fisk of the SPR (Society for Psychical Research), Professor C. W. K. Mundle, R. H. Thouless, ScD, and T. Whitehead, OBE, PhD, MSc, ARCS.

Telepathy, clairvoyance and precognition are today well authenticated facts, based upon as great a weight of observation and experiment as that which supports most other scientific fact. Professor Broad accepted telepathy as happening among normal human beings, but recognised the unconscious unwillingness of the mind to accept this knowledge. 'They (the bulk of the public and most scientists) would no more think of looking into the evidence for telepathy than a pious Christian thinks of looking into the evidence for Mahometanism, or a pious Mahometan of looking into the evidence for Christianity.'

Bergson, who accepted that injury to the brain can result in 'loss of memory' and impairment of the mental faculties, considers this as a further proof that the brain is an instrument. It is as though a television tube was smeared with thick oil. The resultant picture would be blurred and perhaps in places absent from the screen, but it would be an instrumental fault. The brain, on this reading, has to keep our 'consciousness fixed upon the world in which we live: it is the organ of attention to life'.

Our thought habits lie in the world of everyday and we dread anything which may disturb that basis. Tyrrell, in his Presidential Address to the Society for Psychical Research, said:

> It is the constitution of our minds, as a result of biological evolution, which causes us to reject whatever is entirely foreign to the world of common experiences. If we succeed in resisting this psychological tendency even for a moment, we can see quite clearly that there is no reason why our bodily senses should reveal the length and breadth of all existence. There is no reason why nature should terminate at the point where our senses cease to register it, and no reason why, beyond this point, it should not be governed by unfamiliar laws—no reason, but so strong is the self-centredness of our minds that we find ourselves smiling at the idea that anything important can exist in the universe which we cannot either directly perceive or grasp with our existing mental equipment.

Dr Grey Walter pointed out that we use the word 'mind' in the

English language to cover psychic states which would be designated quite differently in other languages. It does seem as though we badly need a distinction between (1) mind which deals with everyday action; (2) mind which is responsive to abstract thinking; and (3) mind which is visited, as will be witnessed by later mystical experience, by an intuitive non-self experience individualised, however, by the participant. For the occultist there is no doubt that mind is a separate vehicle.

Most occultists separate mind into two vehicles, and most psychologists today would accept this differentiation and agree that Man's mind has a twofold aspect. In addition to our physical perceptions and the thoughts that deal with all that relates to Man's physical environment, there is a creative mind which is perhaps far more important in defining what man is. Experimental psychology uses the words 'objective' and 'subjective', and the phrases 'concrete thought' and 'abstract thought' make the same division. Child psychology has taught us that when a baby is born, its thinking is purely subjective; its early lessons consist of learning to think objectively and, by contact with an environment, to come to grips with the objective world. In a series of what are quite rapid stages the infant develops control over its sensory nervous system, obtains governance over the voluntary muscles and learns to live in its objective world.

Modern psychologists divide our mental life into these objective and subjective thoughts, and some modern psychologists split the latter between the subconscious and the superconscious. Most of the really important things that constitute life are done by the subconscious, which attends to such matters as the beating of the heart, the circulation of the blood, the work of the lungs, the necessities of the digestion, and all those human needs which are, in the truest sense of the word, vital, but about which we do not have to think. There is also the wonderfully interesting project of cell replacement. As has been said earlier, our physical bodies are replaced every seven years, and apparently this replacement is also under the control of the subconscious mind, which is continuously renewing man's physical instruments. This consciousness, which is not obsessed by physical environment is, in Jung's exposition, intimately related to the collective unconsciousness. At the beginning of his career he thought this also applied to the reception and sending of telepathic messages and the storing of memories, but in his later life came to place these things as part of our superconscious selves.

There is much misunderstanding of the phrase 'collective unconsciousness', which many people consider does away with 'individuality'. This is not so. The individual mind can share in the group mind; indeed, it is by this method that our small 'I's' can contact the universal, and it is by our contact with the universal and the consequent enlargement of horizons that Man slowly works towards the comprehension of the infinite. By such comprehension man can, and does, rise to heights of comprehension otherwise unobtainable, but he can do this while maintaining an individuality.

Another way of considering the difference between the two facets of our minds is to adopt the terms 'inductive' and 'deductive' as methods of thinking. Inductive reasoning is based upon the study of observed facts and phenomena of a physical universe. Deductive reasoning, on the other hand, accepts a fixed law and then moves from that law to a number of related but foregone conclusions. In short, the objective, inductive, concrete mind is based upon the realities of a plane of consciousness which is intensely personal and which, on our present level, we call 'the physical'. The subjective, creative, deductive abstract mind is itself reality in the spiritual, and demands that Man realises, with old Marcus Aurelius, that he is really a soul dragging about a body. This division is all important, for if our reality is a physical one, we look up towards the spiritual; but if we can reverse this thinking, if we lose the egocentricity of an objective world, we experience conversion and we are able to look down from our true selves at the instruments and the planes of consciousness in which we are manifesting.

'Be ye, therefore, perfect, even as your Father in Heaven is perfect' was said by a Man who had attained that perfection and whose entire life was based upon the reality of the spiritual. It is at the mental stage of consciousness that this division is apparent. The physical life, the etheric life and the astral life, all relate to a particular personality which is only a portion of a real self, but with abstract thinking we touch that wider realm, the spiritual realm, in which, as all mystics have taught us, our true self exists.

The power of abstract thinking is on a higher state of frequency (ie consciousness) than concrete thinking. The latter deals with observed fact and emotion emanating from physical causes. The former, abstract thinking, accepts values which apply to a well ordered physical life but which we think of, quite rightly, as emanating from 'above'; that is from the Oversoul. The abstract, by visualisation, can create in the physical and, by the power of imagination, can create in fact. In our Western world we realise that this is true, when we consider, for example, the creation of a noble building: its layout, its structure, are all, first of all, visualised by the architect, who sees, 'in his imagination', the completed structure as it should look. It is only when this work of the imagination is done that he proceeds to put his ideas on to paper, and they then descend into the physical and are erected in bricks and stone, steel and mortar.

Any noble purpose goes through exactly the same process of visualisation, and it is one of the major tragedies that we have allowed the word 'imagination' to become so debased. This is one of the things that distinguishes Man from the animal, and makes him the master of this earth, because he can create in physical form the product of his thinking, not by instinct but by a process of separate imagination allied to the end in view. As more and more people really use the mental vehicle, so will the earth become a fairer and a more beautiful place.

In the East, however, thought and thought forms, the power of imaginative visualisation, are given a much more concrete meaning, for the Easterner believes that the mind can control and use physical matter in order to clothe its thought forms. A Western savant, in the person of Alexandra David-Neal, has told how the Tibetan mystics actually use the power of thought in meditation to create physically visible things, and this lady, who had, of course, a very high academic standing, tells how she herself created a thought form which could be seen by other people. She says:

> Nevertheless, allowing for a great deal of exaggeration and sensational addition, I could hardly deny the possibility of visualising and animating a tulpa. Besides having had few opportunities of seeing thought-forms, my habitual incredulity led me to make experiments for myself, and my efforts were attended with some success. In order to avoid being influenced by the forms of the lamaist deities, which I saw daily around me in paintings and images, I chose for my experiment a most insignificant character: a monk, short and fat, of an innocent and jolly type.
>
> I shut myself in tsams and proceeded to perform the prescribed concentration of thought and other rites. After a few months the phantom monk was formed. His form grew gradually fixed and life-like looking. He became a kind of guest, living in my apartment. I then broke my seclusion and started for a tour, with my servants and tents.
>
> The monk included himself in the party. Though I lived in the open, riding on horseback for miles each day, the illusion persisted. I saw the fat trapa, now and then it was not necessary for me to think of him to make him appear. The phantom performed various actions of the kind that are natural to travellers and that I had not commanded. For instance, he walked, stopped, looked around him. The illusion was mostly visual, but sometimes I felt as if a robe was lightly rubbing against me and once a hand seemed to touch my shoulder.
>
> Once a herdsman who brought me a present of butter saw the tulpa in my tent and took it for a live lama.

It is emphasised that this experience, miraculous though it may be to our Western minds, is a commonplace of Eastern thinking and, indeed, of many Western mystics.

The mental vehicle perhaps distinguishes Man more than anything else from the animal, despite their common physical ancestry. It is the power of imagination and visualisation that has already given Man the power to create and will lead him, as in occult belief, to that place where it may truly be said that men are like Gods.

The mental plane vehicle (or body) is also an ovoid and lies further away from the physical than does the astral. It differs however from the astral, which is in a state of constant movement, in that its activity is immensely greater than that of the astral but it is an activity that presents an almost static picture. If you will think of the apparent mobility of a 'sleeping' top, say a humming top, it has so complete a 'stillness' as to appear static; but in fact it is the intense movement which gives this illusion. The mental body has such an intense movement.

Whereas in the astral there is constant change as differing emotions reach it from the physical and but little stabilisation, the mental does tend to stabilise, and this means that the kaleidoscopic change of colour in the astral is in the mental vehicle replaced by more definite colour locations. The areas will change but a centre point will represent the person's general tendency of thought—his personality traits.

A further thing may be noticed. The abstract colours which are lighter in shade tend towards the top of the ovoid, whereas the concrete thoughts, often of darker shade, tend to stay at or towards the bottom of the egg.

Many people have written about the meaning of colours apparent in the astral and mental bodies, and the general consensus of opinion concludes that an average, reasonably cultured person of our time will show yellow (intellect), light but cloudy blue (religious or philosophic), and some orange often striated with medium red (sympathy but with personal outlook). Often there is a girdle around the centre of the egg of medium or dark grey showing fear, worry, depression. Green shows adaptability, and shades from lighter to darker green show cunning, even to deceit. The brown of selfishness is likely still to be noticeable. But all the colours are less cloudy than in the lower types of development, and the awakening of abstract thought and selflessness illumines the egg with their respective luminous yellow and light blue.

The mental is probably Man's most important *evolutionary* vehicle, for it is the perfecting and purgation of this vehicle that leads to the higher potentialities of the individual man, as opposed to personality man.

Exercise Nineteen

We are going to 'perceive' your egg.

1 *Preliminaries,* which remember for the *rest* of the course means

posture, breathing, colour flooding, sound. This in effect is 'tuning your instrument' to a state of receptivity and must never be scamped or omitted.

2 Visualise that you are going to recognise your various vehicles and start by slowly breathing in. As you inhale, *feel* your physical self expanding and going outwards to a shell-like ovoid that is both malleable and transparent. Consider this: in fact you are pushing out your consciousness to a limit.

3 When you have fully inhaled, hold the breath and 'perceive' where you have pushed the shell to; it is your starting point for the next breath.

4 As you exhale, expel with the breath all the deleterious emotions and thoughts that are within your 'egg'. Force them to go out with the breath, where they will dissipate.

5 Now breathe in again and start your 'pushing out' from the point you feel you previously reached. Do not try to get too fast a result or to 'expand' too far. 'Many a mickle makes a muckle', says the old countryman, and this is right.

6 Hold and establish the new diameter of the egg and then expel as in (4).

7 Continue this exercise until you 'feel' you can go no further. This is your present limit and you should know how many inches you have got away from the physical centre. *You will know,* it will feel just right.

8 When you have attained this serenity, which is much more than physical 'rest', you must discard your 'shell' armour, so at the last exhalation draw in the egg with your outbreathing until you feel you are back in your physical-etheric, but one much purified by this exercise. *It is very important to dissipate the shell fully.*

9 It is very good to do this exercise and then follow with the retrogression (Exercise Twenty-one).

At first you may find it difficult to conceive the named phases, but one or two efforts will unfailingly produce results and prepare you for the entry into the higher states of perception and understanding which follow.

LESSON 17
The Vehicles of 'Man' — Buddhic (Spiritual)

Exercise Twenty 'Stretch Your Mind'

It is also necessary to remind the reader that Spiritual Evolution means shifting the centre of consciousness towards the Divine Centre of our being and realising our divinity more and more. The spiritual unfoldment of the *individuality* is certainly reflected in the personality but only to a limited extent which is inherent in the lower planes which prevent the full expression.

Dr I. K. Taimi. *Self Culture*

Lord Buddha, on thy lotus throne,
With praying eyes and hands elate
What mystic rapture does thou own
Immutable and ultimate.
What peace, unravished of our ken,
Annihilate from the world of men?

Sarojini Nayadu. 'To a Buddha'

Now know we spirit
Now all life's loveliness and power we have
Dissolved in this one moment, and our burning
Carries all shining upward, till in us
Life is not life, but the desire of God.

Lascelles Abercrombie. 'He'

The Buddhic or Spiritual vehicle is the highest that man uses, and it completes his personality. It is the farthest from the physico-etheric's low vibrations, and movement is at speeds which are beyond our possible comprehension.

The writer has hitherto given statements which are primarily those of the masters of this subject but also to some extent checked by his personal knowledge and observation. As to this vehicle, his experiences are so few that he must quote others.

A great number of names are used in different religions and mystical sciences to express this plane and its vehicles. The Causal body, the inspirational vehicle, the *ego,* what St Paul meant by the *soul* are all attempts to express its wonder. It expresses the three forces of will, of near divine love (what the Christian Master meant by 'charity') and of inspiration. 'Spiritual' must not be confused with that pure 'spirit' which is the 'spark of the divine within us', but the separation is difficult for our comprehension—it is the infinite and the finite of the same.

We are told that the vehicle is of circular shape, and pulses inwards yet at the same time emits beams to the outer that surrounds it. The colours go inwards like the petals of an incurved chrysanthemum (the writer has seen this in operation), and there is an ever-expanding outer rim of brilliance. It is at this level that one finds the Oversoul, Man's expression, which is the store house of all that the various personality lives have gathered from each life.

From this height the Oversoul can control all the materials and all the psychological powers and potentialities of the lower planes—physico-etheric, astral, mental—and from this plane impressions can be conveyed to Man from the reaches of the higher plane's wisdom. (The Individual Divine Spark itself.)

For most men the spiritual body will not be immensely active, but at no time can evil thoughts and impulses enter into it; only the good of the man can find tenure here. We are told that it is the absence of colour (that is spiritual possibilities) that have not yet been awakened which typify the generality of men of our age, but there are also those who have achieved, whom we call 'adepts', and of these some occult teachers have waxed most lyrical. Leadbeater in his *Man Visible and Invisible,* after expressing the impossibility of painting the picture of an adept's spiritual body either by picture or words, says:

> In his case the size of the causal body has enormously increased and shines with a sunlike splendour far beyond all imagination in its glorious loveliness . . . such a body is not only larger than that of an ordinary man but has its colours differently arranged . . . If it is impossible to attempt to illustrate the causal body of a Master it may be worthwhile to give some idea . . . the colours are more delicate and ethereal, yet at the same time far fuller, more brilliant and more luminous.

Another great teacher has likened the 'spiritual' to 'luminous sun in the splendour of a glorious sunset that never happens', and the old Egyptians probably tried to express this in their representations of 'Ra'.

For so simple a book as this, such possibilities may only be glanced at, as our aim is the lower one of purifying and using the lower vehicles. Such an ascent is made through abstract thinking.

With the advent of abstract thinking, Man enters into a different phase. The physical, the astral, and the lower (or concrete thinking) mental vehicle, all appear to be completely immersed in the earth personality which we normally call 'the Man'.

With abstract thinking, however, Man starts upon a higher means of perception. This, it will be noted, has nothing to do with personality: a mathematician, a musician or an artist may be of any creed, caste, colour or religion, yet his work will speak to his fellows of the same craft according to their own ability.

In abstract thinking the personality may be 'inspired' by group consciousness, and very often by inspirations which do not arise from his conscious thinking. 'A.E.', the great Irish poet and mystic, spoke of his own inspiration: 'There was an element of the unexpected in the poetry itself for it broke upon and deflected the normal current of consciousness. I would be as surprised at the rising words which in their combination seemed beautiful to me as I would have been if a water lily had blossomed suddenly from the bottom of a tarn'.

The famous case of Coleridge and his inspiration for 'Kubla Khan' is well known, but a great number of other artists, writers and musicians have experienced these God-given gifts. Stevenson and his 'imps', Socrates and his 'daemon', Paracelsus and his 'Azoth', Joan of Arc and her 'voices' and St Teresa and her 'guidance' are some of the historical instances of this inspiration from above. However, a very modern expression of this inspirational guidance is given by Minnie Theobold, concert 'cellist and mystic, in her autobiography *The Three Levels of Consciousness.* This is a book that must be read and cannot be paraphrased, but it is enough perhaps to say that she consciously lived with inspirational powers; from the first dawn of her intelligence she felt that her life was dictated by them, guided by them, and when at last they came to full realisation, she became what is usually termed an 'adept'. She found that her inspirations, which largely dealt with her mystic development, came as definite orders. They were instructions often quite difficult to perform and from which there was no appeal. Despite this, she found little hardship in following them once her restless personality brain was controlled. She has said: 'All the orders were punctuated with so much wit and humour that however unusual and hard the training, it was both amusing and delightful'. It will be seen how completely there is surrender to the voices.

A further delightful expression about these mentors is that given by

Rosalind Heywood in her book *The Infinite Hive*. By nature and early environment she was a sceptic, and her daily records of what she calls *orders* are therefore the more convincing. The instruction, usually of the most practical type, is heard by Mrs Heywood inside her head. In her nursing career she found 'from now on Orders were inclined to take over', and the resultant benefits to her patients were considerable. Through the whole of her record of a very busy life, she was aware of, almost at the mercy of, *orders*.

For the writer such few intimations as he has been vouchsafed appear as though spoken inside the head. They are not heard in the sense one listens to a spoken word—they are suddenly apprehended as being spoken and accepted.

It is probable that this ability to be influenced by a higher collective power gave rise to the old ideas of the Greek Oracle, of the Hebrew Prophet, of the soothsayer, all of whom appear on occasion to have been furnished with gifts of prophetic utterance which were 'from on high'. There is a great literature regarding mystical illumination, and many people of undoubted integrity have experienced these blinding flashes of illumination, which are probably a higher level of inspiration. When these occur, the individual seems to be welded to something greater than any personal experience could offer. Evelyn Underhill has collected for us much factual information, and speaks also from personal experience. She has said:

> The eyes of my soul were opened and I beheld the plenitude of God, by which I understood the whole world both here and beyond the sea, the abyss, and all other things . . . And in this I beheld nothing save the Divine Power, in a way that is utterly indescribable, so that through the greatness of its wonder the soul cried with a loud voice saying, 'The whole world is full of God'. Wherefore I understood that the world is but a little thing; and I saw that the power of God was above all things and the whole world was filled with it . . .
>
> After I had seen the power of God, His will and His justice, I was lifted higher still; and then I no longer beheld the power and will as before. But I beheld a *thing,* as fixed and stable as it was indescribable; and more than this I cannot say save that I have often said already, namely, that it was all good.

There are, indeed, hundreds of these cases, where the personality was immersed in a consciousness that is beyond expression in earthly words.

Very little is known about this inspirational function of man, and those who do know are perhaps silent. In the East this is called the 'Buddhic power', and there they believe that certain people have reached such a stage of development that they are 'adept' in its use. It may be that a few of our Westerners have also experienced this divine illumination, but enough has been said by men and women of all nations to let us know that this stage of consciousness is there for our future use and even now for occasional 'inspirations'.

Exercise Twenty

No exercise is given as to this vehicle, for the development work required is beyond the scope of this book. It may, however, be suggested that the student prepare for the heights by judicious use of music, poetry and good literature (which does not mean novels, with few exceptions).

In his magnificent *Through Literature to Life* Ernest Raymond says that the purpose of good literature is 'simply this, and exactly this: that you may have life and have it more abundantly . . . A work of literature is not an idle tale to entertain and relieve the reader in his lazy hours but, rather, the cry of a great soul at the spectacle of life he sees before him . . . Literature makes us feel about more things and makes us feel more about them.'

Because the Buddhic is the plane of approaching unity, this is exactly what the student must try to achieve. Nothing is alien to us. All life is sacred, as Schweitzer taught us, and we, as occultists, must endeavour to thrill to *all* life—its joys, its sorrows, its disasters, its triumphs *and particularly those aspects of it which have nothing to do with our personality.*

Poetry 'is the breath and finer spirit of all knowledge'; it 'is the spontaneous overflow of powerful feelings: it takes its origin from emotion recollected in tranquillity', said Wordsworth. 'Poetry is more philosophical and of higher value than history' was Aristotle's comment.

In the great days of religion it was the practice to memorise a verse of the Bible and/or to read a chapter of it each day. It was a practice that could lead to the spiritual heights, although today it is better to suggest perhaps that we memorise a verse of poetry or read *and understand* two paragraphs of a book with spiritual purpose—not necessarily 'dry'. Try Shaw's *Back to Methuselah,* for example.

Of music one may only say that, apart from it being a matter of taste—let it be MUSIC. For the writer this means Bach and Brahms, Beethoven and Mozart (in that order), but you will have your own choice. 'Provided music makes you swell' it is useful, said a great teacher to me, and it was not until I learned how to perceive the 'egg' that I really understood what he meant.

Stretch your mind!

LESSON 18
The 'Oversoul'

Exercise Twenty-one
Very Very Important Retrogression

Fear not, little flock; for it is your Father's good pleasure to give you the kingdom. St Luke, 12: 32

A soul that desires to attain knowledge of spiritual things must first know itself. The Soul does this when it is so re-collected and detached from earthly preoccupations and from the influence of the senses. Then it understands itself as it is in its own nature, taking no account of the body.

Walter Hilton. *The Ladder of Perfection*

. . . he ever bears about a silent court of justice in his breast.
Himself the Judge and jury and himself the prisoner at the bar.

Tennyson. 'Sea Dreams'

I sat alone with my conscience in a place where time had ceased
We discoursed of my former living in a land where the years increased
And I felt I should have to answer the questions it put to me
And to face those answers and questions in that dim eternity.

And the ghosts of forgotten actions came floating before my sight
And the sins I thought were dead sins were alive with a terrible might
And I know of the future Judgement: how dreadful so'e'er it be

That to sit alone with my conscience would be judgement enough for me.

C. W. Stubbs, former Bishop of Truro

All we have willed or hoped or dreamed of good shall exist.
Not its semblance, but itself: no beauty, nor good, nor power
Whose voice has gone forth, but each suffices for the Melodist
When Eternity confirms the conception of an hour.
The high that proved too high, the heroic for earth too hard,
The passion that left the ground to lose itself in the sky,
Are music sent up to God by the lover and the bard;
Enough that he heard it once: we shall hear it by and by.

Browning. 'Abt Vogler'

Geraldine Cummings in one of her books reports that her communicator, F. W. H. Myers, has called Man a 'Sum in Arithmetic', by which is meant that Man's various vehicles must be totalised in order to know what his life has meant. This is the function of the Oversoul.

First we must not confuse this with spirit—the 'divine spark', which is pure spirit, has a permanent relation with the Creator that is beyond words and because of that cannot be engaged in evolution and betterment. Secondly, what St Paul called 'Soul' is the summation of one lifetime's work whose totality is preserved by the Oversoul, which is the projection from pure spirit that synthesises all the Man's experiences in various lives. Thirdly, there are the four planes of Inspiration, Thought, Emotion and Sensation which go to make up each man's full equipment of potentiality. These planes are interpenetrative and in communication with the physical, which acts as the base of the operations.

So far as *Man as Oversoul* is concerned, these four planes of manifestation are his to control. There are still above the four planes three higher planes which complete the Individual, the perfected Man whom Jesus commanded we become.

Man's descent into the four lower octave planes is what we call the 'Fall'. As he passed through each of these planes on his downward thrust into density-consciousness, he made a vehicle or body suitable to the vibrations of that group. When at last he reached incarnation in the physical-etheric (the lowest octave group for Man) he had latent knowledge of all the planes through which he had passed, and moreover had within the physical instrument sympathies arising from the passage and a system of cognisance which could communicate and affect the higher vehicles, *provided that he could raise the vibrations to the requisite level.* Through channels of communication which the Indians call 'chakras' the Persians, 'wheels of force' and our scientists know only materially as the endocrine glands, the higher planes can be reached.

This raising of the vibrations can be accomplished by occult science or it may come involuntarily at certain times. Extra-sensory perception is merely the ability to use, either at will or involuntarily, the 'windows to the higher plane'.

Throughout our lives every action, thought, wish, impulse makes a transmission to the higher vehicles, but for most of us our thinking and wills are capable of creating only such weak impulses as to be almost imperceptible by the higher vehicle. Constant thought upon one subject will, however, create a 'habit track', and then each 'mickle' will end in a 'muckle', as they say; each small stone will end in a road either of good or bad tendencies being built.

At death, when the use of the physico-etheric ceases, the impulses of that life also cease, and an ascent begins, gathering together all the results, the habit tracks on that one life. It would be ridiculous to think that all the experiences, the triumphs and failures, the gains and the reverses could be lost. Much may have happened to us which none knows except ourselves, *but* the impulses have had their effect.

> But all the world's coarse thumb and finger failed to plumb
> So passed in making up the main account:
> All instincts immature, All purposes unsure,
> That weighed not as his work yet swelled the man's amount.
>
> Thoughts hardly to be packed into a narrow act,
> Fancies that broke through language and escaped.
> All I could never be, All that men missed in me
> This, I was worth to God, whose wheel the pitcher shaped.
>
> Robert Browning. 'Rabbi Ben Ezra'

All such thoughts and impulses are graven upon the permanent atoms which pass upwards to the judgement and custody of the Oversoul, which it is helpful to think of as being between the lower groups of octave which mean evolution as a man and the high groups of octaves which mean evolution beyond humanity.

At death then Man will start discarding the various vehicles, for death is but a name for transformation. The breaking of the 'silver cord' means the severance of earth contact through the chakras with the higher vehicles; this can be seen by clairvoyant sight. The totality of the 'sensations' of the physico-etheric are passed on to the emotional body in the form of an 'atom of consciousness' which is the impression, more fine than that of a gramophone record, of all past 'sensations'.

The upward path continues and the emotional is the next vehicle to be discarded. You may remember that the *nature* of this vehicle is swirling movement, and when it feels its severance approaching, it puts all its coarser vibrations (those nearest the earth similitude) on the outside of the egg 'to repel boarders' as it were. These will naturally be the first to disintegrate, and this is the 'purgation' of emotions. It is a time of assessment of all habits which have been acquired by the physical (eating, smoking, drinking, and so on), and getting rid of them may be a very real task. There are also the good emotions pulling the entity upwards, and so at last the astral bequeaths its 'atom' and the twain of physical and emotional pass on to the mental.

The mental vehicle is perhaps the most important for people of our kind. It has probably been the most used. Here the thought life of man is re-enacted. This is a time of recollection of 'gifts misspent and things undone'. It will afford us a panorama not only of our thinking but of the effects of that thought upon others. This is another part of the 'purgation'. But the upward pull will persist and in due course the entity will ascend to the Buddhic plane of love and inspiration, taking with it the permanent atoms of physical, emotional and mental work done.

For many of us the Man has been largely dormant in the Buddhic; he has not reached the intense love which culminates in sainthood or the intense inspiration which results in genius. The St Francis, the Beethoven, the St Teresa, the Einstein or the Simone Weil will at this stage add enormously to the collection of atoms from the lower reaches. For many of us the service we have given to a cause, or the love of an art, or the practice (not profession) of a religion will illuminate the lower atoms. And now we have to pass on the work of the four planes to the eternal Oversoul. The old Egyptian priests pictured this as the 'weighing of the heart'. The Oversoul is to be perfected, that is to assume complete control of the lower four octaves and all manifestations thereon. It will now decide that unless completion and integration have been reached, the entity will descend again into matter, bearing the purified 'permanent atom', which will now include the result of many lessons, the fruits of much work done and the potentialities of many unrealised impulses both in the life just past and lives previous to that, and act as the 'original sin' and potentiality for new incarnation.

> And I shall thereupon take rest, ere I begone
> Once more on my adventure brave and new
> Fearless and unperplexed when I wage battle next
> What weapons to select, what armour to endue.

The verse quoted is from 'Rabbi Ben Ezra' by Robert Browning, and should be read, and in the writer's opinion memorised, by every occult student.

Most obviously the information given above must be but a pale shadow of the actual truth: 'The forceps of our minds are clumsy instruments and crush the truth a little in taking hold of it', said H. G. Wells. But these are truths stated by men of all nationalities, and the central teaching has not altered for 5,000 years of history.

The sum of our real achievement is the sum of our work through these various vehicles of consciousness, and we must again emphasise that all these vehicles must interpenetrate. It is therefore natural that when a man 'dies' in any one of these stages, it means that he has winnowed out the experiences of his 'I' in that particular stage. When the writer's physical life is ended, it will mean that his physical instrument is no longer capable of properly responding to the needs of his real 'self', and that he has begun the withdrawal back to that self. It is logical to think that the physical husk he leaves behind him merely means that the power animating it has been withdrawn. The power would then proceed to winnow out the experiences of the emotional life and leave these also behind it. This would pass on to the thinking life and, in each case, the experiences of physical incarnation will be relayed.

The idea of interpenetration is of scientific interest for physicists. Denys H. Wilkinson, FRS, a leading physicist, is quoted by Rosalind Heywood and reported in the *Listener* as saying: 'Perhaps there do indeed exist universes interpenetrating with ours; perhaps of a high complexity; perhaps continuing their own forms of awareness; constructed out of other particles and other interactions than those we know now, but awaiting discovery through some common but elusive interaction that we have yet to spot.' It may well be that the perception we need is that of the fully integrated man.

The need of Man, according to both psychology and occultism, is that we should integrate all our experiences, preferably while on earth. Certain adepts, both in the East and the West, claim to have done this and to have become 'whole'. By making oneself, in this life, into an integrated whole, and not allowing partial emotions, moods or thoughts to masquerade as our 'Self', we really achieve the purpose of living. In his work Jung refers to this as having secured individuality, but for the occultist that word has an extra meaning.

In regard to this life, please consider how the 'I' uses such phrases as 'my body', 'my time', 'my thinking', 'my wishes', and so on. These represent, in fact, intuitive knowledge that the particular aspects of personality referred to are not the whole self. It would be wrong for us to think that the real self can be assessed in terms of one lifetime or earth personality. It is suggested that there is an Oversoul, an observer who calmly assesses the whole of the happenings of a lifetime, almost as a devoted mother might consider the day in the lifetime of a beloved child.

When my wife was approaching her physical death, and before she went for a crucial operation, she related how, in the semi-dream state in which she lived at this time, and through the mist of known pain dulled by injections, she suddenly became conscious of another state of being, and in that state of being she saw herself looking down upon the tormented physical organism that was lying in the bed. Her own description was that she observed her pain-racked body with a sense of calmness and of kindly aloofness, with the certainty that this too would pass, that it was temporal and not particularly important.

One of the most interesting of all stories of dissociation is perhaps that of Caroline Larsen, the wife of a college professor, who wrote a book entitled *My Travels in Spirit World.* Taken at her own valuation, this presents a remarkable instance of the 'calm Over-self'. One evening in the summer of 1918 she suffered from quite involuntary dissociation: that is, she suddenly found herself looking at her body on the bed. She could hear her husband rehearsing a string quartet and, in her own words, she felt 'airy and delicate', filled with 'unbounded joy and enthusiasm'. She thought she would go downstairs to the music, and found that she at once moved with the freedom of thought. However, as she came to the little platform which divided the stairway into two flights, she saw 'standing before her a woman spirit in shining clothes, with arm outstretched and with forefinger pointing upwards: "Where are you going? Go back to your body".' Mrs Larsen knew instinctively that from this command and authority there was no appeal. Reluctantly she turned, reascended the stairs and with 'feelings of loathing and disappointment' rejoined her physical form. Mrs Larsen was able to have many other experiences which, indeed, rival those of Sylvan Muldoon.

This Over-self has always been the object of the occultist's search; and the various facets of our personality, whether on physical, emotional or mental level, are assessed by, and possibly absorbed into, this majestic individuality. The Over-self is, indeed, the essential being which, eternal in its nature, creates and gives momentum to the personality.

Exercise Twenty-one

This is a very short and simple exercise but perhaps the *most* important in this plan. It consists of an honest, thorough appraisal of each day's actions at the end of that day.

1 Before going to your nightly rest of the physical, it is wise to open your window or go out into the fresh air and do at least five breathing exercises.
2 When you are in seclusion and before going to sleep, review the entire day's work, starting with *that* moment and working *backwards* through the day until the time you awakened. There is a good occult reason why it is important to work backwards.
3 This process means considering at the fullest length you can manage *all* your actions, assessing them, apportioning blame for the wrong ones (this does not mean saying to yourself that you are 'sorry' or rationalising your mistake—it means realising the wrong and

memorising *how you fell* into the trap), and apportioning praise for those things you have done right (you will not be overburdened). It is one of the tragedies of religious tradition that we are not allowed to experience a glow of satisfaction at something well done. This is nonsense! Good actions are to be encouraged, as bad ones are to be condemned.

4 The effect of this exercise if done thoroughly is to
   (a) create in the unconscious mind barriers against the condemned errors and habit tracks for the approved right-doing,
   (b) activate the whole of your vehicles (bodies) before sinking into sleep and leaving the physical, thereby preparing the vehicles you are to use in that period with them already cleansed,
   (c) give you purgation day by day—a very vital thing.

This exercise sounds simple, but if done for only one year, thoroughly and truthfully, it will ennoble your entire entity and illumine your daily life.

LESSON 19
Developing Latent Powers—Auras

Exercise Twenty-two More about the Aura

Magic I felt was no more than a first crude attempt at science and it had been superseded by science.
It now seems to me that the exact reverse is true.
Magic was not the science of the past. It is the science of the future. I believe that the human mind has reached a point in evolution where it is about to develop new powers—powers that once would have been considered magical. Colin Wilson. *The Occult*

With the last lesson, you have completed the necessary elementary philosophical and practical training necessary to develop one or more powers of the 'sixth sense'. It is important to remember that such development of 'signs and wonders' will not bring on your true ego, your true 'self', one iota; the sole advantage of such powers is to confirm that Man is something more than his five-sense brain (the mind's servant) or his physical body instrument.

It is unlikely that you will develop all latent powers; you will have special facilities which will depend upon your ray in this incarnation. The 'sixth sense' (a misnomer) operates because in your present incarnation you passed through the higher planes ('the Fall'). In your physico-etheric there are traces of the higher planes on which you created 'vehicles of expression' (bodies) in that descent. Such high vehicles can be stimulated while still in the physical, and the exercises given assure such contact. *Unless there is regular practice every day and perseverance until an exercise produces a result* you will only approach the higher vehicles (bringing perhaps occasional 'flashes'), but you will not bring them into your full use.

Telepathy, clairvoyance, astral and auric perception and the power of 'thought forms' are all facets of the same ability to use the higher vehicles to create forms at their level of vibration and to experience such results through the physico-etheric.

We propose to treat the various manifestations in the following order, though this is not obligatory; it does, however, show some sequence in a subject where one aspect supports another.

1 Etheric perception (this you should have achieved, and *practice means success*).
2 Auric perception (this is allied to etheric). See this lesson.
3 Creation of thought forms (see Lesson Twenty), leading to
4 Telepathy (see Lesson Twenty-one).
5 Clairvoyance (see Lesson Twenty-two).

The writer's society considers clairaudience to be a meditation result needing a 'stillness' of mind even at the lower levels of that particular power. This will therefore be dealt with under the head of 'Meditation (elementary)'.

Auric Perception

It is essential to have secured some facility of etheric perception before the 'seeing the aura'. When you have achieved etheric perception, develop it by daily use, in your office, at your bus stop, in your tube station and so on. All living things have an etheric—vegetable, animal or human. Gaze at a distant line of trees until their etherics are clear, or, if you live in an industrial area, observe the tall chimneys. The next step is towards the higher and incredibly faster vibratory rate of the astral atoms.

Everyone receives 'perceptions' from the higher vehicles in dreams. This is an occult truism which needs expansion. Let us consider the phenomena of dreaming. From the beginning of recorded history dreams have had a meaning for mankind; the seers of every age have recorded them and their message has always been interpreted by the Josephs among men. With the advent of the 'infidel half century', such meanings were consigned to the rubbish heap as 'old wives' tales'. As often with modern science, the scientists have 'discovered' truths which are age-old, calling their science by the name of psychology.

Sigmund Freud was the great Austrian who led this discovery, and while modern work has far outstripped his initial thesis, everyone should honour his name. His great work *The Ego and the Id* (1923) brought back dreams to their rightful place as one of the illuminating displays of what a man is. He was perhaps obsessed with the sex explanation and 'the old man in the cellar' (repressions), and Jung and Adler disagreed with his dependence on these factors. Jung was especially constructive:

'Something always comes out of the study of a dream if we carry it around with us and turn it over and over.' Dreams he thought 'provide a kind of guiding image which corrects the self devaluating image and bring about a better direction of consciousness' *(General Aspects of Dream Psychology*). He did much work on the question of symbols, installed the 'Mandala' as a scientific figure (*Secret of the Golden Flower*) and even saw that dreams could be precognitive—they 'may act as a kind of prevision or anticipation of the future achievements in the continuance of life, something like a preliminary exercise or sketch or a plan roughed out in advance' (*General Aspects of Dream Psychology*).

Modern depth psychology has moved much nearer to the old occult teachings of 2,000 years ago. P. W. Martin in his *Experiment in Depth* has said: 'Dream analysis is a constructive technique. Most depth psychologists would agree that dreams show, in their own manner, the situation in the unconscious. The number if a figurative one, a picture writing, a language of images.'

'Every dream is a prophecy', says Father Keegan in Shaw's *John Bull's Other Island, but* Martin says in *Experiment in Depth:*

> Most dreams appear to be relatively superficial, a straight reaction of the unconscious . . . at the opposite end to this reaction type of dream is what the primitives call the great dream. The great dream has a reality and vividness all its own—often there is a special type of light about it. Between the reaction dream and the 'great dream', with no distinctive dividing mark are the dreams which show the unconscious as it is at the time.

The occultist thinks that all these manifestations have to do with the various 'vehicles' of man and the perception in and of them. He divides into another quaternion four separate types.

The first type come from the individual, that point of striving Man which amalgamates with the 'divine spark'. Such 'dreams' are called 'visions', nearly all are 'religious' in nature (that is, accepting all religions). While dressed in symbolism, like St Joan and her voices, they are nonetheless categorical imperatives from the highest contact man can know.

The second come from the Oversoul, that dweller in the eternal *now,* who bears the synthesis of our past lives, consciousness of our present state, and limitations and intimations of our future 'needs'. The Oversoul may see plainly the course of our future, but to know is not necessarily to communicate. Such dreams are usually confused by passing through the various planes before entering into our conscious minds; this is why we must write down our dreams immediately on waking, as the first impulse of the physical is to rationalise or dismiss.

The third class come from soul mind, and are expressions of the higher vehicles about this present life. They again will suffer from passage through lower planes, expressing themselves probably in symbols. Many accomplished persons acknowledge indebtedness to 'sleeping on it', and the old theory of so doing has some relation to fact. Such 'dreams' may bring answers to problems, personal prayers, and while they may be answers from any of Man's planes, they will usually be expressed in 'earth' pictures simply because they come from a plane nearer to the physico-etheric.

The fourth class come from the astral or emotional plane, and are usually mixed with distortions of the body's sensations, worries or aspirations of emotive type. They are often wish-fulfilment dreams, particularly of a sexual nature, and are the basis of Freud's thinking. Their expression will usually be vivid and a mixture of earth happenings.

It must be understood that all these dreams may interpenetrate and will, because of their passage through perceptions, undoubtedly be distorted. The skill of the psychiatrist or the occultist is in removing the distortions from the real import. The dream is a nightly contact with the higher vehicles, and as such is an evolving experience—a prophecy of the real hinterlands of the being we call Man.

What is the aura? Everyone has seen paintings of saints and holy persons whose heads are encircled with a ring of translucent light; such 'auras' were depicted from the time of Egyptian 'Ra', but although the aura is usually shown around the head, it does in fact surround the whole physical centre or body, rather like an inverted egg with the broad portion at the top. It is easiest to see around the head, because there are four chakras in that locality (throat, pituitary, pineal and crown); naturally this gives a concentrative power to that area, for all is vibration and electromagnetic in presentation.

The dictionary defines 'the Aura' as a 'subtle emanation from any body: a sensation as of a current of cold air arising to the head (as in epilepsy or hysteria) (pathological): the air current caused by a discharge of electricity from a sharp point (electrical): a vague luminous glow surrounding a figure or an object; it may take the form of a sound, sight, smell or feeling not perceptible to others'.

The occultist might define it as follows:

> The increasingly subtle essences of the vehicles which surround the physical centre and which portray the differing rates of vibration emanating from the denser centre in its contact with and use of the higher vehicles of its electromagnetic field. Such octaves of vibration have their own density of respective prana, and the rate of vibration arouses the colours which are seen as the aura.

We may comment on this definition:

(a) The essences are subtle because, although each octave group has its own pranic levels, from which it creates the form of the vehicle, yet they are not perceptible to five senses at normal level. To be perceived, the vibrations of the normal must be raised, and that is why certain diseases do raise the level, thereby providing the medical definition of the dictionary.
(b) The aura is an egg-shaped form of varying intensities of prana created by electromagnetic force. Remember the analogy of the fountain composed of millions of drops of water which are dependent for form on the energy that activates them.
(c) Each octave group has its own density and vibratory rate, so that to perceive implies raising our vibratory rate to that level. This means following the precepts already taught and using constructively our latent power in full knowledge of the theory of the chakras.

It is important for the student to realise that all is vibration. Our eyes are only sensitive to light that lies between the wavelengths of 380 and 760 millimicrons, but we know that technology has extended this sensitivity, and we speak of 'infra red' and 'ultra violet'. The occultist knows that sensitivity increase can be made without the use of technological instruments, although their corroboration is helpful. There is a process, for example, known as the 'thermographic' technique, which transforms heat radiation into coloured pictures. This system proves that the body radiates on wavelengths outside our normal vision.

Oliver Bagnall, the Cambridge biologist, in his work *The Origin and Properties of the Human Aura* (New York, 1970), has come to the conclusion, in line with the Ancient teachings, that there is an inner and an outer layer (etheric and astral) in which he finds striations and ray action.

It has long been known that people who have lost a limb can still sense reactions from the non-existent physical, and it is taught that this is because the etheric still remains. This seemed to the practical man like fantasy, but a Soviet electrician, Semyon Kirlian, has produced a machine which shows that 'there is an energy matrix in all living things and that it has a shape like that of the organism but relatively independent of it'. This quotation is from Lyall Watson's *Supernature,* which has been used in the above two paragraphs also. The Soviet scientists, who are of course materialistic in approach, have called the phenomena 'Biological Plasma Body', and this in fact reduces the phenomena to occult explanation (Ostrander and Schroeder. *Psychic Discoveries behind the Iron Curtain,* 1971). Increasingly numerous scientific 'discoveries' reinforce the teachings and you may welcome their help while using the greater instruments of Man's own vehicles and perceptions.

The size of the aura in the undeveloped animal man possibly extends only a very few feet from the physical centre, yet for the Adept and the Saint, incredible though it may seem, the aura can extend to enormous distances. It is said that the Lord Buddha's aura stretched over 200 miles, while the Gnostics believed that the aura of Our Lord embraced the whole of his environment wherever he cared to concentrate. 'In Him we live and move and have our being.' The writer can testify that in the case of some he has known, merely to sit in their presence was to feel a calm sublimity. Paul Brunton has explained this beautifully in relation to the Sage of Arunachala, while the disciples of Ramana Maharishi or the flock of Padre Pio speak similarly of this phenomenon of peace within the aura of their Master.

As for the *colours of the aura,* you know that the aura will be seen as colours in vibratory movement, because each octave group has its own special colour, and the more of that octave group there is in our sevenfold make-up, the more will that colour be manifest in the aura. But because of this there will be compounds: for example, a high intellectual, primrose yellow might under the impact of devotion show as light green, the colour of hope and aspiration. This is a specialist subject, and the student will find he soon learns to place his own colour assessment on what he perceives.

The writer was fortunate in that at the age of four he was able to 'perceive' the aura; in his case it was with a sense of shock that this occurred, but he has known other students who have worked for years to achieve this ability. Work, however, will always succeed and the perception of this 'outside the physical' adds great weight to the true psycho-philosophic work of the Ancient Wisdom.

Exercise Twenty-two

You will have acquired the ability to see the etheric and it will be wise to recapitulate Exercises Fifteen, Sixteen, Seventeen and Eighteen thoroughly. You may then proceed to 'perception of the Aura'. This is of course an outer composed of the Buddhic, mental and astral and an inner of the etheric. You will *only* be able to 'perceive' vibrations coming from the subject for which you are able to raise to a corresponding height of vibration. This means for the student that he will certainly be able to see the etheric, lower emotional and mental, and some traces of the higher vehicles. Perception of the Buddhic is rare. You will see the etheric like a haze outside of and roughly in the form of the physical corpus. Outside of that there will be the ovoid, but this will have definite areas. Nearest to the physico-etheric is the astral, which has already been explained as a swirling mass responsive to all emotive thoughts. The colours are also swirling with the impulses felt by the physical (sensation) and the thoughts of emotional content. This coat of many colours will have an edge, a definition, but without breaking off rapidly.

The mental, a much more stable vehicle, will also have many colours, but they will largely stay in one place, although there is a constant play across these background colours as new thinking intervenes and vitalises. Again there is an appearance of limitation, but with the advanced man this higher mental colour fades into the Buddhic.

1 It is helpful to have a fellow student, as suggested in Exercise Eighteen, but you may also practice by observing others without their cognition.
2 The preliminaries are obligatory and a review of Exercises Fifteen to Eighteen most desirable.
3 Sit in Egyptian position with the nightlight before you and in such a place that its rays strike the corners of your eyes, which will be partially closed in the position you have previously established is correct for you. Shield the light from your subject.
4 As soon as you perceive the etheric of your sitter, and while keeping them in view, very slightly turn away so that in fact you are doing the 'Tibetan squint'.
5 You must then wait until the etheric is infused with a ray of colour. At first this may be only a flash, but practice will secure a greater permanence.
6 Never sit for this work at the beginning for more than ten minutes, although, if you have a student companion, it is permissible to interchange—indeed sometimes this helps.

This work will not in most cases be attained quickly, and in all of this effort *practice* is the operative word.

LESSON 20
Developing Latent Power—Making Thought Work for You

Exercises Twenty-three, Twenty-four and Twenty-five
The Talisman   Wish-Willing   Dream Recording

There is nothing either good or bad, but thinking makes it so.
Shakespeare. *Hamlet*

Culture being the pursuit of our total perfection by means of getting to *know* . . . the best which has been thought and said in the world.
Matthew Arnold. *Culture and Anarchy*

For who would lose,
Though full of pain, this intellectual being,
Those thoughts that wander through eternity.
Milton. 'Paradise Lost'

Mind is the Master power that moulds and makes
And Man is Mind and evermore he takes
The Tool of thought, and, shaping what he wills
Brings forth a thousand joys, a thousand ills:—
He thinks in secret and it comes to pass:
Environment is but his looking glass.
James Allen. 'As a Man Thinketh'

Dr Grey Walter, the famous specialist, has said in *The Living Brain* that Man only uses nine-tenths of his power even in the most complex operations. Dr Grey Walter also affirmed that he believed there were no limits to the possibilities of the human brain.

This course has suggested that our earth and its denizens float in a sea of 'undifferentiated consciousness', and that Man (mineral to man) has been formed by two cosmic forces—prana, the form creator, and fohat, the vitaliser—and their evolutionary impulses. Today the popular words are 'Cosmic Mind', but it is quite immaterial what the 'sea' is called so long as we understand that it enters into octaves of vibration, creates a suitable vehicle for each octave and can be vitalised to the fullest use of that octave.

You can use these facts of 'Cosmic Mind', and on three levels: the unconscious, the day to day conscious, and the supra-conscious (which may be likened to the nine-tenths that are above the five-sense brain mechanism).

If you use the collective unconscious, then there are two possible approaches:

1 The appeal for 'gifts', ie by concentration, which centres upon what you desire and will surely find a response (sometimes called 'sympathetic magic').
2 Because the *mind* can control the forces of prana and fohat, we can create (see Alexandra David-Neal's *With Mystics and Magicians in Tibet*). Most people, however, merely wish without using will, and this cannot result in achievement. The principle of *prayer* is exactly this focussing with a known object for attainment. The mere formula of repetition is unlikely to do much for you. If you say the Lord's Prayer (a magnificent exercise), say it alternately as dedicated speech and in the mind, in the silence. Moreover take one sentence each night at the end of your praying and *consider* what it means for you.

You will have to fight against your own training in earthly five-sense environment, for Mother Commonsense admonishes us and says, 'Oh, yes, but of course that is all your imagination'. Of course it is, for imagination is the hallmark of Man's creative ability, of the superior man. 'Well', says she (and there are many scientists who are old women in this respect), 'Well, but it is all your fancy.' Of course it is, a dictionary definition of 'fancy' says to portray in the mind, and this exercise has preceded every great discovery of Man; only then we call 'fancy' by the more sedate sounding word 'inspiration'. The powers of imagination and visualisation are two of the 'I's' chief tools: 'imagination' is the power of expressing through the physical brain the concepts of higher planes; and visualisation is the ability to express such concepts in form at the higher mental level. They are interdependent and call in the aid of the power of concentration to fructify.

It is strange how certain words take on a meaning which is not an accurate one. The word 'imagination' has linkages with being born and valued, but years of considering only those things which we can touch and see as real have debased the importance of this word, with its tribute to Man. Planck, faced with a problem, *imagined* a possible solution, and when the famous 'constant' had been imagined, he declared it took him months to find a mathematical basis for it; he imagined, foresaw, 'guessed' if you like, and then did the material work. Every great work of art is a product of applied imagination. Mozart said that he heard the music in his mind; his job was to copy it down. Stevenson laughingly called his imagination his 'brownies'; they wrote the story, and all he had to do was to copy it.

Please give the word 'imagination' its proper place, for it is man's abstract thinking at its best. 'We discover', said Sir James Jeans in his *Mysterious Universe,* 'that the Universe shows evidence of a designing or controlling power that has something in common with our individual minds.'

'Imaging' as Fawcett called it, is not aimless 'daydreaming', however; it must have a purpose, a concentration. Wise men have always recognised the power of directed imagination. Samuel Taylor Coleridge in *Biographia Literaria* said: 'The primary imagination I hold to be a living power and prime agent of all human perception and as repetition in the infinite mind of the eternal act of creation in the infinite 'I AM.' Professor W. P. Montague said, in *Ways of Knowing:* 'Imagination is the main source of all new ideas and all variations, not only in "the art of life", but in the life of science.' And Professor Wildon Carr, in *Imagination and Reasoning,* went so far as to state: 'Imagination is more original, more fundamental and more essential a factor in the mental life than sensation, understanding or reason.'

In *Essay on Creative Imagination,* Professor A. Ribot says: 'Underneath all the reasoning, indictions, deductions, calculations, demonstrations, methods and logical apparatus of every sort there is something animating them which is not understood, that is the work of that complex operation, the constructive imagination'; and David Hume, the eighteenth-century philosopher, refers to imagination as 'a kind of magical faculty in the soul (Mind) which though it is always most perfect in the greatest geniuses—is however *inexplicable by the greatest efforts of human understanding.'*

Finally, Christian Larson, in *Powers of the Mind,* has written:

> When you use imagination—and see it constructively, extensively and brilliantly—then you are taking steps: then you are giving this faculty real training and causing it to grow by leaps and bounds. When you acquire the power to use imagination correctly it will be a simple matter to train the other faculties in the group—

imagination is the leading factor and always takes the lead, playing the major part at all times.

The difference between imagination and fantasy can best be described by saying that imagination seeks a concrete result while fantasy indulges in butterfly thinking. This is the meaning behind the great saying, 'Imagination is a good servant but a bad Master'.

To control imagination fruitfully, we have to learn to concentrate and visualise. You have already done a small exercise, but very important, in the 'Tulip' growth. You have to learn to train your power of visualisation on every important subject on which you want guidance and result-inspiration. You have to make your aspirations take 'form'.

Please ask yourself the question 'What is form?' Form always means duality, division. Take a sheet of white paper and draw on it a circle with, say, a green pencil—immediately tremendous things have happened.

(a) A circle, an individual thing, has appeared on a sheet of nothing. The circle is divided from the remainder of the sheet, which may be termed by the Indian '*not*-circle'. The terms we use are 'individual' and 'undifferentiated consciousness'.
(b) There is a colour. Now you know that all colour is vibration, and that our vision divides the white ray into seven colours. So what the circle colour has done is to abstract *one* of the seven rays from the all-embracing creative primary white.
(c) By drawing the circle, we have separated from the unity and made a line of limitation, of restriction.
(d) So to create any form, the Divine Unity has to be broken and a duality division made.

The *Upanishads* speak of 'Self' and 'Not self', Gurdjieff taught us that all life is separation, and Pythagoras spoke of 'Two' and 'dark constructor', symbolised by parallel lines which never meet. This is fundamental to all occult thinking; light and dark, high and low, warmth and cold are all dualities which also have complementarity. All human experience depends upon this duality, in which one half of manifestation has a shadow, as Jung called it, of another half.

So when you use prana/fohat to create thought form, you are separating from yourself a portion of your life force; but because this thing is vitalised by you, it is your creation, and you can send it on your messages through higher vibrations to find a complementary on that level of vibration according to your wish and power. Your response in another's thought can be on many levels of vibrations, from the five senses ('a thought just came into my head') to highest vision. Whenever you think, you set up a stress; if your thought was feeble and had no definite end, then it will have little effect on the etheric surround, but if it is powerful and directed, it can effect wonders and affect all in its vicinity. This is why some people can alter the emotional temperature of a room by merely entering into it. Like all forms, thought forms must be energised. Energy from the physicist is the term applied to any mass or body which when moving strikes against another body and sets that also moving. Radiant energy is that type which can be imparted to the medium surrounding it, and the speed with which this is effected depends upon the transmitting power—the sun is a good example of radiant energy, with its poles of negative and positive and thereby the creation of an enormous magnetic field.

'As above so below'. Your mind can use your brain, with its two poles—cerebrum (positive) and cerebellum (negative)—to create a magnetic field. This is what you do when using thought form creativeness. To summarise:

1 Purposive life is the abstraction from a universal 'Undifferentiated Consciousness' into a limited instrument that can use certain of the octaves of vibration of which the mass (Cosmic Mind) is formed.
2 This undifferentiated consciousness uses two forces, called in science gravitation and electromagnetism, and in occult language 'prana', which is the atomic form maker at a particular level of octave of vibration, and 'fohat', which is the urging, energising 'mind' controller behind the evolution from the mineral to the superman.
3 While on earth, we can use the various levels of our physico-etheric, emotional-mental and spiritual structure, and the 'vehicles' which correspond. This is done by a discipline of concentration and of occult meditation. Some mystics achieve it by silence alone.
4 Man is a mortal God—we are, here and now, creatures who live and have our Being in the Universal Mind/Soul.

Exercise Twenty-three

It is proposed to give two exercises. The first deals with the Law of Suggestion, called by some people 'sympathetic magic' but best thought of as an appeal to your own unconscious. It is based upon the belief that if you really ask for something *that is for the benefit of your evolution,* you will receive it through your own unconscious, which is part of the great collective unconsciousness.

A good way to make this appeal is to create a TALISMAN (Fig 8). This *must* be done in entirety by your own hand and brain—it must be your *own* expression of wish-will.

1 On a piece of cardboard or something similar draw an outer circle of 2½in radius and within that circle another of 2¼in radius. Draw

(Fig 8)

THE TALISMAN

both in pencil and lightly, so that later you can colour them, as explained.

2 Draw a centre circle of ¾in radius.

3 Divide the interior between the 2¼in and ¾in circles into four equal parts either by diagonal or vertical/horizontal lines.

4 Into each section put a symbol which *you* understand. It is wise as far as possible to avoid the ordinary English letters, because if you use them, they may distract your mind. Some people use the Runic symbols, Chinese letters, indeed any symbol which conveys a message to their mind and is entirely expressive of their private personality.

5 In the small centre circle draw a picture of what it is you require. You may again have to symbolise. If your wish is an amatory one, then a picture of your choice drawn by your hand is best, but if you cannot draw, like the writer, cut out a small snapshot picture and paste into the middle.

6 Now colour the talisman by lining in the small centre ring in black, dark blue or purple; the next (middle) ring in your favourite colour; and the outer ring with a faint colour wash or wavy line of the other colour of your choice.

This talisman should be covered, so that you can have it with you day and night, and be able to look at it whenever the wish to do so comes—your unconscious will act as timekeeper. Just look at it, mentally phrase your wish-will and put it away. Your five-sense brain needs to do nothing; leave it to the unconscious. You will probably have surprising results.

What happens does not depend upon the piece of cardboard nor its pictures. You are in fact building a thought form of your desire, of your wish-will, and the constant references mean that you reinforce that thought form with an implication to your unconscious. This has power and will give results, so be quite sure you ask for what you really need and you make at most repetitions lasting a couple of seconds each say fifty times a day.

There are hundreds of other ways to use this Law of Suggestion. A mantra like the famous one of Coué, for example—an hourly repetition of 'I'm getting better every day'—will work, *provided* you accept that it will and rely upon your unconscious to make it, so do *try it*.

Exercise Twenty-four

This, second, is a much more potent exercise, and means that you are using all your knowledge of preliminaries, imagination, concentration for visualisation and ability to enter into your higher vehicles. You are in fact trying to use 'prakriti' to build a form of pranic-atomic force, and vitalising it by your control of fohat (your electromagnetic power, which is whole *mind*).

1 Preliminaries of material—either use a black mirror or, better in the writer's opinion, a reversed yantra. Make this on a piece of cardboard, which may be leant up against a support (or furnished with its own, like a picture frame). An outer circle of 12in diameter is needed, in a *light* blue or *light* yellow according to choice, and a centre circle of white or cream and of 3in diameter. All the intervening space between the two circles must be coloured black, and a varnish is best.
2 Preliminaries *must be performed until you are in a state of quiescence.* You need to be alone in the room, and as silent as the environment permits; your breathing must be slowed down to your known lowest level.
3 Decide what you are going to create—a treatment of mental or physical health, an attempt to make 'poise' in some family or business fracas, a successful result to an interview or an examination, money (but remember Jacobs' play, the *Monkey's Paw*). *Only* an initiate like David-Neal can make a 'tulpa', but you must not try this without the personal supervision of a *guru* of standing. This decision is the creation of an *archetype.* Now visualise a symbol of the happening in the white-cream of your anti-yantra: eg, if you wish to pass an examination, *see the certificate* with all possible detail; if you wish to restore harmony to a friendship and you are willing to forgive, as you feel there may be a need for forgiveness, see the person concerned smiling and holding out his hand. Visualisation will have untold

beneficial results on your personality and Oversoul. It is the beginning of that higher vision you are tending towards. Use your *mind* to make the picture and to impress the five-sense brain, and incidentally the unconscious. This is making the *idea*.

4 Now gaze at the yantra in the usual way, and when the eyelids are partially closed, *concentrate on the centre*. If you lose concentration, open your eyes again and recap number 3. *Concentration is a marvellous power,* and you cannot get it without constant practice. Consider the magnificent exposition in Colin Wilson's SF story the 'Mind Parasites' (which you must read, but as fiction only). Wilson says 'that to concentrate one must learn to control the "beam"' (consider the analogy of a burning glass previously given). Consider every word in this extract:

> The secret is this that the poor quality of human life—and consciousness—is due to the feebleness of the beam of attention that we direct at the world.
>
> Imagine you have a powerful searchlight but that it has no reflector inside. When you turn it on, you get a light of sorts but it rushes off in all directions and a lot of it is absorbed within the searchlight. Now you install a concave reflector, the beam immediately becomes ten times as powerful as before. But even this is only a half measure for although every ray of light now follows the same path, the actual rays are 'out of step' like an undisciplined army walking along a street. If you now pass the light through a ruby laser the result is that the waves now march in step: and their power is increased a thousandfold.
>
> The human brain is a kind of searchlight that projects a stream of attention on the world, but it has always been like a searchlight without a reflector. Our attention shifts around from second to second: we do not really have the trick of focussing and concentrating the beam.
>
> Most human beings never realise that life is so dull because of the vagueness, the diffuseness of their beam of attention.

You have learnt to direct the beam, and by your breathing exercises to secure the necessary rhythm.

5 When you feel you have really concentrated for one minute (excellent if you can), rise from the chair (if Egyptian position) or raise and lower arms if Yogic 'tailor' position. Stand to your feet, expel by a cleansing breath and say some Mantra such as 'Thy will be done', 'So may it be', 'Thy will Father not mine', and fill the room with your euphoric light blue.

The results will surprise you after a week of *constant* daily exercise (and it takes in all twenty minutes a day).

Exercise Twenty-five

In fact thought works for you every night, for dreams, while often mere reflexes of the turmoil of the day, have high levels, according to the vehicle which prompts them.

Some years ago a book by J. W. Dunne, *An Experiment with Time,* created a furore. In it Dunne, who was a noted aeronautical inventor and very down to earth, stated he had noted that some of his dreams had a precognitive message. He gave several outstanding examples, and as a result of his work, a group of students scattered all over the country started recording their dreams. The results were astounding. His study created for him a philosophy which he termed 'Serialism', and which is well exemplified in 'Nothing Dies'. The argument was that there must be an 'Observer', and for us this of course means our Oversoul. In his first book there were some charming pictures of an artist painting a rustic scene (the stream, the old bridge, the surrounding trees make a picture of reality). When the artist has finished, he steps back, content, but a moment's thought makes him say to himself, 'I've left something out, however. I should have shown myself painting the scene'. So he now puts in a picture of himself with easel and palette, and steps back again content, feeling that as a realist painter he has done a good job. Although momentarily satisfied, he realises that in fact he has not told the whole story, for there must surely be an observer who watches him, the artist, observing the scene and painting it. This is another expression of the fact that *'Man is a sum in arithmetic'* for each of our vehicles represents a higher degree of reality, and therefore both observed and observer—the individual (the divine spark) from timelessness, the Oversoul from the 'eternal now' and each vehicle from its own vibratory expression. This means of course that when we are free of the physico-etheric, we have experiences in higher vehicles, some of which may be precognitive, as were Dunne's and his followers'.

Every student should keep such a 'Dream Record', expressing as clearly and concisely as possible the dream experienced. This must be done immediately on waking—notice how soon your dream is forgotten. Dunne recommended a notebook and pencil by the bed, and (with as little physical movement as possible) an immediate recording.

The dream of import (and you cannot fail to have them) has of course to filter through the various vehicles and express itself through the physical brain when you write it down. Nonetheless you will find you have results; very often a dream will fulfil itself months after you have dreamt and recorded it. *Very* occasionally you will get the dream of symbols. This is the basis of the latest psychological development called

'Depth Psychology', and those interested will find an excellent exposition in P. W. Martin's *Experiment in Depth*.

Start keeping a record book tonight. Your thought at all your levels is always working for you and may sometimes feel despairing because *you* will not listen to it.

LESSON 21
Developing Latent Power—Telepathy

Exercise Twenty-six Practical

> By magical power a person on this side of the ocean can make another person on the other side hear what he wishes to communicate. Just as the physical body can hear and understand the voice of another at a hundred paces so the ethereal body can hear the thoughts of another at a distance of a hundred miles or more.
> Paracelsus

> Man has found the tools with which to handle the intricacies of nuclear physics; perhaps the basic principles of the mind are more evasive and intricately involved because they are not entirely physical and the mind of man has not yet come to accept the Spiritual as a field offering desired reward for research capital invested.
> Sir Hubert Wilkins. *Thoughts through Space*

From what has been said in the previous lesson, you will know that all the latent powers of the sixth sense (such as telepathy, clairvoyance, clairaudience) are those of the Mind/Soul controlling the five-sense brain. Moreover, in each of the named subjects, the sender will create a thought form and send it to a designated person. The thousands of 'death bed' visions, of appearances from soldiers killed in action to their dear ones, are so well known as to need no repetition. Please note what has happened: under the stress of a supreme emotion, the sender has made a mind image and instructed it, probably unconsciously, to seek out a certain person to give a message. There are also many thousands of cases where both sender and recipient are hale and hearty on this earth.

Telepathy is proven as well as any scientific subject can be, and yet many scientists and philosophers are afraid to accept the proofs because if they did it would strike at the very base of the materialist conceptions of Man. But their ostrich-like posture does not obliterate the facts.

In this lesson we shall deal with telepathy. One of the most interesting books you can read is that written by Sir Hubert Wilkins, who demonstrated practical telepathy with one Harold Sherman although they were *continents* apart. If you want some definite facts about this, read his book *Thoughts through Space*.

Professor Gilbert Murray of Oxford carried out 'family' experiments and his results were carefully tabulated (over 800 records), with the astounding result that, although the senders mixed living and fictitious characters, real scenes and made-up ones, he was successful in describing accurately 35 per cent of all the efforts tabulated. Indeed many of the remaining 65 per cent were partially successful.

It is possible to bring myriads of instances, and the obtuseness of science in not recognising this fact was castigated by Professor C. D. Broad, who said:

> It is hardly necessary for me to reiterate my often expressed conviction of the extreme importance for philosophy and psychology of the well established results of psychical research, and my regret that most philosophers and psychologists are content to remain in ignorance of them. Telepathy, both simultaneous and precognitive, is now experimentally established fact.

While many scientists still resist the evidence, which might easily upset their established mechanistic positions, Governments have grant-aided investigations. This is true of both the USA and Russia. The latter has, through books and magazines, revealed many of its findings, and established an enquiry known as the 'Popov Group'. The group has evidenced a connection between telepathy and the alpha rhythm, and the results seem to come when the student is thinking of 'nothing at all'. Indeed the yantra exercise is ideal for the introduction into this state. Among the subjects examined by the group were Karl Nikolaiev, an actor, and Yuri Kamensky, a biophysicist, who after some preliminary trials were placed under control some 400 miles apart, one in Moscow and one in Leningrad. Their results were completely unaffected by distance. The Russian scientists have established that the brain, during telepathy, was unusually activated 'one to five seconds after the beginning of telepathic transmission. We always detected a few seconds before Nikolaiev was consciously aware of receiving a telepathic message'.

So it is indeed scientific to call telepathy an 'experimentally established fact'. It is probable that a very high percentage of persons today could be using this faculty, indeed do use it unconsciously, but the methods of private investigation will increase the possibility.

The convincing proof of telepathy can best be found in a harmonious home circle or duality. Belief is not necessary; open-mindedness and willingness to accept evidence is. Moreover the experimenters have to realise that results may not always be exact, yet near enough to prove something occurred. The writer had an experiment with some beginners who were sending to him; he received the impression of a violin but it kept changing into a 'cello. He had told the student not only to send a picture of the object thought about but if possible to give a clue in sound or voice. In fact the sender had sent a violin *but he had hummed a well known 'cello aria.*

Telepathy is comparatively easy, but like all such work demands patience and harmony to produce the best results. If you can get a collaborator—someone you know well, whose respect, even affection, you return—then try this exercise.

Exercise Twenty-six

Preliminaries will include all the stages which you should now be using automatically when trying to contact latent power.

In addition the following suggestions may be helpful:

(a) It is better for beginners to work at night, when the sun's rays have not to be overcome. The *sun* is penetrating all your bodies.
(b) Practise to begin with at a regular time and preferably with a regular assistant.
(c) At the beginning work in the same room but *not* facing each other. Later you can ignore time and space as the words are used in an earth sense.
(d) Try to convey either actions or words.
(e) It is wise to alternate the roles of sender and receiver.

1 Preliminaries. It is better if both persons do the Complete Breath, and in unison as far as possible. *Avid expectations will destroy.* Both persons must be calm and poised and not overly expectant. The writer had a pupil who could never get any impressions until he had finished the exercises, when he found ideas entering by the score—he also was very telepathic when *not* expecting it. In other words, he was too tense to operate when performing consciously; latent powers either come unexpectedly or in a state of composed acceptance for the beginner.
2 The two participants should slowly close their eyes and visualise the other. *See* every feature of your *vis-à-vis;* a link of amity should

connect you. When you have visualised, *and not before,* send your message. *Never hurry.*

3. *Send your message in concrete form.* You may, for example, request that the receiver goes to the window, or you may convey a word or a short message. Whichever you do, *visualise it.* If a movement, see your comrade doing it. If a word, try to use the law of the triangle—that is, pick a word which you can convey by form sound and word name. A good example is a bell. Mentally repeat to yourself over and over the name *bell;* as you do so, 'see' the bell, note its shape, and when you have done so, hear the sound it makes when rung. As you will know, what you have done is to create a thought form. When you have done this, you must let it go—forget it, let the form go on its way, for the other will not normally receive until you have done so.
4. The receiver may hear a sound, see a form or 'know' a word, a name, or more likely a combination of these. *It is very important to accept the first suggestion.* The moment you get it, the five-sense rationalisation will confuse the issue; you will doubt and hesitate. *Accept the first impression* and remember that telepathy is *proven.*
5. Practise, and remember all that word means.

It helps to keep a record. The writer uses a points system. He gives minus three for a complete miss, minus one for no response, plus one for a near success. A sender sent him the word 'triangle', as applied to the actual instrument used as a dinner gong in Western films ('Come and get it'). He received the impression of a kitchen and of a frying pan being beaten; this was a disguised message, and you may count it either as failure or partial success. The previous instance given, concerning violin and 'cello, was a plus three for a correct forecast but also, in the writer's opinion, rated the exceptional plus five, as it was really a double success in reception.

At the end of each week over, say, a three-monthly period assess your plus or minus result. Normally you will find that for the first three months you will vary between plus one and minus one. Suddenly you will find yourself consistently in the pluses, but do not think you have achieved much until you are plus three or over. *Then* you are telepathic and can proceed without formality.

Repeat the above exercise at a distance. In the store, bus or theatre queue mentally tell someone to turn round and look at you, to put their hand to their hair or to mop their brow with a handkerchief. You will be surprised.

LESSON 22
Developing Latent Power—Clairvoyance

Exercise Twenty-seven Practical

He who doubts from what he sees
Will ne'er believe, do what you please.
If the Sun and Moon should doubt,
They'd immediately go out.
William Blake. 'Auguries of Innocence'

Are intimations for the elected soul, dubious, obscure and of unauthentic power
Since ghostly to the intellectual eye, Shapeless to thinking?
Nay but are not we
Servile to words and usurping brain, Infidels of our own high mysteries
Until the senses thicken . . .
Until the imprisoned soul forgets to *see* . . .
Edward Dowden. 'By the Window'

The student will know that there is a linkage between all latent powers. Telepathy may be thought of as a means of communication which demands a 'receiver' and a 'sender'. Indeed Professor C. D. Broad prefers the term 'telepathic interaction' to that of 'telepathy'.

Just as Jung divided us into 'extroverts' and 'introverts', so some people are better at receiving than sending, and vice versa. Like Jung's famous classification, however, there are traces in all of us of both abilities, although one may be dominant. Professor Gilbert Murray, although perhaps the greatest exponent of systematic telepathy, while recording some almost unbelievable successes as receiver was not apparently equally as successful as a sender.

As you proceed upon your quest, you will undoubtedly meet information about the rays, and while this subject is beyond the scope of this elementary 'textbook', we may glance at the subject. Just as white light passed through the prism splits into seven colours, of which three are primary, so the cosmic light or ray passed through humanity's consciousness splits into seven rays, of which three are primary (like red, yellow and blue in colours). While we all also have secondary rays, we shall be found to be on one main primary ray, which will bring its own special powers; some latent powers, therefore, will come easily to you, whereas others can only be acquired at the cost of much harder work.

Clairvoyance (a compound of two French words best translated perhaps as 'clear sight') is in fact a type of telepathy, or of telepathic interaction, which expresses itself in seeing 'forms'—usually a 'thought form' made voluntarily or involuntarily by a person who wishes to communicate some fact to the receiver. Very often the receiver sought is wrapped in five-sense obliviousness, and merely 'feels' something about the sender, but a person who is 'open' will 'see' for a moment the form of the sender or a symbol which bears relation to that person. The records of war apparitions offer many thousands of cases, and there are well accredited instances of contact between living persons, where one of the two (or more) has been a voluntary 'sender'.

Clairvoyance may have come upon you during any of the later exercises you have recently completed, but if you desire this faculty, it can be aided by the right exercises. The power is one that, like nuclear power, can be used for good or bad purposes, and if you seek this power, it should be with the aim of helping your fellows.

Bishop C. W. Leadbeater, whose book *Man Visible and Invisible* still remains one of the great clairvoyant expositions, has said in *Some Glimpses of Occultism:* 'It is not difficult to see that this is a power that may be misused. The additional information about others which it puts into the hands of its possessor may be employed for personal gain.'

Rudolph Steiner is an outstanding example of one who possessed clairvoyance in a remarkable degree and used it for the help and guidance of his fellows. It has also been well said by Leadbeater that a prime test is whether the clairvoyant is using his or her power for money: 'The moment he [the clairvoyant] takes money for any service which professes to be of an occult nature—that moment he brands himself as having no true occultism to give.' So we offer the following exercise with the certainty that you, the student, will be entering into the exercise of this power not only for your own illumination but on occasions for the benefit of another.

Exercise Twenty-seven

You will need one of the concentrative aids—a black mirror, a yantra, a crystal ball or a coloured goblet filled with a dark liquid (diluted blackcurrant wine is excellent). Do not, however, worry too much about apparatus; excellent results were obtained by one who used a postcard painted black and fitted into an ordinary light-coloured picture frame. So long as you have a focus of attention, its nature does not really matter.

You will also need complete privacy and the utmost possible silence. You will also need to be in a state of quiescence in all three lower vehicles—physical, emotional, mental. The light in the room should be minimal (a small blue globe in the electric light; the writer used a nightlight). Remember that in the old days of photography we had to dive into our 'dark room' to develop our picture because the white light affected the emulsion and obliterated the latent markings on the film or plate.

One other need is imperative—that you keep a record of your experiences. You will enjoy seeing how the power unfolds, sometimes apparently being lost altogether and then reappearing in greater strength. *Recording of all exercise work is of immense value to you, and later to your Master.*

1 The room preliminaries have been enumerated above.
2 Usual preliminaries, particular attention to breathing and creating a feeling of gentle warmth and euphoria in the room.
3 Gaze at your yantra or mirror, which needs to be at a comfortable height for you to see steadily in a more or less straight line. You will most probably enter into a 'drowsy state'. Many people have a species of clairvoyance every night before drifting into sleep. The scientists call this the 'hypnagogic' state, and give no explanation of it. In these states one often sees faces and places in a series of 'stills', as it were—ie the face will appear to you for a moment, most probably in the form of someone you do not know, and then it is gone. As you gaze into your black mirror, you will probably find a 'drowsy state' occur, and a white misty cloud appear. Maintaining your concentration, you may find this cloud break up into portions—some very dim, some more or less static and some 'whirling'.
4 These manifestations are formative to clairvoyance, and may turn into faces or scenes just as in the hypnagogic state.
5 Once this has been achieved, possibly in a further attempt, you will begin 'scrying' and see faces quite clearly. In your records do not attempt to personalise or dramatise what you have seen, but just record; the meanings will appear later, although of course they may not have any meaning for you, but just be 'passers-by' in the astral.

6 After some successes you will start to 'perceive' in earnest, and find appearances which symbolise for you definite events that affect the present personality. There are hundreds of cases where such visions have had a very helpful message to convey.
7 Like all occult work, the exercise demands patience and continuity, until finally you will be able to open your 'clairvoyant perception' almost as easily as you open your physical eye. If you can do this, then you may be sure this is your ray; for others of us it only comes after much effort and if it is greatly desired.

LESSON 23
Meditation (1)

Exercise Twenty-eight Semi-trance (Self-hypnosis)

The life of the soul in thought . . . is called Meditation. The meditation is the means to supersensible knowledge . . . rather must he permeate himself with the lofty thoughts with which men already advanced and possessed of the spirit were inspired, in such moments . . . Through such a meditation a complete transformation takes place in the student. He begins to form new conceptions of reality. All things acquire a fresh value for him. It cannot be repeated too often that this transformation does not alienate him from the world.

Rudolph Steiner. *Knowledge of the Higher Worlds*

Have we not stood here like trees in the ground?
Have we not grovel'd here long enough, eating and drinking like brutes?
Have we not darkened and dazed ourselves with books long enough?
Sail forth—steer for deep waters only

O my brave soul!
O farther, farther, sail!
O daring joy, but safe; are they not all the seas of God?
O farther, farther, farther sail!

Walt Whitman. 'Passage to India'

The soul within me; it is lighter than a corn, a barley, a mustard seed or the substance within it. The soul within me is greater than this earth and the sky and the heavens and all those united. That which performs and wills all, to which belong sweet juices and fragrant odours, which envelops the world and is silent and is no respecter of persons—that is the soul within me.

Chandogya. *Upanishad*

This much publicised but little understood path to power needs clarification. When a chairman at a meeting gets up and asks his audience to meditate for a minute on some word, he is, quite frankly, talking nonsense. Meditation means a gradual and general attunement of the various vehicles—sensation, emotion, mental and, if one can reach so far, Buddhic (spiritual). No 'Self' can meditate at a higher level than it has reached in its evolution. So while such a chairman's plea may help to steady vibrations, it can have no other effect.

It is much better to think of the foundations of this work as entry into a special type of prayer, a prayer of stillness, awaiting for 'the Voice of the Silence'. It follows that to meditate needs stillness of body, mind and spirit, a linkage with the unconscious and also with the Oversoul. It is unification. This course has no sympathy with those who believe that all one has to do is sit. If your mind is entirely passive, it is open to many influences which, whatever they may masquerade as being, are certainly not those you wish to evoke. So in meditation it is necessary to control one's thoughts, in other words to concentrate.

There are four degrees of meditation, of which two are beyond the scope of this elementary course and for which the help of a capable tutor is most desirable. We shall write of two stages.

The first requirement in all meditation is to raise oneself above the five-sense brain levels, and to open oneself to one's highest potencies. The student will find it a good exercise, therefore, to practise what may be termed 'self-hypnosis'.

There are many ways in which this can be done. The charcoal walkers do it by days of abstinence, during which chanting and breathing exercises prepare them for the walk on burning charcoal without hurt to their feet (this has been shown on the new God, the TV screen). The Dancing Dervishes use another method of rhythmic and sonorous exercises until they 'experience'. The Yogi reaches it by means of abstracted thought—meditation. Alfred, Lord Tennyson used to walk down country lanes saying his name over and over again, just loud enough for himself to hear, and was rewarded by 'states of mystical similitude'. The repetition of the Rosary, the chants of the monks of all religions, are basically the same idea—release from the thralldom of the five-sense brain and a journey into mind.

The following exercises will state an easier way, which, of course, nonetheless demands effort on your part. This way is *absolutely safe,* and amounts to self-hypnosis under the control of your own will and directions. The writer, who has some hypnotic power, is nonetheless averse from the use of hypnotism except in certain medical cases. This is because he believes that we have no right to interfere with another's mind processes, and any hypnotist must to some degree *control* another's mind. This is not good for either party. But self-hypnosis, repeat *self,* and the ability to use it is invaluable, not only for the pursuit of knowledge, not only for self-evolution and experience, but for relief from daily cares and illnesses of the nerves. Taken in conjunction with the retrogressive exercise already given (Exercise Twenty-one), the process is a cleansing one of great value.

Some further comments are desirable:

1 It is absolutely safe. Except for the adventurous few, this reassurance may be necessary. You are never out of your own vehicles, although you are free from your five-sense brain; you are held all the time most safely by the Silver Cord, which permeates and anchors all your vehicles. The method is *completely* safe.
2 You are in control. You will give the orders and obey your Oversoul. The method in psychology is referred to as instructing your subconscious, and the work of Dr Assagioli (psychosynthesis) uses the technique most efficiently.
3 You can enter this wonderland of extra-sensory perception for the length of time *you* desire and stipulate. Beginners would do well to limit this to five minutes at the most, and for the first essays perhaps only a minute.
4 The method is simple, so simple that at first most people cannot believe they have achieved the self-trance state. It is easily provable *but the directions must be obeyed in detail.*

With these four guidelines understood, the following exercise should be attempted with absolute certainty and freedom from five-sense-brain fear tendencies.

Exercise Twenty-eight

Venue and equipment. You need a room where you will *not* be interrupted, a comfortable chair with arms, and sufficient heat so that you will not feel cold. Ensure the *maximum possible silence.* Have your yantra in good position or choose some other focal point.

1 For the first few minutes before sitting down do your breathing, colour and intoning exercises. You may care to have a gramophone playing something slow and somewhat repetitive.
2 When you feel you have sufficiently prepared your room (what you are doing is highering the vibrations), sit down in your chair and fix

your gaze upon your selected point of focus—your yantra, some photograph or such—which must not be too large.

3 Having got your *self* into the right mood for exploration, issue precise instructions that you will enter into semi-trance and experience higher perception

(a) that your immersion in this superconscious state shall last for one earth minute of time (this is enough to begin with, and you will be surprised what can be experienced in one minute);

(b) that at the expiry of that minute you will return to normal consciousness but with recollection of what you have experienced.

4 Now give your *self* to meditation. Some phrase like 'All's love but all's law', 'Truth is with ourselves', or some verses of the Twenty-third Psalm, or similar verses, may be useful. While you are doing this,

(a) keep your gaze on your yantra;

(b) breathe in and out in slow rhythm. Count your breaths, breathing 'in' to the even numbers and 'out' to the odd numbers. It is essential to make and keep a steady flow with each breath, in or out, at the same length. You should aim at one to ten, the first breath being out and cleansing the instrument.

5 Somewhere along the route your eyelids will start to feel heavy and close. Surrender to this—after all it is what you do every night in sleep. It is the Self's way of shutting out the five-sense perceptions; it will remove them and replace by higher vehicle perceptions.

6 You need have no fear. You are doing by will what nature does for you each night *but* you are directing your escape from the physical.

No one can tell you what you will experience—usually at first colour healing for your tired self, later perhaps colour healing for others. Some people see other folk and scenes known in this life or a previous one. When you awake, you will find you doubt whether you have been in a trance, so easy is it all. This is excellent, because next time we do the semi-trance we will prove it to ourselves. *For beginners, however,* as in most things, practise moderation. A trance every third day is ample, and for one minute only. As you achieve expertness you may work much longer.

7 For succeeding sessions *ask* for some specific question to be solved or for some specific experience (not at this stage one that necessitates you getting out of the chair physically to perform a task). So when you give instructions, ask your question—out loud of course as you do all instructions, and repeat it in rhythm to the breathing. As you progress, you will find your own developments.

After you have practised this exercise with devoutness and *moderation* for some time, you will find you have a Shangri-La of your own, and moreover, like its namesake, the treasures will appear to be inexhaustible.

LESSON 24
Meditation (2)

Exercise Twenty-nine   Mantric Word of Power

If thou wouldst hear the Nameless, and wilt dive
Into the Temple-cave of thine own self,
There, brooding by the central altar thou
May'st haply learn the Nameless have a *voice*
By which thou wilt abide, if thou be wise.

Tennyson. 'The Ancient Sage'

He who would hear the voice of the Spiritual Sound and comprehend it he has to learn the nature of intense and perfect concentration.

Before the soul can comprehend and may remember, she must unto the Silent Speaker be united as the form to which the clay is modelled is first united with the potter's mind,
For then the soul will hear and will remember
And then to the inner ear will speak
The voice of the silence.

H. P. Blavatsky. 'The Voice of the Silence'

By one pervading spirit
Of tones and numbers all things are controlled,
As sages taught, where faith was found to merit
Initiation in that mystery old.
The heavens, whose aspect makes our minds as still
As they themselves appear to be
Innumerable voices fill
With everlasting harmony.

O Silence! are Man's noisy years
No more than moments of thy life?
Is Harmony, blest queen of smiles and tears
With her smooth tones and discords just
Tempered into rapturous strife
Thy destined bond-slave.
No though earth be dust
and vanish, though the heavens dissolve, her stay
is in the *word,* that shall not pass away

Wordsworth. 'On the Power of Sound'

Meditation is an individual thing transcending the confines of personality. Let us give some negative definitions. It is *not* the following:

1 *Concentration,* for while this is an essential preliminary to all occult knowledge, it is *only* a 'preliminary', although the doorway to all power.

2 *Visualisation,* for this is a step nearer in that it not only teaches how to concentrate but how to enter into the inner meanings of such concentration. Alexandra David-Neal tells an amusing story about concentration in her *With Mystics and Magicians in Tibet:* 'A young man begs the spiritual guidance of a mystic anchorite. The latter wishes him to begin by exercising himself in the concentration of the mind.

'"What kind of work do you usually do?"

'"I keep yaks on the hills", answered the man.

'"All right", replies the gonchen, "meditate upon a yak".

The novice repairs to a rough cave and settles down there. After some time the master goes to the place and calls to his pupil to come out of the cave. The pupil hears the master's voice, gets up and wants to walk out of the cave of which the opening is large enough to allow the passage of a man but is too narrow for a big bull. So, struggling against an imaginary obstacle, the young man answers his guru, "I cannot get out, my horns prevent me".' Remember too the exercise on the Tulpa (Exercise 24, p 166); both of these were powers in control of the lower instruments, not spiritual illuminations, which you are seeking in true meditation.

3 *Prayer* is not meditation, though this is a more controversial statement, for undoubtedly many who really pray reach the heights of the Buddhic and link with the Oversoul. Prayers of asking or those that are in any way personality-based cannot achieve this, but the prayer of surrender or adoration undoubtedly has so done. Meditation gives *you* a new power and a new horizon; it moves into the higher triad and forgets personality.

Most occultists and mystics have experienced this, but few have been able to define it in words. For the writer the best expression is that of Plotinus, the third-century philosopher, who said:

> Many times it has happened: lifted out of the body into my Self; becoming external to all other things and self centred; beholding a marvellous beauty; then, more than ever, assured of a community with the loftiest order; enacting the noblest life; acquiring identity with the divine—stationing within *it* by having attained that activity poised above whatsoever in the intellectual is less than the Supreme.

Many of the great Masters of the Arts have experienced being caught up into the Supreme: for example, Wordsworth, Tennyson, Browning, Goethe, Vaughan and Traherne, among poets, have testified to this experience. Tennyson, who had his own approach, a mantra one, has said: 'the individuality seemed to dissolve and fade away into the boundless and this is not a confused state, but the clearest of the clearest, the surest of the surest, the weirdest of the weirdest, utterly beyond words'.

Warner Allen in *The Timeless Moment* has told how he entered this beatitude (after years of work) while listening to the Seventh Symphony of Beethoven:

> I closed my eyes and watched a silver glow which shaped itself into a circle with a central focus brighter than the rest. The circle became a tunnel of light proceeding from some distant sun in the heart of the Self. Swiftly and smoothly I was borne through the tunnel and as I went the light turned from silver into gold. There was an impression of drawing strength from a limitless sea of power and a sense of deepening peace—I came to a point where time and motion ceased.

The student will find thousands of other comparable instances. (Two recommended books are Raynor Johnson's *The Imprisoned Splendour* and Underhill's *Mysticism,* although the latter confounds occultism, scientific religion, with Black Magic.) Perhaps one may close with a sentence from Radhakrishnan's *Eastern Religions and Western Thought:* 'The oldest wisdom in the world tells us that we *can* consciously unite with the Divine while in this body, for this is man really born. If he misses his destiny, *nature* is not in any hurry; she will catch up with him some day and compel him to fulfil her secret purpose.'

Occult meditation is at a still higher spiritual stage. It is the 'third Heaven', of which St Paul spoke, and discussion is beyond the elementary stage of this course.

Now it will be seen that a tutor may aspire towards teaching something of the first two steps of concentration and visualisation. For the ascent to meditation, however, it is the 'I' only that can teach. The presence of a Master may assist, as Brunton found in Arunachala, but only your own divine 'I' can be reached and used at these sublime heights, and by your own efforts, 'for this is Man really born'.

St Matthew (6, 6, *New English Bible*) gave us the great Master's instructions. Re-read them. They tell that we must go into a secret place—a silent place. This is an essential, for if you are to hear 'the Voice of the Silence' you must have immersed in that silence. So you must perform all the preliminaries you know—breath, colour, sound—to attune your vibrations, and then you must be ready to hear. As stated in Exercise Twenty-eight, this means making the physical instrument as comfortable as possible. You may find complete relaxation in a Yogic posture, or you may prefer the Egyptian—the essentials are a straight spine and such posture as leaves the physical without *any* irritations. It sometimes helps to concentrate on an object—a yantra, a black mirror, a symbol such as the cross, and to endeavour to visualise what that object means. From this will come a meditatory state.

Now as St Matthew has said, 'your Father who sees what is secret will reward you'. As occultists we believe that man is a divine spark and therefore may 'wait upon the Lord' (*Isaiah*) in confidence. 'Truth is within ourselves'; we have no need to search for it, we have only to clear away the veils and to perceive it. It is already there. The level of perception that you attain will depend upon the level of your spiritual evolution. For the Adept or the Saint this will obviously be much higher than the writer and probably the reader has attained. The Divine and our realisation of it will be there at the highest level *at which we can comprehend it;* it will bring the Wisdom and Certainty which the student needs to inspire to the higher of comprehension, of achievement, of illumination. No man knows the limit of this search; but whatever your level of attainment you will *know* the spiritual Wisdom, which will remove any fear of physical death, any doubt of your divine potentiality, any mistaking of Man's real mission on earth (the Lord told us that we cannot serve two masters). It is the truth 'whispered in our ear', to quote Browning's phrase.

Exercise Twenty-nine

If you have well practised Exercise Twenty-eight, you will probably have had several instances where you have known you were 'seeing' through another vehicle of consciousness than the eye. We are now to proceed further with this exploration into the heights of our 'Self'. We repeat, 'Cast out Fear'; *all vehicles are yours to use,* all are under the control of your Oversoul; and from the subconscious to that height of the Oversoul all is held by the Silver Cord, which will always bring you 'back'. This may often be to your annoyance. Sir Auckland Geddes in an address to the Royal Society of Medicine expressed the views of a friend of his as follows:

> . . . as the heart began to beat more strongly, I was drawn back and I was intensely annoyed, because I was so interested and just beginning to understand where I was and what I was 'seeing'. I came back into the body really angry at being pulled back, and once I was back all clarity of vision or anything and everything disappeared.

You are in fact trying to link with the vibrations of your highest attained level and to experience your life at that level. Most of you will have attained the sublimity and use of the higher mental vehicle, and some few the Buddhic. The experiences there awaiting you are beyond description.

In performing the exercises it may have happened that a direct 'ORDER' has come to you from the Oversoul. A classic example of such guidance is of course Socrates and his 'daemon'. Minnie Theobald in *Three Levels of Consciousness* has called these orders 'imperatives', which come with all the definiteness of a command. Rosalind Heywood in *The Infinite Hive* says: 'I want to emphasise that they come out of the blue, as if from another person and always as a surprise to the conscious mind. One has not wittingly thought it out, so to speak.' She gives many instances from her experiences of this power. While these 'Orders' come unbidden from the heights of the Oversoul, you can facilitate such experiences and others by practice.

Alice Bailey in her *Letters on Occult Meditation* says that what you are seeking is 'reciprocal vibration'. You already know that the physical has traces of those higher vibratory levels through which the self passed on the way to incarnation in the physico-etheric. You are now establishing linkage between those traces and the actual vehicle which is your 'Self' in those higher vibrations. Myers has well called man a 'sum in arithmetic' and the physico-etheric is but one of the groups we have to add up to reach the true total of the Oversoul. This means we can use 'reciprocal vibrations', and true meditation means leaving the lower triad to experience *your* heights—it is the domination of the Personality by the higher triad, the majestic Oversoul.

If you have had some success with Exercise Twenty-eight (and this is necessary before proceeding to this work), you will have found that your rhythmic breathing became more or less automatic; you probably forgot to count and certainly you found that you were breathing steadily, probably more slowly (everyone has their own pace) and more deeply. We are now going to practise adding the power of sound to the rhythm and the breathing.

You know that all teaching emphasises the power of sound (or 'the Word' as the Bible calls it) and you will appreciate that each vehicle of your 'self' will respond slightly differently to the use of sound. In your later studies you will find everyone has a key note, and most of us find this without tuition. Sound is of course vibration. The use of 'Words of Power' runs through every religion and all occult societies. The repetitive prayer, the litany, ritualistic intonings are all based on this knowledge.

At this stage one must choose one's own 'Word of Power'. There is today a great cult of the Mantra, which is simply the repetition of certain words over and over (similar to Tennyson). It is best, however, at this stage to choose one single word which symbolises for you all your effort, eg Harmony, Unity, Love, Success, Service or one of a thousand others. Having chosen your word, *think* what it means. Say it, and analyse it and its manifold observances. *Understand* your word in the deepest sense. You are then ready to do this exercise.

1 Usual preliminaries, which you should now use automatically.
2 Flood your room with colour and repeat the word you have chosen loudly and sonorously. As you do so, try to take a cloud of your colour to your higher chakras—pineal, pituitary and thyroid (see Frontispiece).
3 Now repeat the rhythmic breathing you have done in Exercise Twenty-eight, but when exhaling mentally or in a whisper, repeat your mantra word. This will at first produce no observable result because you are aligning your subconscious to your high vehicles and your Oversoul.
4 But soon you will find that all has become 'habit', there will be no need for organised breathing or repetition of the Mantra. You have entered into the silence.
5 No one can tell what you will find there, except that it will be joyous. What has happened is that your line of vision has changed; you are now looking at things down from your viewpoint as Oversoul. Your perception is now in reflex from your normal five-sense earth consciousness. Whatever happens, you will have euphoria, wisdom and certainty.

Do these exercises with regularity, once or twice a day, and within weeks you will have achieved that certitude which has been called 'the Islands of Bliss'.

LESSON 25
Meditation (3)

Exercise Thirty Dissociation

Hemmed in by petty thoughts and petty things,
Intent on toys and trifles all my years,
Pleased by life's gauds, pained by its pricks and stings,
Swayed by ignoble hopes, ignoble fears;
Threading life's tangled maze without life's clue
Busy with means, yet heedless of their ends,
Lost to all sense of what is real and true,
Blind to the goal to which all Nature tends: —
Such is my surface self;
        but deep beneath
A mighty actor on a world-wide stage,
Crowned with knowledge, lord of life and death
Sure of my aim, sure of my heritage—
I—the true *self*—live on, in self's despite
That 'life profound' whose darkness is God's light.
    Edmond Gore Alexander Holmes. 'La Vie Profonde'

Beneath this world of stars and flowers that rolls in visible deity,
I dream another world is ours and is the soul of all we see.

It hath no form, it hath no spirit; it is perchance Eternal Mind;
Beyond the sense that we inherit I feel it dim and undefined.

How far below the depth of being, how wide beyond the starry bound,
It rolls unconscious and unseeing and is as Number or as Sound.

And through the vast fantastic visions of all this actual Universe
It moves unswerved by our decisions and is the play that we
rehearse.

Agnes Mary Frances Duclaux. 'The Idea'

In this last lesson of our elementary course the student is requested to pass the teachings in review. The progression is the following:

1 There is a choice for all men to make. We may accept that life finishes with the physical and there is no purpose behind it—that we are in fact 'accidents' of an accident. In such a case the pessimism of Bertrand Russell is justified, and the whole of our life journey is indeed 'a tale told by an idiot'. On the other hand, we may accept that there is purpose in the Universe, and Man is indeed a mortal God, for he has a spark of divinity within him that owes no homage to the Sun.

2 If there is purpose, then the path must be an evolutionary one. In material affairs this is taken for granted, but when it comes to consciousness, to the sign-manual that raises man above the beasts, we tend to ignore evolution. Teilhard de Chardin has pointed out
   (a) Throughout time there has been a tendency in evolution in matter to become increasingly complex in its organisation.
   (b) With increase in material complexity there is a corresponding rise in the consciousness. In fact Man's physical evolution appears to have reached a stage of completion, and it is in the consciousness, in the evolution of Soul/Mind that Man may expect further advances.

3 Such Life Force as enters into the physico-etheric shows this constant urge towards more consciousness. The 'building bricks' of prana are vitalised by the electromagnetic force of fohat, their functions determined by vibrations—*'all is vibration'*. Vibrations in scientific and in occult thought are divided into groups—the Law of the Octaves.

4 Man during his fall into incarnation as a physico-etheric entity passes through all these higher states of vibration and creates 'vehicles' in each octave, whose enormous rates of vibration puzzle our understanding (as do the latest astronomical ideas or the 'gas of matter' which seems to lie behind the atomic causation). Man's fall from the 'Paradise' of the Oversoul to physico-etheric creates,
   (a) Vehicles capable of using the rates of higher vibrations.
   (b) Traces of such vehicles, which are kept by the incarnating entity and brought to the physical vehicle, so that Man can, while in the physical, experience 'reciprocal vibrations' which are in fact latent powers.

5 In order to experience such latent powers two things are necessary:

(a) We have to overcome the barriers which every age builds for itself. To quote Chesterton, 'we are all too inclined to think of our time not as merely another Age but as the Day of Judgement'. History shows us how all great men are cramped by the environment in which they live: Gibbon could doubt if any further improvement could be made in the human condition as he saw it in 1780.

(b) We have to develop latent facilities by practice combined with knowledge, as an athlete does to 'put up' a body muscle. We must know how to alter vibrations, how to focus attention away from the earth environment, to seek in the 'Silence' for those higher manifestations of our true selves (breathing, concentration, meditation).

6 The thirty steps given in this little book are culled from the experience and teachings of hundreds of sages who have practised and understood the Ancient Wisdom. The writer but recapitulates what he has learned from his Masters, as they in turn learned it from theirs.

Each person who enters into the *path* becomes both teacher and scholar, both exponent and learner. It is probable that science and occultism will continue to move towards each other (notably this is happening now in physics and cosmic astronomy), and the near future may see a revival of the Ancient Wisdom dressed in new scientific theory, and in technological machinery and abilities. Such an evolution is due; the New Age is at hand and the results will explode pessimistic mechanistic thinking as though it had never been.

7 The beginning of all power has been given in our thirty steps: correct breathing, the understanding of vibrations, the ability to concentrate rhythmically, and the entry into the wonderland of meditation. The rest is practice, and an inner certainty of achievement which will not be betrayed. Do not, however, expect to have *every* power; according to your ray you will find some comparatively easy of achievement, and the rest will come with knowledge. And *finally* remember that the 'signs and wonders' are only aids to the understanding of a philosophy that, as the Master said, will enable you to enter into the Kingdom of Heaven, when all these other things shall be added unto you.

Introduction to Exercise Thirty

You will have had some experiences in dissociation from your physico-etheric in Exercises Twenty-eight and Twenty-nine—slight perhaps but encouraging. *Remember that practice means success;* make it regular and wholehearted.

This exercise deals with an extension of meditatory power, which has been called by many names—the mystic 'Union', the Yogi, 'out of the body', the psychic 'Astral Travel'. We prefer to consider it as the culmination of this course, as an entire journey to latent power. While your five-sense brain exerts great power, because Mother Commonsense sticks close to her earth consciousness, yet you know that there lie realms beyond, as indeed the physicist and the astronomer have told you. Some realisations are necessary before you do this exercise.

1 *Full* understanding that where your consciousness is, there will be your 'seeing'. If you listen to a piece of music which 'entrances' you, you will become oblivious to your physical surroundings. Whenever you concentrate properly, you will have the same unconsciousness of physical surroundings and desires. Perception is where you focus attention.
2 Whatever 'vehicle' you reach in your exercises, youı Oversoul is in complete command. Therefore 'Cast out fear', which is ludicrous.
3 Keep a record book. Be absolutely honest with yourself. Neither rationalise away the 'intimations' which will undoubtedly come, nor dramatise experiences into inflated importance. Write down *what* actually happened—you will be amazed and strengthened in the work.

Exercise Thirty

1 Privacy is essential, as are also the preliminaries which you have found suit you best. It may be of use to use the 'pranic breath', Exercise Six, as the more your room is charged the easier it is to get the correct vibrations. The writer usually spends 10-15 minutes.
2 Now lie on your bed, or on a blanket on the floor. A minimum of clothing is essential, and if privacy and warmth permit, none at all.
3 You should lie with your arms at the sides of the body, palms upwards, fingers stretched out and separate.
4 Now move your consciousness away from your surroundings. Stare fixedly at some place on the ceiling and slowly close your eyes. When the eyelids are down, focus your seeing to the root of the nose—it helps if you 'squint' behind the closed eyelids. You will feel some result, known to the Yogi as the 'tickling of the ant'.

It is always recommended that you practise this for several nights until you are sure of the procedure, and have felt the sensation at the root of the nose. Breathe as slowly and rhythmically as possible. On the night when you feel secure in this knowledge, proceed as follows:

5 Slowly raise your arms and your consciousness of the 'tickling of the ant' together, so that you are making a triangle of force. Keep the fingers extended. The three must move up as though you were ascending in a slowly moving lift—you may even feel the tremor that affects some people when they are 'airborne'.

6 Proceed until you 'feel' (know) that you cannot go any higher on this occasion. Lower the arms slowly and at the same time open the eyes in the same rhythm.

It is always recommended that you now make a rough sketch in your record book showing how high you believe you reached, and also any notes of 'feelings' during the exercise.

7 The next night proceed as before, but you will now find that you can raise a little higher. It is essential to keep the etheric triangle intact, ie hands and 'ant' all on the same plane. Go as high as you can and then slowly lower all forces.

It is always recommended that you make fresh notations in your Record Book.

8 After at least twelve nights of *regular* practice (a 'broken night' makes it necessary to start over again), and having attained the highest you can reach, *think of yourself as being on the plane you have reached and look down at your body*. Remember that, in the Astral, you can see all around you like a fly.
9 Continue until suddenly, perhaps after twenty evenings of work, you will find it suddenly happen, and *your astral* is looking down at *your physico-etheric*.

The usual reaction is to panic and dive back into the physical, which is pulling you back into habit circumstances that men call 'normality'. But of course, once you have achieved, you can do it again (not necessarily on the next try). You know now it is quite, quite safe, and proceed with the exercises as follows.

10 Before you start, give orders, spoken normally but very slowly, to impress the following on your unconscious:
   (a) That when the experience occurs, you will return to your physical within forty seconds, but very slowly, so that you fit easily into the physico-etheric. If this is done properly, you will find a euphoria pervade your 'self', and this is likely to last for many hours.
   (b) That when you glance down at your physical, you shall move away from the plane reached, where your astral is supported by the hands (etheric) and 'ant' (mental), and stand at the foot of your bed.

   Having given these orders slowly and absolutely authoritatively, follow with procedures 1 to 8. *Never force.* Make haste slowly. You are acquiring a 'soul' habit as opposed to mere earthly ones.

It is always recommended that you do not go outside the confines of your own room when you once find you have astral locomotion, until an *order* instructs that you can or your own decision is overridden. The writer believes that you ought not to go outside your own magnetised area (your room) without a teacher being present, but most people seem to do so.

When this exercise is achieved, then this book has fulfilled its purpose. A word first to those who have not succeeded at all—if you have had no result, then you have not followed the exercises. It is impossible to do them thoroughly and wholeheartedly without a result. If, however, your success is minimal, it is suggested you do the sensible thing and start again right at the beginning. You will find the exercises come much more easily, and you will probably make extremely rapid progress.

One barrier that *must* be overcome is that you must *not* 'skip' the theory. You cannot 'do' until you have convinced your unconscious mind that this basic thinking is right, for it has been trained for many years to accept 'earth' barriers. *The theory is more important than the exercises, the philosophy than the signs and wonders.*

When you succeed, you will have gained the following:

1 Knowledge that physical death is a nonsense—you merely transfer to other vehicle of perception.
2 Your higher vehicles are now in touch with the earth body and therefore you may rely upon 'orders', inspirations and also answers to your *non*-personal questions.
3 You have moved towards true integration, towards the Oversoul. You have achieved a high level of poise and knowledge, and you may feel kindly towards Mother Commonsense and her progeny. *You know.*

God be with you!

BIBLIOGRAPHY

From some of the 1,000 books the writer loves he has selected 30, as one has to stop somewhere. He has divided but *not* evaluated them into two groups. Read to stretch your mind. 'Be sure that you go to the author to get at *his* meaning, not to find yours', said Ruskin in *Sesame and Lilies.*

Please make your own library of books. 'Some books are to be tasted, others to be swallowed, and some few to be chewed and digested', said Bacon. Find those which you wish to chew over, and do so until they become part of your way of life, your philosophy.

MUSTS (Preferably in the order given)

WALKER, Kenneth. *The Diagnosis of Man* (Jonathan Cape, 1942)

TYRRELL, G. N. M. *Grades of Significance* (Rider & Co, 1931)

JOHNSON, Raynor. *The Imprisoned Splendour* (Hodder & Stoughton, 1953)

HEYWOOD, Rosalind. *The Infinite Hive* (Chatto & Windus, 1964)

PAYNE and BENDIT. *The Psychic Sense* (Faber & Faber)

BESANT, Annie. *The Ancient Wisdom* (Theosophical PH, 1910)

WATSON, Lyall. *Supernature* (Hodder & Stoughton, 1973)

HIGHLY RECOMMENDED

ALDER, Vera S. *Finding the Third Eye* (Rider & Co, 1938)

BRUNTON, Paul. *Search in Secret India* (Rider & Co, 1933)

BRUNTON, Paul. *The Secret Path* (Rider & Co, 1938)

CHARDIN, Teilhard de. *The Phenomenon of Man* (Fontana Books, 1959)

CROCKELL, R. *The Study and Practices of Astral Projection* (Aquarian Press, 1970)

CUMMINGS, G. *The Road to Immortality* (Nicholson, 1932)

DAVID-NEAL, A. *The Secret Oral Teachings* (City Light, New York, 1967)

DAVID-NEAL, A. *With Mystics and Magicians in Tibet* (Penguin, 1936)

EDDINGTON, A. S. *The Nature of the Physical World,* The Gifford Lectures (Everyman, 1928)

EVANS-WENTZ, W. J. *Tibetan Yoga* (OUP, 1935; revised 1957)

FEURSTEEN, George, and MILLER, Jeanine. *A Reappraisal of Yoga* (Rider & Co, 1971)

HAIGH, Elisabeth. *Initiation* (Allen & Unwin, 1965)

HAPPOLD, F. C. *Adventure in Search of a Creed* (Faber & Faber, 1957)

LANGLEY, Noel. *Edgar Cayce on Reincarnation* (Paperback Library, 1970)

LEADBEATER, C. W. *The Hidden Side of Things* (Theosophical PH, 1920)

OUSPENSKY. *Search for the Miraculous* (Routledge & Kegan Paul, 1950)

PAUWELS and BERGIER. *Morning of the Magicians* (Mayflower Books, 1963)

RAMACHARAKA, Yogi. *Fourteen Lessons in Yoga Philosophy* (L. N. Fowler, 1964)

SOLOMON, Joan. *The Structure of Space* (David & Charles, 1973)

STEINER, Rudolph. *Knowledge of the Higher Worlds* (Anthroposophical Publishing Co)

THEOBALD, Minnie. *Three Levels of Consciousness* (J. E. Watkins, 1949)

WEATHERHEAD, Rev. Leslie. *The Christian Agnostic* (Hodder & Stoughton, 1965)

WILSON, Colin. *The Occult* (Hodder & Stoughton, 1971)

Entry of the Cosmic Homogenity (Prana/Fohat 'Undifferentiated Consciousness) into Man's Chakras

Endocrine Glands	*Wheels of Force*		*Vehicle*	*The Path of Vitalisation entry*	*Indian names*
PINEAL	CROWN	BUDDHIC	HIGHER TRIAD	ENTRY INTO INCARNATION FROM OVERSOUL TO PHYSICO-ETHERIC / INCARNATION / DISSOCIATION / return from physico-etheric to Oversoul DEVELOPMENT OF LATENT POWERS SHEDDING OF VEHICLES AT 'DEATH'	SAHASRARA
PITUITARY	BROW	MENTAL			AJNA
THYROID	THROAT	HIGHER EMOTION			VISHUDDHA
THYMUS	HEART	EMOTION & FEELING	POISE		ANAHATA
PANCREAS	NAVAL	SENSATION	LOWER TRIAD		MANIPURA
ADRENALS	SPLEEN	ETHERIC			SVADHISTHANA
GONADS	ROOT	PHYSICAL		KUNDALINI (CREATION)	MULADHARA

INDEX OF NAMES

INDEX OF SUBJECTS

These indices were compiled by fellow students Mary and Geoff Joyce to whom the Author proffers fraternal thanks.

The Author will endeavour to answer readers' queries, particularly as to Exercises. In these days of high postage and clerical costs he requests a *small* coverage. Address: 'Croton House', Tintern, Gwent, Wales.